MOTHER EARTH, MOTHER AFRICA
&
AFRICAN INDIGENOUS RELIGIONS

EDITORS
Nobuntu Penxa Matholeni
Georgina Kwanima Boateng
Molly Manyonganise

This volume is dedicated
to the 'giantess'
on whose big shoulders every African woman theologian
and women globally are standing,

MERCY AMBA EWUDZIWA ODUYOYE,
daughter of Anowa
and the founder of the
Circle of Concerned African Women Theologians.

CONTENTS

ACKNOWLEDGEMENTS

Over the years, the Circle has benefitted from the various contributions of its members both in kind and cash. Dr Musimbi Kanyoro is one of those who has supported various fundraising opportunities including investing her time and money. At the time of the conference in Botswana in July 2019, she was wrapping up her responsibilities as the president and CEO of the Global funds for women, and she was unable to attend. She instead took a leap of faith by contributing a significant amount towards the celebration of the 30th Anniversary of the Circle. She contributed her service bonus and the funds she raised through Global Fund for Women. For this, we are grateful to Dr Musimbi Kanyoro and Global Fund for Women.

In addition, many thanks go to the University of Botswana, the Circle of Concerned African Women Theologians (Circle) the Global Challenges Research Fund, World Council of Churches and Ecumenical HIV and AIDS Alliance for their financial support, not only for the 5th Pan-African Circle of Concerned African Women Theologian Conference but also for the funds that made this volume possible.

This volume is not the product of a single person's efforts, but the joint effort of a collaborative team. I, therefore, wish to extend my gratitude to all the chapter contributors, and everyone involved, including my fellow co-editors, Molly Manyonganise and Georgina Kwanima Boateng, who played an instrumental role in the production of this book. Your wisdom, focus on detail, energy and enthusiasm are woven into the very fabric of this volume. You are the embodiment of teamwork!

A special thanks to Musa WenKosi Dube and her team for trusting us with the conception of this baby – from the initial stage of morning sickness to the eventual birth of this volume. You certainly know the meaning of the word 'mentoring'. I enjoyed sharing this experience with you.

Much appreciation also goes to Selene Delpoort and Dr Lee Anne Roux for their outstanding job on the proofreading and editing of this volume – thank you!

To God be the glory!

Nobuntu Penxa Matholeni

PREFACE

Mercy Amba Oduyoye[1]

Earth and Africa are both referred to as 'Mother'. This feminisation of Africa and the Earth was captured by E. Bolaji Idowu in his *African Traditional Religion: A definition* as follows:

> Where she (Africa) behaves herself according to prescription and accepts an inferior position, benevolence, which becomes her 'poverty', is assured, and for this she shows herself deeply and humbly grateful. If for any reason she takes it into her head to be self-assertive and claim a footing of equality, then she brings upon herself a frown, she is called names; she is persecuted openly or by indirect means; she is helped to be divided against herself ... a victim who somehow is developing unexpected power and resilience which might be a threat to the erstwhile strong. (Idowu, 1975:77)

Whereas this account may fit Africa and African women closely, Mother Earth escapes some of it but still has her own way of responding to human aggression. The chapters in this volume apprise us of this activity of Mother Earth. What the Akan say of Mother Earth makes her a totally inert phenomenon. The Akan say, "*Asaase Nkyiri Fun*" (the Earth does not refuse a dead body), meaning she does not react to the most obnoxious of treatments. Earth can be 'dumped upon' by all and sundry and at all times. Currently, we are experiencing how Earth makes herself felt.

Mother Africa, however, is slow to respond to aggression and African women are also very slowly raising their voices in opposition to demeaning words and actions directed against them. These chapters offer several examples of the current words and actions of African women.

African Traditional Religions (ATRs) was the designation crafted to describe what is now accepted as African Indigenous Religions (AIRs) because of the ambiguity of the word 'traditional'. I have heard the question 'How long should something exist in Africa before it becomes traditional?', but this is not being debated here.

Given the complexity and wide-ranging nature of the offerings stimulated by this title, I have offered to echo some of the language of the authors in this preface, while I offer some reflections of my own on the subject. When moved to do so, I have

---

1   Prof. Mercy Amba Oduyoye is a teacher, theologian, author and international speaker.

made a comment here and there so as not to do the work of the editors, who will be offering their own introduction to the anthology. I intend this preface to serve as an hors d'oeuvre.

The reference to Mother Earth in the title recalls the picture of Earth as a woman exploited and expected to be silent, just as colonial Africa was seen by both Africanists and colonialists. The contribution 'Liberating Earth…' explores the spirituality of indigenous Ghanaian society, women's involvement, and the place of Earth, *Asaase Yaa*, the Twi name of Earth, which depicts it as female. Being an Akan myself, this resonates with me and gives me the starting point for this preface. *Asaase* is feminine as God; *Onyame* is Kwame and masculine. According to the Akan, the whole Earth is sacred, and any place can be a place for worship. Mother Earth, therefore, is a sacred space.

If the Earth is a sacred entity in the African world view, then the de-sacralisation of Earth and the rest of creation is a key contributing factor to environmental degradation. The environmental crisis facing all of humanity needs to be approached from the perspectives of all the resources that all humanity can muster, and this includes what we can garner from the primary religious imaginations of those who people Mother Africa.

The science of ATR is still being developed; the research and discourse on the current challenges to the integrity of creation, the Earth and the environment in which creation struggles to thrive are moving forward. The notions of community, the interconnectedness of all creation, and the practice of communal existence are supporting the attempt to understand what is happening to the environment, human participation in the crisis, and what can be done to right the wrongs we are perpetrating.

The reverence accorded to Earth and nature, as well as to humanity's past, present and future in ATR, makes the crisis a religious and spiritual challenge. In ATR, the interaction between humans and the rest of creation is a reality that is honoured and lived, and so enjoins deep respect for nature. This close relation and reverence are what led earlier scholars of religion in Africa to coin names such as animism and pantheism, which were viewed negatively as the worship of creatures instead of the Creator. But this view of nature as living, animated and calling for care and respect is not only found in Africa. It is evident in several primal religions globally. In the Christian Bible Paul of Tarsus, who first attempted to 'theologise' the life and teaching of Jesus of Nazareth, observed that faulty human thinking and living were causing creation to groan, waiting for humans to be responsible as enjoined in Genesis 1:26-30.

We are now beginning to recognise that "the ecological problems faced by the world today are due to the loss of traditional knowledge, values and ethics of behaviour that celebrate the intrinsic value and sacredness of the natural world and that give the preservation of nature its prime importance" (Daniel, 1980, cited by Sipeyiye in the current book, page 101). From the standpoint of ATR, we have to agree with Taylor (1998:1) that "radical environmentalism understands environmental degradation as an assault on a sacred, natural world". The Earth is not an inert thing; it is sacred, living, and can get back at us.

The traditional African religio-cultural designation of Earth as female has led researchers, beginning with Idowu, to work out what this means in the life experiences of women. This leads us to a reflection on the challenges of understanding gender on the platform of human relations. In Africa, the mention of woman evokes notions of marriage and children. It is, therefore, not surprising that the subject of women, Earth and environment should lead to a discourse on marriage, wedding rites and the rites associated with death.

The language at marriage ceremonies in Ghana paints the woman to be married as an inert, voiceless commodity. She is described as a beautiful flower to be uprooted from the natal home and transplanted in the affinal compound. The Mfantse have what, for me, is the most obnoxious description. They describe the woman as being taken from her natal home to the husband's to be 'reared'. The Mfantse term, *Waapa no abayen*, says just that: it is like taking a lamb or chick from its mother to be reared elsewhere. The woman is described as 'immature' and lacking socialisation, which is to be provided by the marriage experience. It even suggests that the natal home had done an unfinished job. Worse, the word *yen* (to rear) is only used for persons who lack wisdom. They have only been fed for their physical development, but not socialised (*tsetse*), which means to become a well-integrated human being. This, for me, is even an insult to the natal home. The Yoruba view has its own problems. The new wife has her feet washed before she enters the affinal space and is then given new names by her in-laws. The imagery is that she is a rough stone that is going to be smoothened to fit into that affinal space. In all of this, the man does not change. This is what the Western/Christian marriage ceremony does when it asks: "Who gives this woman to be married to this man?" The man is an autonomous person; the woman is a 'gift' and, in some people's view, a commodity that is sold.

Puberty rites give space to men to roam and explore. In several African cultures, women do not own land; they only work on it at the pleasure of the husband. Even in the matrilineal communities, where married couples do not have community of property and where there is therefore no fear of its being alienated because of marriage, it is the men of her matriclan who are the direct custodians of the family land. So, by and large, the culture treats both women and Mother Earth as belonging to the men of Africa.

Marriage relocates a woman to the husband's home and, all else being equal, she stays there, dies there and, in the patrilineal clans, is buried there. Burying a woman in the husband's home is an indication that she leaves her natal family and joins the husband's even in death. 'Till death do us part', however, operates in the matrilineal system. A wife's body as well as the fruits of her womb belong to her matriclan. In the patrilineal system, the children belong to the man. Operating these two systems has its own challenges, but the overlay of Westernisation and Christianisation compounds the situation and has by and large favoured the patrilineal system. The end result is that today the operating gender construct ensures gender inequality between men and women according to patriarchal norms.

The woman relocates to the man in body and spirit. A woman's grave belongs to her husband's home village. A woman stays in marriage and comports herself as one who 'belongs' to the man. Patriarchy insists on this, but married matrilineal Akan women are buried with their matriclan, hence there is a tension. Resolving this in terms of the principle of 'mirror imaging', which has hardly begun, is for me the way forward in gender relations.

The Earth is the final resting place of the bodies of all humanity. But the challenge of the limited availability of burial grounds is beginning to hit several communities, especially in urban areas. Is the concept of cemeteries as we know them sustainable? The cemetery is linked with birth. At birth, one's umbilical cord is buried in Mother Earth and it awaits being joined to the rest of the body at death. When we are young, we sleep on our mother's bosom; when we die, we find comfort in Mother Earth. Ways and means are being devised not to separate the spirits of the dead from their ancestral lands. When people die outside their natal land, their ashes or nails and hair are brought to be buried at home. Urbanisation has impacted on the relation between Earth and humans, especially with regard to burials. Several people have been severed from their homelands by migration and displacement. This has disrupted people's spiritual, economic and cultural heritage.

A key factor in modernisation is the availability of new technology. Women working the land in Africa have by and large stuck to the traditional hoe and cutlass, and even at home still hold on to the mortar and pestle. The absence of technology keeps women wedded to the land and its traditional uses. On the other hand, travel and communication have been revolutionised, challenging the culture that enjoins women to stay connected to land and husband. The total dependence of women on men economically and spiritually is being eroded, taking gender discussions to new levels.

While women are generally enjoined to live by traditional values, men seem free to choose when their personal and individual interests are on the line. Men in Africa seem to have opted for technology over traditional ways. But neither Mother Africa nor African women can opt out of the technological revolution. The challenge is for both women and men to learn the judicious use of technology. Traditional taboos may help us think of how to use technology in a way that will not jeopardise the sustainability of the Earth and its environment that we shall bequeath to future generations.

Technology, in the form of social media, is widely prevalent in Africa in its usage, even if not in its creation. We can now Google to access a vast vista of know-how, including environmental best practices. But we have yet to use this medium to share our traditional knowledge with regard to herbal medicine and sustainable agricultural practices. Rather we use technology in mining to pollute our waterways and poison the Earth with harmful chemicals.

The role that religion played in how we traditionally related to Mother Earth is gradually being set aside, because the Earth is no longer considered sacred and living. We need to challenge ourselves to do theological reflection on our relation to Earth and its environment. Revisiting the rituals and taboos that have a bearing on environmental sustainability should be encouraged and promoted. We tend to promote religious beliefs that hamper women's development. Instead of asking menstruating schoolgirls not to cross a river on the path to their school, we should be asking why not? And we should then find ways of dealing with the reason for the taboo that does not jeopardise the education of women and keep them subordinate. The education of women is what is at stake here, not menstrual blood. We should be interrogating the fear of menstrual blood as being a pollutant. We have to interrogate Christian communities that use menstruation to marginalise women and keep them subordinate. The mix of African culture and Christian practices requires critical investigation if Mother Earth, Mother Africa, and gender relations are to become life-giving and life-enhancing.

A gender analysis reveals how local unequal ritual spaces set the tone for the future imbalances of space and unequal sexual relationships. When girls reach puberty, they are quarantined, and their movements supervised. Boys, on the other hand, are let loose for long periods in the open country and women are prevented from going near these spaces. While culture limits women's spaces, it expands men's spaces. It is on the basis of such practices that patriarchal practices are maintained and unequal relations emerge. These incongruent spaces disadvantage women, who mostly respond with silence or develop coping devices to survive. For a sustainable environment and relationships, women have to 'remake' themselves. When women are being 'protected', we need to ask whether this is to discriminate against them and give men more room to exhibit their negative masculinities? Such assumptions and a great deal of unexamined African oral wisdom should attract the attention of women and men of Africa.

Christianity has been charged with an attempt at erasing indigenous African epistemology. It has been charged with the 'domination' of the Earth, which has resulted in environmental degradation and climate change. Doing theology in Africa should entail investigating both the African indigenous religious imagination and Christianity, as well as Islam and all other religions that hold sway in Africa. The centrality of the Bible in African Christian spirituality and its pervasive influence, even outside the Christian community, should be put to positive use to liberate Mother Africa, Mother Earth, and African women and men.

It is my hope and expectation that this volume will contribute to this conversation so that Africans, women and men, will be found at the global table where issues such as environmental degradation and sustainability are being investigated. It is my hope that the research and discussions around deep ecology, radical environmentalism and the UN's Sustainable Development Goals will include Africans who will bring the poetry, folk tales, proverbs, philosophy and creativity of Africa to the table.

My hope is that this volume will be a worthy beginning and that it will stimulate more wisdom and more creative action that will answer the many questions about the integrity of creation that are confronting us.

References

Daniel, B. 1980. *Discordant harmonies: A new ecology for the twenty-first century.* New York: Oxford University Press.

Idowu, E.B. 1975. *African traditional religion: A definition.* 3rd Edition. Maryknoll, NY: Orbis Books.

Taylor, B.R. 1998. Religion, violence, and radical environmentalism: From Earth First! to the Unabomber to the Earth Liberation Front. *Terrorism and Political Violence,* 10(4):1-42. https://doi.org/10.1080/09546559808427480

INTRODUCTION

Nobuntu Penxa Matholeni[1]
& Georgina Kwanima Boateng[2]

This volume grew out of the conference 'Circle of Concerned African Women Theologians 5th Pan-African Conference', hosted by the Department of Theology and Religious Studies at the University of Botswana, Gaborone, 2 to 4 July 2019. The theme of the conference was 'Mother Earth and Mother Africa in Theological/Religious/Cultural/Philosophical Imagination'. It is from this theme, that we ultimately derived the title of this book, *Mother Earth, Mother Africa & African Indigenous Religions*. The book is a compilation of revised papers that were presented by the respective authors at this conference.

The words of Musa Dube (2000:8) resonate strongly with me and helped inform my avenue of inquiry:

> I came to realise the sad implications of reading and living with or by stories written for me and not by me. This is a crucial issue, given that oral sub-Saharan black African people who live in the age of the information superhighway, do not own the means of producing and disseminating information about themselves. Most of what we read about ourselves and other subjects is not written or published by us.

The sentiment in Dube's reflection is also taken to heart by many of the scholars of the Circle of Concerned African Women Theologians, especially the authors who contributed to this volume. Over time they have come to realise the limitations, errors and omissions in their stories as they are retold by others and recognise that they have their own her-stories, their own experiences, and their own personal stories to tell. So, by adopting a 'positioned' perspective here, they write about their own (once silenced) stories of African Traditional Religions (ATRs) – on their own terms and from their own perspectives.

In Africa, religion is central and perhaps the most important aspect in the lives of Africans. Yet, the foundational principles of rich African world views and beliefs are too often dangerously misunderstood by predominantly non-Africans, or "outsiders".

---

1   Rev. Nobuntu Penxa Matholeni is a lecturer and researcher at the Faculty of Theology at Stellenbosch University. [Email: nobuntu@sun.ac.za]

2   Rev. Georgina Kwanima Boateng is a reverend minister of the Presbyterian Church of Ghana. [Email: gynaboat@yahoo.co.uk]

Moreover, Goduka (1999) succeeds in explaining that the disdain for ATRs by European missionaries who brought Christianity to the Eastern Cape in South Africa around the 1820s is testament to "the othering" and misunderstanding of amaXhosa customs. This occurred because of the contextual insensitivity arising from the construction of European definitions of appropriate gender roles in an indigenous context. Goduka further claims that the missionaries considered themselves as the embodiment of a superior religion, race and gender; therefore, any aspects of amaXhosa indigenous traditions that did not fit into their European standards were considered offensive and abhorrent, or even primitive, savage and barbaric. In fact, Mthethwa (1996, in Louw, 2008) mentions that ATRs or spirituality pervades and permeates every facet of the life of African people and therefore cannot be examined in isolation. Instead, they must be examined conjointly by those who study the practice of religion and pastoral care. In different ways, the contributors of this volume take this petition seriously and together seek to debunk some of the myths about ATRs, including the belief that Africans do not embrace or care for the environment or Mother Earth – the core theme of the aforementioned conference and of this book.

Furthermore, the instructive viewpoint of Africans, the indigenous education process, covers all spheres of life, including religion, commerce, agriculture, weather, medicine, preservation of the environment, and so on. More specifically, Africans are not only shown to care for and or embrace the environment, but women are at the forefront of advocating for environmental issues. What we can do today is to be more proactive in taking the contributions of ATRs more seriously, something which was completely overlooked by the Western missionaries. The stories about African religion were not told by us, but by the Western missionaries who condemned most of the African rituals, which in their minds were not Christian enough. What they failed to appreciate is that African life is not divided into "sacred" and "secular". But for the African, life is consolidated – everything seems to have meaning only in terms of the religious (Ongong'a 1983, in Muyomi, 2014:346). This notion reinforces the need for us to tell our own stories from our own unique African perspectives and personalities, with our own voices and reactions to contemporaneous circumstances, expanding and making our truths known.

Africans embrace all of life, the humanity of each person, the world, and the creation of God. Consequently, the plenitude of African indigenous education reflects the completeness of life itself (Goduka 1999). This volume brings together voices from leading proponents of ATRs and African religious heritage, bonding us all together, to help us appreciate how values are richly entrenched in African religious life. This volume demonstrates the detailed richness of ATRs and culture and showcases how far the academic study of ATRs in Africa has come.

The various chapters in this volume recount religious events and experiences from individual perspectives as they are unfolding on the continent. The different voices show how modernity, colonisation, urbanisation, Christianity, and technology have sidelined beliefs and practices of ATRs to the detriment of the environment. The book therefore calls for concerted effort through a partnership between these various actors to ensure environmental sustainability.

The many conversations that took place at and after the conference have produced this phenomenal body of work. The book is organised in ten closely related chapters, although they follow no specific sequence, and can be read in any order. Since the book is a diverse collection of chapters that share a common theme as reflected in the title of this volume, I invite the reader to read each chapter individually, taking in the topics addressed by the authors.

Penxa Matholeni sets the tone for this outstanding volume as she makes a gendered analysis of initiation rituals for boys and girls. She considers the unequal allocation of spaces amongst amaXhosa rituals and gives particular attention to the impact of this on relationships within this society, especially between women and men. She concludes that these rituals are sacred and have their place, but they have been used to disadvantage women.

Masaiti Mukuka explores how gendered narratives in ATRs have been absorbed into and entrenched within Christian religions in Africa, and how this has affected environmental conservation. In doing so, she reviews the experiences of the wives of *Bashi Cingo* in the Sweetheart of Nimbi Church.

Boateng picks up on this theme in her chapter as she scrutinises the changing place of Earth in the journey from indigenous pre-Christian African worship to contemporary African Christian worship in the particular case of Ghana, and looks especially at how this has affected the space and place of women. She proposes a rediscovery of African Christian worship as a place for Earth participation by introducing Jesus into African indigenous Earth-centred worship.

Molato examines how the abolition of indigenous religious practices and the imposition of Christianity in the postcolonial period has impacted on environmental conservation using the particular case of the rainmakers in Setswana cosmology.

Manyonganise and Museka critically examine the Fast Track Land Reform Programme (FTLRP) of 2000 in Zimbabwe. They describe the negative impact of the FTLRP on what was left of the taboos amongst the various Shona ethnic groups and contend that the FTLRP has had the effect of 'sedating' the sacred as people have violated the taboos related to the environment with impunity. In their contribution, they devote particular attention to the critical role of women in environmental conservation.

Sipeyiye examines the Ndau notion of 'communal existence' to explore the themes of interconnectedness, reverence, embeddedness, and reciprocity with nature to advance the agenda of environmental sustainability. Sipeyiye thereby supports the conception that ATRs are biocentric, as they see all living beings as elements of one interdependent spiritual community.

Phili takes this further by accentuating the interconnectedness between the African and the land through an examination of burial rituals in Southern Africa. He shows that, even in death, Africans are still connected to the community through the land by means of a proper burial ritual. The land is very much a part of Africans' communal existence through a relationship that does not get severed – even by death – although urban burials have the potential of severing the ties that Africans have with their ancestry.

Nkomazana writes to cement the notion that attitudes, and perceptions influenced by religion play a crucial role in environmental sustainability. She does this by examining the role played by indigenous religious practices and beliefs in the contexts of the Kalanga in the north-east of Botswana. In her chapter, she also explores the effects that modernity and Christianity have had on indigenous beliefs and practices and concludes that all are necessary partners in environmental sustainability.

Nyaga examines how technology diffuses into society and changes its traditional values, thereby establishing how important it is for communities to live according to their traditions and culture, partnered by technology, in ensuring environmental sustainability. Governments' role in ensuring such partnership to create sustainable economic conditions for African communities is emphasised.

Chilongozi concludes this volume fittingly with her chapter that emphasises the necessary role of religion, especially ATRs, in the achievement of the UN's Sustainable Development Goals (SDGs). She reflects theologically on the SDGs and Mother Earth by engaging the theologian and founder of the Circle of Concerned African Women Theologians, Mercy Amba Oduyoye. Mwawi uses Oduyoye's four central themes as a theological lens for doing theology in Africa: (1) community and wholeness, (2) relatedness and interrelationships, (3) reciprocity and justice, and (4) compassion and solidarity. Through her thoughtful contribution, she draws attention to the need for appropriate planning and action to push us towards evolving into good stewards of creation.

We would like to close this introduction with the words of Guba and Lincoln (2005, cited in Chilisa, 2012): "We stand at the threshold of a history marked by multivocality, contested meanings, paradigm controversies and new textual forms.

At some distance down this conjectural path, when its history is written, we will find that this has been an era of emancipation: emancipation from hearing only the voices of Western Europe, emancipation from generations of silence, and emancipation from seeing the world in one color."

References

Chilisa, B. 2012. *Indigenous Research Methodologies*. Los Angeles, CA: Sage.

Dube M.W. 2000. Batswakwa: Which traveller are you (John 1:1-18)? *Journal of Theology for Southern Africa*, 108(November):79-89. https://doi.org/10.1080/03768350120045330

Goduka, I.N. 1999. Indigenous epistemologies – ways of knowing: Affirming a legacy. *South African Journal of Higher Education*, 13(3):26-35.

Louw, D.J. 2008. *Cura Vitae. Illness and the healing of life*. Wellington: Lux Verbi.

Ongong'a, J.J. 1983. Life and Death, A Christian dialogue. *Spearhead*, 78. Eldoret: AMECEA Pastoral Institute, Gaba Publications.

1

KWANTONJANE

The indigenous rites of passage amongst amaXhosa in relation to prejudiced spaces

Nobuntu Penxa Matholeni[1]

Abstract

KwaNtonjane is an isiXhosa concept that refers to the space that a young umXhosa girl occupies from initiation to adulthood. During this time, she is called an *intonjane* – an initiate transitioning from girlhood to young womanhood. Some parallels can be drawn between the two initiation practices, *Kwantonjane* and *ulwaluko*, with the latter term referring to an initiation ritual for boys.

These rituals are similar yet distinct. To illustrate this point further, both male and female initiates receive counselling on their transition and society's expectations. Yet despite the similarities, there are also conspicuous differences in how the initiates are counselled and how much space they are allowed to occupy during and after the initiation process. For instance, on the one hand, the mother of the young man and the significant women in his life are not allowed to be a part of *ulwaluko* or in the spaces surrounding the ritual. On the other hand, the father of the young woman is allowed around and close to the girl's initiation hut. There seems to be prejudice regarding the ritual spaces that amaXhosa women in general are allowed to occupy. This chapter investigates how the location of unequal spaces sets the tone for future imbalance in ritual spaces and unequal social relationships. This will be addressed by making use of the relational indigenous research paradigm, which considers how reality is collectively constructed and the connection that people have with each other from birth to death. The chapter will also discuss and explain the purpose and meaning of these rites of passage.

Introduction and background

KwaNtonjane is the sacred space of amaXhosa, where the ritual is performed to prepare young girls for womanhood. This ritual seeks to teach a girl about the proper and important aspects of womanhood of umXhosa, preparing her for a life of marriage and the responsibilities and rights of being a wife, a mother and a leader.

---

1   Rev. Nobuntu Penxa Matholeni is a lecturer and researcher at the Faculty of Theology at Stellenbosch University. [Email: nobuntu@sun.ac.za]

The *intonjane* ceremony (the initiation school for girls) has three segments, namely: *umngeno* (joining), *umtshatiso wentonjane* (slaughter of a cow), and the final stage, *umgidi* (welcoming home ceremony). Normally the ritual takes place after a girl has had her first period; however, the ritual can also be performed even if the woman has passed the stage of puberty. In fact, the first time I witnessed the ritual, it was my aunt who was in her late 30s. Moreover, Anele Mdoda (television personality) was recently seen shaving her hair for cultural initiation (ALL4WOMEN, 2014). This ritual is symbolic of a girl's sexual maturity and ability to conceive, as mentioned before; it is not just a symbol of sexual maturity and the ability to conceive, but the ritual is performed as needed, as indicated in the two illustrations above. However, Mills (1980) contends that if the woman is married and unable to conceive, or her children are sickly or face any other misfortune, the Sangoma might point the in-laws to the omission of the ritual by her father's household. The misfortunes not only happen to married women, but they can also affect the unmarried women with healthy children. That is why my aunt had to go through *KwaNtonjane*.

The *intonjane* ritual takes three to six weeks. Some parallels can be drawn between the two initiation practices for boys and girls. However, in *ulwaluko* the ritual takes four to six weeks. The *ulwaluko* ceremony also has three segments, namely: *umngeno, ukojiswa* and *umgidi*. This ritual also prepares the young man for manhood but is very different from the *intonjane*. *KwaNtonjane* is built in the proximity of *undlunkulu* (the main house) behind *ubuhlanti* (kraal). Inside *KwaNtonjane* there is a small space that is covered by a curtain which is where the *intonjane* will stay. The initiation school for the young man takes place in the bush, preferably in the mountains where there is ample space to allow sufficient privacy, because women are not allowed in his territory. A direct comparison of the two rituals reveals a number of similarities as well as differences. For instance, both initiates receive counselling on their transition and society's expectations. However, despite the similarities, there are also conspicuous differences, for example, between how they are counselled and how much space they are allowed to occupy during and after the initiation process. The question that arises is how does the location of unequal space set the tone for the future distribution of unequal spaces and unequal social relationships? This is the question this chapter seeks to address. This will be done using the relational indigenous research paradigm, which considers how reality is collectively constructed and the connection that people have with each other from birth to death, as well as the connection between the living and the dead. This chapter will also discuss, explain and theorise the purpose and meaning of these rites of passage.

Methodology

The methodology of this chapter is inspired by the work of Professor Bagele Chilisa on indigenous methodologies, which has resonated strongly with me (Chilisa, 2012). First, I will locate myself within this study. Kovak (2010:110) asserts that self-locating entails cultural identification and "is a powerful tool for increasing awareness of power differentials in society and for taking action to further social justice". Nadar (2014) also confirms that narrative research calls on us to be reflexive about our positioning. Riessman (2008) takes one step further by acknowledging that the construction of any work always bears the marks of the person who created it. I position myself within Black South African culture. I am an umXhosa black woman. I grew up in the province known as the Eastern Cape, where women fetch water from the river early in the morning and early in the evening with their babies on their backs. Like many women and girls, I fetched wood from the mountains to make fire to boil water, cook, and warm our homes. As a young girl I did not go through *KwaNtonjane*, however, I witnessed it personally and was told many stories about this indigenous ritual.

Indigenous knowledge has a specific way of being passed on; it is an element of the oral tradition of sharing information and past experiences (Kovach, 2010). Chilisa (2012) argues that Western ways of doing research involve paradigms that are not always acknowledged (colonising epistemologies, methods and methodologies) cannot exist side by side in African culture. She thus asserts that indigenous languages can contribute to the advancement of new knowledge, concepts, theories, and techniques in research that are rooted in the community's ways of knowing and perceiving reality (based on the African paradigm).

Elabor-Idemudia (2002:230) confirms this when she says that "[i]f we fail to recognise the ways in which subjective factors such as race, class, and gender influence the construction of knowledge, we are unlikely to interrogate established knowledge which contributes to the oppression of marginalised and victimised groups". Cilliers (2018) acknowledges this when he states that local knowledges stand a better chance of resisting, totalising and normalising power, if only for the fact that they tend to be more transparent in their association with, and more self-conscious in, their use of power, and more open to being unmasked by the promptings of the aesthetic of freedom. Bruner (1990) argues that to make sense of the experiences of any individual is to cast it in narrative. Stories are data with soul, explains Nadar (2014). Kovach (2010) establishes that stories remind us of who we are and where we belong; they also hold knowledge within them. Elabor-Idemudia (2002:103) takes this further when she says that "oral forms of knowledge, such as ritualistic chants, riddles, songs, folk tales and parables not only articulate a distinct cultural identity, but also give voice to a range of cultural, social and political, aesthetic and linguistic systems – long muted by centuries of colonialism and cultural imperialism". Chilisa (2012) believes that indigenous epistemology is viewed as knowledge that has a relationship with the people and has a place in the culture and the daily life experiences of the people. Moreton-Robinson (2017:72) brings this home when she says that relational principles "are a way of thinking, a way of learning, a way of storing knowledge, and a way of debating knowledge". This chapter seeks to do just that.

Similar yet distinct

AmaXhosa is one of those tribes that have many sacred rituals. They pride themselves on keeping and preserving these rituals. These rituals existed in precolonial times, and the arrival of the missionaries in the second half of the nineteenth century opposed a number of amaXhosa rituals as pagan practices. Their converts were faced with exclusion from the church if they did not abstain from observance and/or participation in the rituals (Mills, 1980). *Kwantonjane* and *ulwaluko* were amongst the rituals that were repudiated; however, *ulwaluko* has stood the test of time right up to the democratic dispensation in South Africa.

KwaNtonjane, efukwini, ukuzila and *ulwaluko* are a few more examples of amaXhosa rituals. However, for the purpose of this chapter, I will only focus on *KwaNtonjane* and *ulwaluko*, in relation to the prejudiced spaces that are allocated to them by amaXhosa.

Ncaca (2014) asserts that amaXhosa initiation schools are institutions that seek to carve an identity. They consist of procedures and processes, such as religious and cultural rituals, that play an active role in identity formation. It is during these rituals that the lines are drawn between who one is as a person and where one belongs.

Both of the rituals in question have an element of space and time. It seems that time and space are allocated according to gender binaries. To illustrate this, both groups are located in a secluded area within a time frame of three or four to six weeks, depending on the clan. The *ulwaluko* space, as mentioned earlier, is completely secluded from the society, whereas the *KwaNtonjane* space is in the middle of the homestead, behind *undlunkulu* (the main house) and in front of *ubuhlanti* (kraal). Both groups of initiates are allocated guardians.

During the *umngeno* ceremonies, the initiates are to remove their clothes and wrap themselves in a blanket; this is done in private. The young man is given a white blanket with a red strip sewn on the edge of the blanket, which denotes the spilling of blood that will happen (Ncaca, 2014). In addition to being covered with a blanket, the young woman initiate is also given a *doekie* (headscarf) to cover her head and face.

The first seven days of both rituals are critical. During this time, the young man is not allowed to consume any liquids, because it is believed that this will hinder the healing of his penis after the foreskin is removed on the first day of initiation. The young woman, on the other hand, is allowed to eat or drink anything. The young man is allowed to have visitors, while the young woman is not allowed to be seen by anybody except her guardian.

During *umojiso*, which is a ceremony that takes place during the first seven days of the initiation, a sheep is slaughtered for the young man. The young initiate is only allowed to eat a certain part of the animal, which is fed to him by his guardian. After that, they are allowed to eat and drink anything without restriction. The similar ceremony for the young girl is called *umtshatiso*; it also takes place during the first seven days of the initiation. During *umtshatiso*, a cow is slaughtered. As in the case of the young man, the young woman is also fed a certain part of the animal by her guardian. At the end of both initiation schools, both groups of initiates receive counselling by members of their respective genders. There is no slaughtering of an animal during the *umphumo womkhwetha* (the end of initiation of a young man), but for the *intonjane* there is, and this celebration takes place over a number of days.

During the initiation school, the father of the young man and significant other men are present throughout the process. Only if absolutely necessary do they provide the mother with information, as the particularities of the process are strictly confidential. There is less secrecy around *KwaNtonjane*, since this ritual takes place in close proximity to the men's territory. The father of the young woman is able to see and observe what is going on, as the space is not entirely secluded. He is able to hear and enjoy the singing and dancing[2] that takes place every night outside the initiation hut. Cilliers (2016) notes that singing and dancing in African spirituality bring people to the rhythm of life. Music in African spirituality brings those who sing back to their origins; it gives meaning to the present and acknowledges the sacredness of the event. It is worth noting that in Africa there are no lines drawn between the sacred and secular.

The young village women sing and dance every night. Throughout this time the young woman initiate remains inside the initiation home. If she does go out, she is accompanied by her *impelesi* (guardian); they are then both covered with the same blanket, so that it cannot be seen who is who . The young man, on the other hand, experiences much more freedom; he is free to explore his natural surroundings and hunt because he has the land to himself. The emphasis on *ulwaluko* is on being an umXhosa man who will be in charge of talking to the ancestors on behalf of his

---

2   It is worth mentioning here that during singing and dancing, the emphasis is on putting the foot on the soil (Mndende, 2002).

1

father's house (Ntombana, 2011) and officiating in ritual ceremonies (Ncaca, 2014). For the *intonjane*, the emphasis is on her beauty, how to please a man, what it means to have a menstrual period, and what her place in the household is.

However, in *ulwaluko*, the young man is instructed to shout "*Ndiyindoda!*" ("I am a man!") immediately after the removal of his foreskin. This declaration marks a significant shift in his social status. He is no longer an *inkwenkwe* (a boy), but also not yet an *indoda* (a man), which occurs only after the ritual is fully completed. The young woman, conversely, must cover her face, look down and be silent for a while. Furthermore, seclusion from society takes place in both rituals. The young man ventures off into the bush, preferably to the mountains, while the young woman's space is located in the home and around the kraal. This draws attention to the issue of space and freedom. The young man has much more physical space and freedom to move around naked, because no women are allowed in that space. The young woman's space behind the kraal, on the other hand, is much more limited as it is the man's territory; no women are allowed in the kraal. However, the father of the young woman and some men are allowed in the space of *KwaNtonjane*, because the location of the young woman's space is next to the man's territory.

Prejudiced spaces

"Spaces denote roles and relationships. Spaces can speak of privileges, authority, and power. Space separates the doers, the actors, from the audience, the 'in group' from those pushed out to the margins at the edge of the significant space so that they are at risk of having no place at all" (O'Loughlin, 2019:23). This quote speaks directly to the first part of Kobo's (2016) title of his article, *Umfazi akangeni ebuhlanti emzini*, meaning a woman is not allowed to enter the kraal. This dichotomisation of spaces by amaXhosa disconnects women from other spaces such as *ebuhlanti* in the initiation school for boys, etc., completely disempowering them. These prejudiced spaces violate the life of a child who is brought up in such a situation. Kobo (2016) further argues that power is a social structure in which some people are regarded as superior and have the right to exercise control over the lives of others by virtue of the position they hold within the structures of society. She further contends that power is not only limited to political structures, but is also found in the home, as well as at all levels of society and community.

In Cilliers's (2018) view, space and power go together. This is acknowledged by McFadden (2019), who states that space is gendered and highly politicised as a social resource in all societies. She further states that some spaces are culturally, religiously, and politically reserved for either males or females. To emphasise McFadden's point, in many isiXhosa-speaking church congregations, there is a side specifically for women and a side specifically for men. Similarly, in each and every amaXhosa ritual there is a transparent wall separating the men and women on opposite sides. In the same manner, the *intonjane* and her *impelesi* have their faces covered; they are expected to keep their faces bent to the ground and speak softly when they talk. This is interesting because it is exactly what happens when the woman gets married. Her face is once again covered, and she is allocated a very limited space behind the door (literally). She also has *impelesi* with whom to go outside and she is expected to speak softly. The young man, on the contrary, is now a man with space and power.

The spaces where these rituals take place are symbolic of the power that privileges men. Kobo (2016) wondered about the life of a girl who is brought up in an environment where there are gender binaries, where she is told that her place is with her mother. The answer to this question is the beginning of a learning process for these girls. Penxa Matholeni (2019) calls this process "re-posturing", as they transition from one stage of life to another. Additionally, the girls must realise that they are inferior to boys and that these spaces are socially constructed.

Cekiso and Meyiwa (2015) concur that rites of passage, such as initiation and others, are performed to mark the transition from one stage of life to another, and to signify significant changes in the lives of individuals, while confirming their identity and status in the community. The status of the young man, therefore, is elevated. However, the status of a young woman is elevated in a private space; in other words, when she is married, she is expected to be a mother. My argument here is that an umXhosa woman has limited space, and therefore limited power, while the umXhosa man has unlimited power and the space to use that power.

Women are not allowed in *ebuhlanti*, which is a sacred space for amaXhosa; it is the place where the father or the first-born son speaks with the ancestors. Yet their initiation hut is built behind the sacred space; power is at play here. This means, even if the women are in charge of the *intonjane*, they do not own the space; the power is still in the hands of the father and the significant men in a young woman's life. There are spaces in the culture of amaXhosa that are more sacred than others are. These young women are unable to make this temporary space their home, because their space is limited. The young men, on the other hand, can make fires outside their *bhuma* and *boje inyama* (braai the meat).

The father of *intonjane* and some other men, as mentioned earlier, are permitted to walk around the girl's initiation hut, as well as go very close to it to choose a cow or goat to slaughter. Yet the mother of the young man and the significant women in his life are prohibited from the *ibhuma*. If she trespasses, she is deemed a witch and accused of wanting to bewitch the boys. For the young man, this boundary creates the impression that women are inferior to men. The mother of the young man has no authority or power to make any decisions concerning the boy she carried in her womb for nine months.

Black women, particularly isiXhosa-speaking black women, have to undergo the process of what Samura (2017) calls remaking themselves. In this process, they renegotiate their expectations and aspirations to better fit into these limited spaces. In other words, they experience what Penxa Matholeni (2019) calls the migration of identities to increase their belongingness to fit the limited spaces they have occupied. They have to re-orient themselves, as Samura (2017) says, to take control of these small spaces.

No one really knows what is going on behind the closed door or curtain – perhaps nothing. Even though they are not harmed in any physical way, they are expected to stay there and remain silent. Gendron (2011) indicates that silence does not necessarily mean absence of verbal communication. She insightfully argues that stillness and silence are communication methods in themselves. Wajnryb (2001) further states that silence cannot be communicated. There is a mystery in this method of communication; when they look down with their mouths shut, they are indeed communicating with power. Silence can be used as a tool to deny the recognition of an experience or event (Gendron, 2011). Who said that because they are told not to speak, they are powerless?

Reposturing involves beautifying themselves for themselves and the spaces they occupy. *KwaNtonjane* is a beautiful thing to watch as they come out of the initiation school. Before the end of the girl's seclusion, a celebration begins for all the women in the village. This event is referred to as *umngqungqo*. During this event, women are dressed in *imibhaco* (amaXhosa traditional attire) – beautiful beaded necklaces and bracelets. In the morning, after the last day of *umngqungqo*, the initiate goes to the river to wash the white clay off, which is replaced with yellow clay, referred to as *umdike*. The initiate and her assistants wear new clothes upon their return from the river. The celebrations continue, marking the end of the *intonjane* ritual. The dress code of the women and the lyrics of their songs tell a story of resilience and power. They have wisdom to continue to re-posture themselves on their own terms, in different prejudiced spaces, and silently own the spaces of Mother Earth and Mother Africa.

Conclusion

In this chapter, particular attention was given to *KwaNtonjane* and *ulwaluko*, two very sacred amaXhosa rituals. It was argued that these treasured rituals, albeit deliberate, impart patriarchal tendencies and generate hierarchical and unequal relationships of power, undermining the richness of amaXhosa culture. The rituals, along with their similarities and dissimilarities, exemplify the sacredness and aesthetics of amaXhosa rituals. Although a comparison of the two rituals was presented, the intention was not to highlight their common features and differences, but rather to expose and challenge the inherent gender binaries that are used to disadvantage women. These ritual spaces, as distinct and similar as they are, can be a compelling tool to emancipate young men and women to be responsible, equal members of their families, societies, and the nation at large. Unfortunately, as this chapter has shown, prejudice and power still prevail in these ritual spaces. Notwithstanding this limitation, the chapter endeavoured to reveal the resilience and transparent power of amaXhosa women, who have transcended these prejudiced spaces by means of their silence as a communication tool, which was initially intended to oppress them. But instead of remaining subjugated, they have managed to transcend their oppressive circumstances and turn their silence into their greatest weapon. At the very heart of these rituals is preparing young women and men for life and uniting them with their clan and community. These rituals therefore no doubt play a pivotal role in amaXhosa culture.

References

ALL4WOMEN. 2014. Anele Mdoda shaves hair for cultural initiation. 13 June. https://bit.ly/3fchDXY [Accessed April 2020].

Askland, H.H. & Bunn, M. 2018. Lived experiences of environmental change: Solastalgia, power and place. *Emotion, Space and Society*, 27:16-22. https://doi.org/10.1016/j.emospa.2018.02.003

Cekiso, M. & Meyiwa, T. 2015. Gendered naming and values inherent in the Xhosa *amakrwala* (graduate-initiates): Implications for teaching a multicultural class. *Journal of Social Sciences*, 40(1):75-82. https://doi.org/10.1080/09718923.2014.11893304

Chilisa, B. 2012. *Indigenous research methodologies*. Los Angeles, CA: Sage.

Cilliers, J.H. 2016. *A space for grace: Towards an aesthetics of preaching*. Stellenbosch: African Sun Media. https://doi.org/10.18820/9781920689940

Cilliers, J.H. 2018. Power, space, and knowledge: Theological perspective on Michel Foucault's contribution to Post-colonial theory. Paper presented at the Humboldt University Summer School on Postcolonial Theories as a Challenge for Theology. Berlin, 28 May–2 June.

Elabor-Idemudia, P. 2002. Participatory research: A tool in the production of knowledge in the development discourse. In: B. Chilisa (ed), *Indigenous research methodologies*. Los Angeles, CA: Sage. 97-231.

Gendron, R. 2011. The meanings of silence during conflict. *Journal of Conflictology*, 2(1):1-7. https://bit.ly/3eCuYIU

Kobo, F. 2016. *Umfazi akangeni ebuhlanti emzini…* A womanist dialogue with Black Theology of Liberation in the 21st century. *HTS Teologiese Studies/Theological Studies*, 72(1):1-6. https://doi.org/10.4102/hts.v72i1.3268

Kovach, M. 2010. *Indigenous methodologies: Characteristics, conversations, and contexts*. Toronto: University of Toronto Press.

McFadden, P. 2019. Why women's spaces are critical to feminist autonomy. *Isis International*. https://bit.ly/2Wwm9dm [Accessed November 2019].

Mills, W.G. 1980. Missionaries, Xhosa clergy & suppression of traditional customs. *International Journal of African Historical Studies, X111 'The Roots of African Nationalism in the Cape Colony: Temperance, 1866-98'*, 2:197-213. https://doi.org/10.2307/218873

Mndende, N. 2002. Signifying practices: AmaXhosa ritual speech. Doctoral dissertation, University of Cape Town.

Moreton-Robinson, A.M. 2017. Relationality: A key presupposition of an indigenous social research paradigm. In: C. Andersen & J. O'Brien (eds), *Sources and methods in indigenous studies*. New York: Routledge. 69-77.

Nadar, S. 2014. Stories are data with soul: Lessons from Black feminist epistemology. *Agenda: Empowering Women for Gender Equity*, 28(1):18-28. https://doi.org/10.1080/10130950.2014.871838

Ncaca, M. 2014. *Yithi Uyindoda!* (Say, you are a man!): An ethnographic study on the construction of religion and masculinities in initiation schools in Cape Town Townships. Master's thesis, Stellenbosch University, Stellenbosch.

Ntombana, L. 2011. Should Xhosa male initiation be abolished? *International Journal of Cultural Studies*, 14(6):631-640. https://doi.org/10.1177/1367877911405755

O'Loughlin, T. 2019. Space matters. *Liturgy*, 44(1):22-26.

Penxa Matholeni, N. 2019. *Endleleni*: A construction of the diasporic space for black women in South Africa. Unpublished.

Riessman, C.K. 2008. *Narrative methods for the human sciences*. London: Sage.

Samura, M. 2017. Remaking selves, repositioning selves, or remaking space: An examination of Asian American college students' processes of 'Belonging'. *Journal of College Student Development*, 57(2):135-150. https://doi.org/10.1353/csd.2016.0016

Wajnryb, R. 2001. *Silence: How tragedy shapes talk*. Crows Nest, New South Wales: Allen & Unwin.

2

BEMBU RITUALS AND THE ENVIRONMENT

Experiences of the wives of *Bashi Cingo* in the Sweetheart of Nimbi Church

Bridget N. Masaiti Mukuka[1]

Abstract

This chapter seeks to investigate the rituals around the wives of *Bashi Cingo* by using a feminist narrative. The chapter examines the experiences of the wives of *Bashi Cingo* in relation to their cultural beliefs that forbid them to cultivate the land. I explore the rituals' links with the wives and the environment and, of course, their spiritual connection with the Sweetheart of Nimbi Church in Zambia. I will employ Mercy Amba Oduyoye's (1995) and Elisabeth Schüssler Fiorenza's (2011) feminist methods of inquiry to guide this chapter. I found that some wives of *Bashi Cingo* have fairly low levels of support from the Sweetheart of Nimbi Church and from the community. Also, it took some months to bury the founder of the Sweetheart of Nimbi Church, because he came from the lineage of the Bemba chief, *Chitimukulu*, in the Northern Province of Zambia. This demonstrates the influence of Bemba[2] culture and biblical scriptures in formulating some church policies that reinforce the rituals. It also uses a measure of feminist narratives that may be of much benefit to some feminists as well as many African women.

Introduction

Bashi Cingo are men who are assigned to preserve the bodies of some Bemba chiefs when they die. When a Bemba chief dies, such as *Chitimukulu* and *Nkula*, his body is not buried within a few days, but it is embalmed until the harvest of the following

---

1   Dr Bridget N. Masaiti Mukuka is Dean of Research at the United Church of Zambia University, Lusaka Campus. She is also a research associate at Stellenbosch University. [Email: nondeb@gmail.com]

2   In referring to 'Bemba women and culture', this chapter uses Bemba as an umbrella term. The reason is that within the Sweetheart of Nimbi Church of Zambia there are different groups of Bemba people, coming from various provinces. For instance, the Luapula people(s) are also part of the large Bemba-speaking group in Zambia. The differences within the other groups are due mainly to the Luapula Bemba-speaking tribes being primarily fishermen. The Bemba people hold in common the feature of being organised in matrilineal clans. They include the Bemba, Bisa, Aushi, Ngumbu, Chishinga, Mukulu, Kawendi, Shila, Tabwa and Lamba, to mention a few (Cunnison, 1959). All these occupy much of North-Eastern Zambia and extend into South-Eastern Katanga. This also includes the whole of Kasama, Mpika, Chinsali, Luwingu and Mporokoso. To the west, south and east are the Bisa. To the west, further into the Democratic Republic of Congo (DRC), are the Aushi and their subgroups. The Mambwe-Lungu are found in the northern provinces of North-Eastern Zambia (Cunnison, 1959; Whiteley, 1950).

year. The process of embalming is done traditionally using soup made from *ilanda* (black-eyed beans). Research conducted in an African Initiated Church (AIC), namely the Sweetheart of Nimbi, indicates that some male members of the church are appointed as *Bashi Cingo*. It is believed that when *Bashi Cingo* are performing their duties, they are not allowed to sleep with their wives. The wives are forbidden to work in the fields, because it is believed that they will pollute the land.

Guided by the feminist method of inquiry of Oduyoye (1995) and Fiorenza (2011), the chapter reports on a qualitative investigation of some rituals and taboos around the wives of *Bashi Cingo* from the Sweetheart of Nimbi Church. The chapter concludes by positing that women should deconstruct the rituals and taboos that are formulated in terms of male power, because they hinder the women from achieving their full humanity. The sample size of the research was six, two men and four women. This chapter utilised numbers such as 'woman number 6' (W6) to identify the participants in the text and analyse the data. This was done to protect the anonymity of the participants. Hence, this chapter is elucidated by in-depth original research on the responses of some pertinent church members.

Theoretical frameworks

In order to better understand the rituals or taboos around the wives of *Bashi Cingo*, the discourse is investigated through the theoretical lenses provided by Oduyoye (1995) and Fiorenza (2011). In Oduyoye's (1995) book titled *Daughters of Anowa*, she narrates the history of secret societies in West Africa, where it is believed that women were once keepers of certain secrets of divinities and had powers like those of some avenging spirits and of the Great Mother, who was believed to be the Supreme Creator.

She points out that while men were entitled to carry out all tasks, women were in charge of shrines belonging to the Great Mother. This was referred to as 'the cult of women'. However, as the years went by, the shrine belonging to the Great Mother was eventually captured by men. Women had no option but to hand over knowledge of the cult's secrets to men. Men ensured they had full knowledge of the shrine, although they had to behead the priestesses in order to possess the shrine. Oduyoye (1995) continues that to this day the cult's priests have maintained the custom of plaiting their hair and their dresses are like those of women. Because the secrets of the farms were mainly linked to the cult of the Great Mother, men taught themselves techniques of farming, while women were forbidden to take part in planting yams. She explains that the festival of the yam, originally performed by women to appease the Earth goddess, was also taken over by men. The goddess became the deity of the men's secret societies. To date, whenever the goddess's statue is in procession, women are advised to remain in hiding, since they have to remain silent and are forbidden to be seen. According to Oduyoye (1995:32), "the Mother Goddess, who used to be the source of power for women, has been appropriated by men and is now the reigning deity of men's secret societies that demand that women remain voiceless and out of sight." The role of women that was once in power has been sidelined. Women's voices have been silenced. Oduyoye (1995:31-32) asserts that

> [s]everal West African communities have exclusive men's secret societies associated with creation and agriculture that provide the means for keeping order in the society. This is true of the Ogboni and Oro of the Yoruba and the Poro societies of Sierra Leone. The annual demonstration of power over women in these religious festivals helps to perpetuate women's inferiority in the minds of growing boys and girls and to ensure that patriarchy reigns where once there [was] parity or, perhaps, even female leadership.

With reference to Oduyoye's (2015) statement, the majority of secret societies in West African communities reaffirm the silencing of women and make them depend largely on their male counterparts. This also indicates that some men amongst the Ogboni and Oro of the Yoruba and the Poro societies believe that because of the nature of a woman, she should not be allowed to take part in farming for fear that she may "pollute the land". Thus, the power of societal norms prevents the participation of women in agriculture and other leadership positions. This is similar to the rituals around the wives of *Bashi Cingo* that prevent women from farming.

To this end, Oduyoye (2001a) is calling on both men and women to examine African culture with gendered lenses, thereby inviting both of them to create a culture of inclusiveness. Oduyoye (2001b) argues that in Africa, particularly in the AICs, "women are the keenest participants in the religious provisions or regulations that link women with evil and make men the innocent victims of women's sexuality" (Oduyoye, 2001b:19). Oduyoye's (2001b) concern corresponds with that of some African women theologians. They observe that the authority and interpretations of the Bible have been exercised with a focus on the oppression and subordination of women. Some African churches, in their quest to 'absolutise' the Bible, have preached the story of Eve to emphasise the wrong things that have been caused by women. The story of Eve allows human separation from God, thereby allowing human beings to respond to God out of their own free will. She argues that the narrative of the Eve story needs to be examined critically so that it allows inclusiveness in the church and society (Oduyoye, 2001b). The answer to Oduyoye's (2001b) call for inclusiveness could be seen in the latter part of Genesis 3:6b. However, the role of Eve is in consonance with Oduyoye's (1995:32) contention that "women were in charge of shrines belonging to the Great Mother".

In her publication titled *Transforming vision: Explorations in feminist theology*, Fiorenza (2011) divides her work into four sections. The first section deals with feminist theory and theology. The second section outlines feminist theology and struggle. The third section deals with Catholicism as a site of feminist struggle, and the fourth section concentrates on feminist revisions of the divine (see Fiorenza, 2011:198). While it is not the intention of this chapter to explore the entire book, the chapter focuses mainly in the fourth section. Here, Fiorenza (2011:198) explores a wide range of issues, such as violence against women, anti-Judaism in feminist theology, the concept of Mariology, and the concept of monotheism.

Fiorenza (2011) indicates that many churches have developed a very positive image of Mary, mother of Jesus. I use an example from the Sweetheart of Nimbi Church, where members admire Mary's characteristics; they imitate these characteristics and venerate her. They believe that Mary is the mediator, because she is the mother of God. However, Fiorenza (2011) is critical of some churches, such as the Sweetheart of Nimbi, that imitate the role of Mary, arguing that this is mainstream Mariology that continues to inscribe a weaker sociocultural image of the feminine and sanctifies the marginalisation and exploitation of women. While Fiorenza (2011) sees this as one way of exploiting women, some women in the Sweetheart of Nimbi Church believe that this is positive, because it empowers some women to appreciate their motherhood. Furthermore, Fiorenza (2011:198) argues that "in holding up to women the image of the perpetual virgin and sorrowful mother Mary, churchmen are preaching a model of femininity that ordinary women cannot imitate". Fiorenza (2011) advocates the abandonment of a Mariological type of preaching, since imitating Mary in a modernist society has turned into a postmodern issue. But this is a paradox, since Mary and her characteristics are unique symbols that ordinary women cannot reach, yet Emilio (a founder of the church) teaches them to his members.

Such conceptions are ideological. Fiorenza (2011:199) argues that "it is overlooked that these ideologising and mythologising forms of *kyriarchal* Mariology often go hand in hand with a conservative politics of ecclesiastical and societal restoration that is contrary to the vision of the discipleship of equals". I argue that in a church like the Sweetheart of Nimbi, the possibility of finding a vision of the discipleship of equals amongst members might be rare. This is because the doctrine/s often seem to surpass the members' natural human understanding. It is, therefore, considered a privilege for the Sweetheart of Nimbi Church members to direct all their prayers to Mary, whom they strongly believe is their senior Saviour.

Women, male power and the environment

In the same way, secrecy in the Sweetheart of Nimbi Church is a custom that is attached to Emilio, and it has found symbolic expression when all the members respect and honour Emilio. This is reflected in the saying "*ubufumu bucindikwa kubene*", literally meaning "honour is given to whom it is due". As the church founder and having been born from the lineage of Bemba chiefs, whatever he ideologises is not questioned. It is in situations such as these that Scott (1990) suggests ideological and symbolic dissent are similar. In a metaphorical manner, the hidden transcript determines the acts that should be performed on stage. To uncover the hidden transcripts of the people, it is important to assess the circumstances that are experienced by subordinate groups and what these would mean within the public transcript. Scott (1990:14) points out three dimensions in which these may occur. "First, the hidden transcript is specific to a given social site and to a particular set of actors" (Scott, 1990:14). Second, "… it does not contain only speech acts but a whole range of practices … for many peasants, activities such as poaching, pilfering, clandestine tax evasion, and intentionally shabby work for landlords are part and parcel of the hidden transcript" (Scott, 1990:14). Third, there is a thin line between public and hidden transcripts, and this exacerbates the struggle between dominant and subordinate groups. The capacity of dominant groups to define what may be called public transcripts and to maintain that which is hidden remains in their power to control. This struggle between the dominant and dominated groups is one of the common conflicts that exist in our daily lives (Scott, 1990:14). Thus, if there is not much pressure from the subordinates to reorder the pattern of domination, "others will exploit that breach and a new, de facto limit governing what may be said will have been established incorporating the new territory" (Scott, 1990:196). In the same way, members exalt Emilio for being the 'Parent of Truth' and receiver of divine revelations. It is in this way that his own children will also rise and establish their own territories.

Using the words of Fiorenza (2011:200), the Sweetheart of Nimbi Church members "have developed a very positive image of Mary". They revere Mary. The members of the Sweetheart of Nimbi Church exalt Mary. They believe that Mary mediates between humanity and God, inasmuch as Mary is both their liberator and their mother. They admire Mary's characteristics; they imitate them, and they venerate her. They believe that Mary is the mediator because she is the mother of God. Mary is referred to as *Mayo Nakabumba*, literally Mother of the Creator, Seat of Wisdom or *Namfumu*, meaning Mother of the King or literally *Nyinefwe*, which means 'Our Mother'. All these are titles of exaltation for Mary in the Sweetheart of Nimbi Church. The Sweetheart of Nimbi Church uses the symbol of Mary in many forms. First, Mary is used as a symbol of purity because they have been taught that she had no sin. Mary received no temptation from the devil. Second, Mary is used as a symbol of fertility. It is from this premise that the wives of the *Bashi Cingo* are forbidden to go to the fields, for they may pollute the environment. Instead, they should remain in their given homes so that they do not pollute the land or contaminate others. Mary cared for and maintained her pregnancy without thinking of an abortion. Third, Mary is used as a symbol of life. She gave birth to Jesus. She nurtured Jesus and taught him God's ways. The Bible does not state that Mary went to the fields (interview with W6).

Fourth, Mary is seen and portrayed as a symbol of humility. It is through Mary that the Sweetheart of Nimbi Church members believe that God has both feminine and masculine characteristics. This is revealed through Mary, since she is the 'Senior Redemptrix' over Jesus. Mary is used as the mediator between humanity (Emilio) and God. Fifth, it is through Emilio that Mary has established her own church with Black people, that is, the Sweetheart of Nimbi Church (Burlington, 2008). This is because through Mary's saviourhood and her relationship with her favoured child, Emilio, and her children, the Africans, there was something that was hidden from the Europeans, just as the messiah-ship of Jesus was also hidden from the Jews (Burlington, 2008). These are some of the reasons why Mary is revered. Loades (1996:128) is of the view that "Mary is taken into dialogue with God, as a woman of courageous choice, proclaiming God's vindication of those who need it, surviving poverty, flight, exile and so on". To the Sweetheart of Nimbi Church members, Mary's conversation with the angel Gabriel portrays how she humbled herself. It is for this reason that church members portray Mary's humility in songs and prayers, as they believe that Mary obeyed God's command and she was highly favoured because of that.

From this perspective, Fiorenza (2011) observes that male dominance, Mariology, and the cult of Mary degrade both men and women in four ways. First, they emphasise that virginity is detrimental to sexuality. Second, they do this in a unilateral manner; for example, they associate the model of 'true womanhood' with that of motherhood. Third, they do this in a religious manner. For example, they valorise obedience, passivity, humility and submissiveness as being the cardinal virtues of women. Fourth, this is done by constructing an essentialising gender complementarity that sustains the structural oppression of women (Fiorenza, 2011). For instance, while the Roman Catholic Church had various orders under the patronage of Mary, they did not have 'nurses of Jesus'.[3] However, Emilio, using the

---

3   It was highlighted that in the Sweetheart of Nimbi Church all the priests, as well as the other members of the church who have leadership positions, undergo a three-year training course that is done within their Parishes. During this training, both men and women are called Nurses of Jesus (NJs). This is where

Bemba culture, has initiated one – the 'nurses of Jesus'. In the Sweetheart of Nimbi Church, this is blended with Christian traditions and Bemba cultural perspectives. It is embedded within Bemba culture.

Fiorenza (2011) explains that because of the brokenness and inadequacy of the human language, some readers read 'woman' as a subject and/or object of inquiry. She refers to her own work as decolonising the human language. She insists that women do not share a unitary essence but are multiple and fractured in many different ways by race, class, age, sexuality, and gender (Fiorenza, 2011). Fiorenza's (2011) use of the term "wo/man" is one way of indicating this fracture.

Background of the founder of the Sweetheart of Nimbi Church

The founder of the Sweetheart of Nimbi Church, Emilio Chishimba, was born in Ipusukilo, Zambia in the Luwingu district around 1921. This was the time the Society of Missionaries of Africa (SMA), hereafter the White Fathers, made strategic plans to establish themselves within the largest tribe, which was the Bemba. Emilio's mother and father became Roman Catholic converts. His mother's name was Chilufya (Chishimba, 1976). They embraced Catholicism to the extent that Emilio joined the minor seminary at Lubushi when he was ten years old and was later sent to the major seminary of Kipalapala in Tanzania in 1940. He spent three years studying scholastic philosophy and theology. During that time, he was increasingly beset by the fear that he was not holy enough to receive the priesthood of Jesus Christ (Hinfelaar, 1994). Emilio's mother, Chilufya, came from the royal clan of *Chitimukulu* in Kasama that is purely matrilineal. Chilufya had eight children.

Chitimukulu simply means 'a big tree with many branches'. In Kasama, the Paramount Chief of the Bemba people is known as *Chitimukulu*. Some Bemba paramount chiefs, just like many other Zambian chiefs, look after their mothers. In most Bemba tribes, whether the Bemba-Bisa, Bemba-Aushi or Bemba-Lunda, mothers are very important and significant because it is believed that they are the ones who give birth to and nurture the chiefs. Some mothers of the Bemba chiefs hold leadership roles in society. Since they are consulted about carrying out some tasks, they have the final say and are honoured by their subjects. That is the reason they are regarded as mothers of kings. In Bemba, this is referred to as *Banamfumu*, literally mothers of kings. For instance, Burlington's (1998) article has discussed how Chilufya is elevated and, in some sense, equated to Mary, Mother of Jesus. Although Chilufya gave birth to Emilio, honour is also given to Emilio's grandfather and grandmother.

they are trained to observe the characteristics of Mary, Mother of Jesus. (For more information on this, see Bridget Masaiti, PhD dissertation, Stellenbosch University.)

In many African cultures, such as the Bemba, the grandfather and grandmother represent figures of authority.

In some of the Bemba documents that he wrote for his church members, Emilio explains how his attention was caught by the Sacred Heart of Jesus Christ. Gazing at the Sacred Heart of Jesus Christ made Emilio see himself as a searcher for truth, known in the Bemba language as *Ukufwaisha ichishinka* (Chishimba, 1976). Emilio initiated families into the practice of gazing at the Sacred Heart, an image that was found in most Christian homes. As Hinfelaar (1994:104) writes:

> Emilio exhorted the members to fast from time to time, to abstain from alcohol, and amidst the noise of life in the compounds to spend long hours in deep silence in order to create an atmosphere of peace and harmony ... The white missionaries, whose primary goal was to plant the visible church and had little time to introduce their neophytes to the mystical aspect of Christian prayer, had taught them to express their new religion through the recitation of long prayers and singing of hymns.

In trying to integrate Christianity and traditional religions, many Bemba people acknowledged his preaching and admired Emilio's teaching. Hinfelaar (1994) asserts that Emilio attracted the cream of the teachers, catechists and other lay leaders of the Catholic Church who were trying to integrate their own religious background with the teaching of Christian belief and morality. Emilio established some parishes that, in the Bemba language, are still referred to as *Namfumu/s*, meaning 'Mother/s of Kings'.[4]

Death of the church founder

In the Sweetheart of Nimbi Church, ritual practice is the norm. Arbuckle (2010:82) defines a ritual as "any prescribed or spontaneous action that follows a set pattern expressing through symbols a public or shared meaning". A ritual is a repeated expression of some symbolic nature; for instance, in the Church, members bow or lie prostrate before they greet Emilio. Some leadership roles are generally associated with rituals. Rituals tend to portray the power of leaders over their subordinates.

Emilio died in Lusaka in February 2015 and was buried in his village in September 2015. Emilio died at one of his *Namfumu* steads (parishes) in Lusaka. He was buried in his home village in Luwingu in September 2015. In many instances, when a Bemba chief dies, burial takes place after one year. The body of the chief is kept

---

4   Emilio used the Bemba titles, where sisters of the Bemba chiefs and their girl-children are called *banamfumu*, meaning mothers of kings (Whiteley, 1951; Richards, 1940). He also derived this from the concept of Mariology, since Mary, Mother of Jesus, is referred to as Mother of King in the Council of Ephesus (Rakoczy, 2004; Fiorenza, 2011).

in a separate hut, where some special men (*Bashi Cingo*) are assigned the duty of traditional embalming. Since Emilio came from the royal family, his body was embalmed using soup made from *ilanda* or black-eyed beans.

This meant that the *Bashi Cingo* and their wives had to move out of their houses and were camping within the *Namfumu* steads, the congregations that were initiated by Emilio. In fact, they are kept near the *Namfumu* steads and not within them, because there are some other members who live near these congregations. The wives accompanied their husbands because they were supposed to be cooking for them, but were not allowed to engage in farming. Since farming is linked to fertility, the wives of the *Bashi Cingo* are not supposed to interact with other members of the community or the church, or engage in farming or water drawing for fear of polluting the land and the water wells. This issue of not allowing some wives to engage in farming where they can cultivate their own food or clean the water wells is linked to the environment. This has an impact on the environment.

Since Bemba culture is matrilineal, it means many women own the land. They do more of the farm work than their husbands, who mainly trim the trees. Women clear the fields with their children and till the land. Women take turns to clean the water wells. They even water some of their crops. They draw water and collect firewood. But if they are meant to stay indoors because they may pollute the land, it is certain that the environment and the children will suffer the most, because there will be no experienced women to clear the fields, clean the water wells, tend to the children and draw water. If, for example, some wives insist on going to the farm, the church will acquire a small portion of land for them that is situated far from the other fields. Because of the nature of the rituals, the *Bashi Cingo* and their wives leave their children to be looked after in other *Namfumu* steads until the cultural process of embalming and burial of the chief has been completed. In terms of the wives who have not asked for their own fields, the *Bashi Cingo* take turns in taking care of the wives by providing food for them.

In response to the interview, W4 highlighted that after eight months of mourning their chief, she found it difficult to attend prayers while being excluded from both farming and her family members. Some church superiors approached her. They asked W4 to go for prayers, since she knew the call of her husband was divine and from God. In contrast, W2 stated that "Emilio was guided by the Spirit of God to formulate all these rules that are even found in Leviticus and he was from the royal family ... I was excited because I knew God would not fail me ... being *Bashi Cingo's* wife, I left my five children and my family, and went to live in isolation."

In other cases, some of the male members of the church explained that the death and preservation of Emilio's body should not be viewed as a taboo, because many people are aware that their leader originated from the royal family. They revealed that there are a number of cultural procedures to be carried out before the chief is buried. For instance, M3 indicated that there are some men who are assigned to preserve the body of the chief and there are some men who are assigned to bury the chief. The two are separate. By the time the chief is declared dead to the *Bashi Cingo*, it is the duty of the *Bashi Cingo* to inspect some of the chief's body parts, such as fingers, toenails, teeth, eyes and other body parts. According to M3, "[t]he reason for doing this is to ensure that no one has removed some parts from the chief's body, such as a tooth, a nail or to cut some of the hair." Asked why people would do such a thing, M3 indicated that there are many reasons people do this because they have different beliefs, some of them being issues connected with authority or power. It is important to note that Emilio's preaching also underlies issues of knowledge and power that he acquired from both the seminary where he studied and from the Bemba chieftaincy from where he comes.

Knowledge and power

Comaroff and Comaroff (1991) argue that power operates within three interrelated modalities. These are hegemony, ideology and culture. The religious beliefs and values in the Sweetheart of Nimbi Church fall within these three spheres of power; hegemony, ideology and culture. For instance, when we examine the role of the Bemba Paramount Chiefs, they hold authority in their hands. Some Bemba chiefs do not marry one wife, but many women. The wives of Bemba chiefs are referred to as *Abasano*, literally meaning belonging to the royal clan. There are many reasons for the men to have several wives. It may be because they hold authority in their hands or because of prestige (Mbiti, 1999); furthermore, a chief has the liberty to choose which woman he wants to marry.

As knowledge is generally linked to power, this chapter argues that power is also related to knowledge and influences specific people in social situations. Purvis (1993:20) defines power as "the ability to accomplish desired ends and social power [or] the ability of one individual or group to affect the behavior of another individual or group". This chapter defines power as an instrument used by a male person to impart knowledge or teachings to others. An African priest with power and knowledge has acquired such knowledge from certain sources and is therefore using knowledge as a skill to teach and convert people to African Christianity.[5] Becker (1996:164) defines power as "the capacity to produce change". This means there are possibilities for changing or influencing the mind-set of others. This kind

---

5   The term 'African Christianity' in this chapter indicates the good news of Jesus Christ and the world views of some Bemba people in the Sweetheart of Nimbi Church.

of power is what is known as silent and subtle (Comaroff & Comaroff, 1999). It is silent in some way and positive, because members are being taught how to read and understand the Bible and imitate the kind of lifestyle lived by the Israelites in Old Testament times.

Malina (1983:26) defines power as "the ability to exercise control over the behavior of others". He views power as a symbol that should not be confused with physical force. For Malina (1983), power is also associated with the weak. He states that some parents and teachers often control the behaviour of children without the use of physical force. But, in exercising their power, these characters create very real unpleasant consequences for those under their sway (Malina, 1983). However, Malina (1983) does not view power as a form of violence such as applied by some teachers and parents.

For Nuckolls (1996), cultural goals (similar to those of Emilio) cannot be reached, since they represent values that contradict each other. Such kinds of contradictory cultural goals "generate dialectics, and such dialectics become the framework of knowledge systems" (Nuckolls, 1996:117). In this sense, Emilio was motivated to reach a cultural goal that could not be reached. His aim to teach the concept of Mariology to his members could not be achieved, unless he welcomed and exploited a dialectic (instead of a static position) whereby members imitate the lifestyle of Old Testament times when they are amongst themselves in the *Namfumu/s*, which contrast with their preference to live and experience a modern kind of lifestyle.

While polygamy may not be practised widely amongst commoners, polygamous marriages do occur amongst the Bemba chiefs, who "may have as many as several dozen wives" (Whiteley, 1950:18). Richards (1940) observes that the Bemba people regard married life as the only possible existence for a normal man and woman, and in this way they resemble other African peoples. Bemba men and women desire children passionately, for there is a craving for offspring. Richards (1940:17) argues that "to produce and possess children is one of the strongest ambitions of Bemba life". Richards (1940) was a missionary who lived and researched widely amongst the Bemba people during the colonial era. The wives of chiefs are well secured, because they live in huts fenced around a common stockade (Whiteley, 1950). In the midst of all this, there is an issue of power that is designed to control the wives of chiefs. The Bemba chiefs do not live in the fenced huts with their wives, but have their own palaces where they live. In Bemba language, the chiefs' palaces are known as *Kumusumba wa Mfumu*. However, it is from these palaces that the Bemba chiefs control their wives and children's huts by assigning guards to be in charge of them.

2

Unmasking the rituals and symbols

Fiorenza (2011:198) argues that "feminist criticism has unmasked the images and symbols of hegemonic Mariology as the religious projection of a celibate, male priestly hierarchy – a projection which has ideologically legitimized male domination in church and society". In the Sweetheart of Nimbi Church, however, this still needs to be unmasked. Emilio's teachings lean on the Bible, thereby propagating holy patriarchy, which is reinforced by African culture, particularly the Bemba patriarchy (Ramphele, 1989).

Fiorenza's (2011) publication is key to this chapter, because it offers a theory that aims at dismantling the distortions of relationships between men and women as a result of masculine exegesis of the Bible. In the Sweetheart of Nimbi Church, more pressure is applied on girls than on boys that they should be virgins before getting married. If a virgin marries but experiences difficulties to conceive, it is permissable for a man to choose another woman or even a sister, who may bear children for him. This is why Fiorenza (2011:199) argues that this is a way of "associating the model of true womanhood with that of motherhood". It does not matter if a woman is hardworking or not, because in many African contexts true womanhood is associated with hard work, while childbearing is associated with motherhood. In contrast, women in many parts of the world may not be allowed to take another man if her husband does not embody a model of fatherhood.

In many cases, this is a religious ideology that Emilio preached to his members. His members are taught to be obedient, humble and to submit to and valorise Mary, mother of Jesus. But one may observe that this kind of teaching lands more in the ears, minds and hearts of women than men. It is because of the duty of their husbands, the *Bashi Cingo*, that the wives have to obey the rules of accompanying their husbands and being isolated from the entire community. While the *Bashi Cingo* will be busy with their traditional embalming job, their wives are restricted from working in the fields or cleaning the wells or drawing water. The *Bashi Cingo* take turns in providing food for their wives. This means that the *Bashi Cingo* are allowed to go to the fields and draw water from the wells even though they may be on duty. The *Bashi Cingo* cannot pollute the land, but the women can. This shows that the church has sustained the structural oppression of women, which relates to issues of religion, culture and power.

All these are issues of power, because religion, including Christianity, is a manifestation of power, just as Bemba cultural values are symbols of power. Emilio saw his role as part of the Bemba royal lineage, where his Mother (Chilufya) was like *Namfumu* (proto-Mary). These two powers and belief systems operate concurrently but not without tension. Tensions exist because the wives of the *Bashi Cingo* are excluded from performing some duties, although the job done by the *Bashi Cingo* is so intense that they are the ones who should be excluded from performing the duties, such as going to the fields and interacting with other community members. One could point out that Emilio was the patriarch (Saviour) in the Sweetheart of Nimbi Church, and a 'Father of Truth', a patriarch who is the protector of women in a way that discriminates against them in the Bemba cultural dispensation. The men perform the duties assigned to them, yet the women bear the consequences of leaving their loved ones and working in the fields. The church disempowers women, in the sense that they remain voiceless. They do not share the happiness with their husbands and other family members, as well as being restricted from going to the fields, drawing water and other things.

However, the role of the *Bashi Cingo* should be questioned in their act of preserving the chief's dead body. Questions, such as 'How do they feel?' and 'Who appoints them?' were asked during the interviews. Some of the answers to the questions were that appointment to becoming *Bashi Cingo* is passed on in the family lineage and that it is a great honour to belong to the *Bashi Cingo* clan. These rituals have been brought into the church because, according to the church members, they are part of the Bemba tradition and culture. However, they dehumanise and diminish the roles of women in a number of areas such as limiting their husbands' sexual desires, having no interaction with family members and friends, and the worst part is that they are not allowed to fetch water from the wells or go to the fields or farms. This, therefore, means that they are both spiritually and culturally disconnected.

These are ideologies. Fiorenza (2011) is of the view that these ideologies and dogmas that were articulated during the time of the Greco-Roman imperial form of Christianity were institutionalised and have remained historically operative. She argues that "indeed, it is overlooked that these ideologizing and mythologizing forms of kyriarchal Mariology often go hand in hand with a conservative politics of ecclesiastical and societal restoration that is contrary to the vision of the discipleship of equals" (Fiorenza, 2011:199). As Emilio is also considered a sacred person by the members of his church, he is the one who established the structures in his church. It should be noted that members of the Sweetheart of Nimbi Church might be referred to as a group of subordinates. Scott (1990:27) stresses that "the hidden transcript of subordinate groups, in turn, reacts back on the public transcript by engendering a subculture and by opposing its own variant form of social domination against that of the dominant elite. Both are realms of power and interest."

Fiorenza (2011) and Oduyoye (1979) have argued that Christianity should take into consideration the African belief that God delegates authority to intermediary beings.

Arguing from an African woman theologian's perspective, Oduyoye (1979:112) stresses that there is a widespread belief in the "divine right of kings". This view is most often sanctioned by African religions. She states that, in most cases, the divine rulers or kings are cultic individuals and their personalities are considered sacred. Such is the case with the Sweetheart of Nimbi Church's founder, who is considered sacred and all that he says derives from the divine. Hewitt (2016) points out that the mission of the church should focus on the life-giving, life-saving, and life-sustaining character and mission of the triune God pertinent to the contextual realities of the world. To this end, the task of the church is to evangelise a message that gives life and joy to all of humanity (Bevans, 2016).

Oduyoye (1995) advocates that women should not close their eyes and seal their lips if they need to denounce injustice. Such injustice may be evident in the that way the wives of the *Bashi Cingo* are excluded from the community and from performing other duties that assist with providing food. Oduyoye (1995) explains that prophetic works are not just meant for men in communities. She advises that denouncing social and religious injustices is necessary to allow the prophetic works that call on communities for healing. Oduyoye (1995:33) observes that, as nurturers of the generations, women should mediate the sense of urgency where they should "share the powers and mysteries of life without resorting to violence". In Oduyoye's (1995) view, women are not created to be violent, but they should work peacefully to restore their position and power. By doing this, women will save not only themselves and their families, but will save and heal the whole community, since "it is one person who kills the elephant for the whole people to feast on" (Oduyoye, 1995:33). This resonates with the fact that women too are bearers of knowledge, power and wisdom, since they are the nurturers of generations.

Conclusion

This chapter has demonstrated that some African rituals and power affect some wives of the *Bashi Cingo*, who are also church members. It illustrates how issues of power intersect with those of sexuality, humanity and the environment. These findings are unique to the Sweetheart of Nimbi Church. The chapter illustrates the role of the *Bashi Cingo*, who are assigned the task of embalming the dead body of the chief, in the church. Traditionally, the soup made from *ilanda* (black-eyed beans) has been used to smear over the body so that it does not rot. Because farming is linked to fertility, the wives of the *Bashi Cingo* are not allowed to be intimate with their husbands or to work in the fields or to draw water for fear that the women may pollute the land.

The findings show that Mary is one of the symbolic figures adopted by the Sweetheart of Nimbi Church. The chapter has portrayed how members imitate the characteristics of Mary as a form of humility. The findings also show that both holy patriarchy (a biblical-derived patriarchy) and African (Bemba) patriarchy are at work in the church founder's teachings and structural formulation. These teachings and formulation of the church structures are embedded in patriarchal ideologies, which include biblical, cultural and hegemonic values. In addition to the arguments by some feminist theologians outlined in the chapter, I have shown that these patriarchal ideologies are power structures that interlock with each other amongst the Bemba. In the biblical traditions, the church founder has portrayed himself as a patriarch, while in the royal Bemba tradition he projected himself as royalty.

In his teachings, Emilio has incorporated some Bemba cultural values to put across his biblical message. In the same way, members of the Sweetheart of Nimbi Church might be portrayed as enriching their beliefs with a Bemba culture associated with their spiritual beliefs. This is a paradox. For example, the members' imitation of Mary shows how they have received the preaching from their founder. They believe that Mary and the other women never went to draw water; they never went to the fields during the crucifixion of Jesus. It is a paradox because members of the church are motivated to imitate religious and cultural goals that cannot be reached, thereby imitating the unseen gestures.

References

Arbuckle, G.A. 2010. *Culture, inculturation, and theologians: A postmodern critique.* Collegeville, MN: Liturgical Press.

Becker, C.E. 1996. *Leading women: How church women can avoid leadership traps and negotiate the gender maze.* Nashville, TN: Abingdon Press.

Bevans, B.S. 2016. Transforming discipleship: Missiological reflections. In K.R. Ross, J. Keum, K. Avtzi & R.R. Hewitt (eds), *Ecumenical missiology: Changing landscapes and new conceptions of missions.* Oxford: World Council of Churches. 404-422.

Burlington, G. 1998. Topography of a Zambian storyland. *International Journal of Frontier Missions,* 15(2):75-81. https://bit.ly/3eGWK71 [Accessed 20 May 2017].

Burlington, G. 2008. God makes a world of difference: The dialectic of motivation and meaning at the creation of an African theistic worldview. *Missiology: An International Review,* (4):435-445. https://doi.org/10.1177/009182960803600403 [Accessed 12 April 2015].

Chishimba, E.M. 1976. Full image of God revealed in Africa: The keys to the full Bible. Unpublished.

Comaroff, J. & Comaroff, J. 1991. *Of Revelation and revelation: Christianity, colonialism, and consciousness in South Africa.* Vol. 1. London: University of Chicago Press. https://doi.org/10.7208/chicago/9780226114477.001.0001

Cunnison, I. 1959. *The Luapula peoples of Northern Rhodesia: Custom and history in tribal politics.* New York: Manchester University Press.

Fiorenza, E.S. 2011. *Transforming vision: Explorations in feminist theology.* Minneapolis, MN: Fortress Press. https://doi.org/10.2307/j.ctt22nm87s

Genesis. 2012. *ESV Global Study Bible.* Wheaton, IL: Crossway Publishers.

Hewitt, R.R. 2016. Together towards life and the context of the Global South. In: K.R. Ross, J. Keum, K. Avtzi & R.R. Hewitt (eds), *Ecumenical missiology: Changing landscapes and new conceptions of missions.* Oxford: World Council of Churches. 473-483.

Hinfelaar, H.F. 1994. *Bemba-speaking women of Zambia in a century of religious change: (1892-1992).* New York: Brill.

Loades, A. 1996. Mary. In: L. Isherwood & D. McEwan (eds), *An A to Z of feminist theology.* London: Sheffield Academic Press. 128-129.

Malina, B.J. 1983. *The New Testament world: Insights from cultural anthropology.* Atlanta, GA: John Knox Press.

Mbiti, J.S. 1999. *African religions and philosophy.* Nairobi: East African Educational Publishers.

Nuckolls, C.W. 1996. *The cultural dialectics of knowledge and desire.* Madison, WI: University of Wisconsin Press.

Oduyoye, M.A. 1979. The value of African religious beliefs and practices for Christian theology. In: K. Appiah-Kubi & S. Torres (eds), *African theology en route: Papers from the Pan-African Conference of Third World Theologians, December 17-23, 1977, Accra, Ghana.* Maryknoll, NY: Orbis Books. 109-116.

Oduyoye, M.A. 1995. *Daughters of Anowa: African women and patriarchy.* Maryknoll, NY: Orbis Books.

Oduyoye, M.A. 2001a. *Introductions in feminist theology: Introducing African women's theology.* Sheffield: Sheffield Academic Press.

Oduyoye, M.A. 2001b. The search for the two-winged theology. In: M.A. Oduyoye & M.A. Kanyoro (eds), *Talitha Qumi: Proceedings of the convocation of African women theologians 1989.* Accra-North: Sam-Woode Ltd. 31-56.

Purvis, S.B. 1993. *The power of the cross: Foundations for a Christian feminist ethic of community.* Nashville, TN: Abingdon Press.

Rakoczy, S. 2004. *In her name: Women doing theology.* Pietermaritzburg: Cluster Publications.

Ramphele, M. 1989. On being Anglican: The pain and the privilege in England. In: E.L. King, F. England &

T. Paterson (eds), *Bounty in bondage: The Anglican church in Southern Africa: Essays in honour of Edward King, Dean of Cape Town.* Johannesburg: Ravan Press. 177-190.

Richards, A.I. 1940. *Bemba marriage and present economic conditions.* Livingstone: The Rhodes-Livingstone Institute.

Scott, J.C. 1990. *Domination and the arts of resistance: Hidden transcripts.* New Haven, CT: Yale University Press.

Whiteley, W. 1950. *Bemba and related peoples of Northern Rhodesia.* London: International African Institute.

3

LIBERATING EARTH AND WOMEN IN POSTCOLONIAL WORSHIP SPACES IN GHANA

Georgina Kwanima Boateng[1]

Abstract

"The African is notoriously religious and takes his religion everywhere", says Mbiti (1969). Africa had solid religious beliefs and institutions, before colonisation brought Christianity. It was an all-embracing religion that was at the very fibre of the lifestyle of the African. Having revered Earth as the substance of creation, amongst other things, and seeing women as like Earth in the formation of life, the destinies of women and Earth have been linked together in the religious spaces of indigenous African worship and culture. In the sites of worship, in the language and objects of veneration, Earth was prominently featured and hence the lifestyles of the people would reflect this kind of veneration of Earth. This chapter seeks to interrogate the changing place of Earth in the journey from indigenous African worship from the time before the introduction of Christianity to contemporary African Christian worship, as well as how it affects the space and place of women. This will be addressed through an ecowomanist approach. This chapter proposes a rediscovery or reimagination of African Christian worship as a place for Earth participation by introducing Jesus into African indigenous Earth-centred worship. This proposition will be viewed through an ecowomanist reading of John 11:18-20, drawing attention to the garden as the site of the first worship of Jesus after his resurrection, woman as the first worshipper, and the gardener imagery as the first object.

Introduction and background

When I initially encountered ecotheology at the World Communion of Reformed Churches' Global Institute of Theology (GIT) a few years ago, I was a first-year student at the seminary. It was my first meeting with the field of theology. I was very enthused and sufficiently confused. I was also very curious and mortified at the same time. First, I was not familiar with ecological issues; secondly, I had never considered

---

1   Rev. Georgina Kwanima Boateng is a reverend minister of the Presbyterian Church of Ghana. [Email: gynaboat@yahoo.co.uk]

3

that ecology was or could ever be a theological issue, much less a church concern. I was utterly surprised, however, to see how much they would interact, theology and ecology. I felt many things – chagrin at my pastors for never mentioning issues around this in church, for keeping me and others stuck to a heaven-bound theology, upset with my one-year's worth of theological education for not having awakened me to this earlier – and then an urgency to go back and let everyone know about it. And then I returned to Ghana fresh from the GIT …

How was this 'letting everyone know' supposed to be accomplished? I had no idea. How was the church to be informed? I was lost and reflected on the question for a long time. This situation accounted, in part, for engaging in an ecological study of my church liturgy for my Master of Divinity studies. During my research, I came to the realisation of yet another intersection, the issue of gender and gender-based violence and how it is linked with violence against Earth. This chapter, therefore, is an attempt to engage the three areas of gender, ecology and worship by exploring the spaces of indigenous African worship, with particular reference to Ghana. It examines the link between women and Earth, and the role of women in the sacred worship with a focus on cultural practices that embrace or reject gender-based violence. Employing an ecowomanist approach, the chapter also examines the participation of Earth and women in colonial and postcolonial African Christian worship spaces by looking at Western mission churches and African Initiated Churches in Ghana.

This section of the chapter will interrogate how the postcolonial worship space accepts or rejects violence against women and Earth. Finally, the chapter will suggest a reimagination of African Christian worship as a liberating space for women and Earth by offering an ecowomanist reading of the resurrection narrative in John 20:11-18. This reimagining will draw attention to the garden as the site of the first worship after Jesus's resurrection, and the gardener imagery as the first object, noting also a woman as the first worshipper in this setting. I will propose revisiting the Earth-centred worship of indigenous Africa in Christian worship today by re-looking at our sites of worship, our language as well as our veneration of all of God's creation as co-gardeners with Jesus, the Christ, hoping to generate a theology that liberates both the Earth and African women from violence of any form.

Ecowomanism as a framework

Harris (2017:27) explains that ecowomanism "centers the religious, theological and spiritual perspectives of black women and women of color as they confront multilayered oppressions such as racism, classism, sexism, and environmental injustice". This chapter, in exploring the spirituality of indigenous Ghanaian society as well as women's involvement and Earth participation, will employ an ecowomanist perspective in its analysis. The research will lean towards a postcolonial ecowomanist analysis of Ghanaian worship spaces and will propose that we revisit indigenous religions in our Christian worship spaces, but from a liberating perspective for women and Earth. An ecowomanist reading of John 20:11-18 will be offered as a theological starting point for the research. An ecowomanist reading has been defined as entailing a multidimensional approach that seeks to read texts in the light of the intersection of the domination over Black women and other women of colour and the domination and abuse of nature (Kebaneilwe, 2015).

This methodology is appropriate for this research, because it deals with a particular case of women in the context of Ghana and their experiences of subjugation and its link to the exploitation of Earth. The research concerns itself with the spirituality of Africans, specifically Ghanaians, and the place of women and Earth, and how these have seen changes through the period of colonialism to the modern age. An ecowomanist perspective will help the research in its exploration of the multi-layered oppressions that comes from within the spirituality of the indigenes, that comes about as a result of the social location of a Ghanaian black woman in the colonial milieu, and that comes about as a result of a colonial heritage in the midst of half-hearted indigenous practices.

The spaces of indigenous African worship

Africans are as much a product of their religion as they are a product of culture, because the two are inseparable. As Kanyoro and Oduyoye (2005:1) note, we live on a "continent where religion shapes the life and thinking of the people". No wonder Mbiti (1969) would remark that Africans have been known to be notoriously religious and that Africans do not know how to exist without religion. African Traditional Religions (ATRs) have variously been misunderstood by colonial Christianity as savage, polytheistic and pagan (Okeke, Ibenwa & Okeke, 2017). This colonial view was derived from ATRs' belief that the spiritual dimension of life permeates the entire natural world and their awareness of human beings as part of a spiritual complex where each component of the natural world has its place. This belief leads to assigning sacramental value to things in nature such as bodies of water, forests, trees, hills and mountains. African indigenous traditions have, therefore, always had a healthy reverence for everything in nature, which has culminated in a culture which usually takes care of Earth. This is because some of the so-called ritual demands of nature (or gods) stem from indigenous knowledge of the land and what it requires to keep it fruitful and improve its capacity to support humanity. Examples can be seen in the allocation of certain forests as to be treated as sacred groves where no one could cut down trees or farm, land areas where only certain crops should be

MOTHER EARTH, MOTHER AFRICA & AFRICAN INDIGENOUS RELIGIONS

.3

planted, water bodies whose spirits abhorred impurity and would visit punishment on whole townships if filth were put into them, etc. (Acheampong, 2010).

Alolo (2007:47) notes that "[i]n ATRs, though both men and women generally participate in religious activities and make spiritual contributions to the wellbeing of their lives, families and societies, these religious roles are often distinct, operating on different planes". In many cultures in Africa, men are traditionally the spiritual leaders of the society at various levels (Afisi, 2010). Scholars are divided on the validity of this assertion, with some holding the view that women had equally prominent leadership roles in the religious, political and economic structure of traditional society (Amoah-Boampong & Agyeiwaa, 2019; Akyeampong & Obeng, 1995), yet others would acknowledge these roles but still affirm that men ultimately took the leading role (Oduyoye, 2005; Oduyoye, 2000; Kilson, 1976), a position that this chapter argues from. Falola and Amponsah (2012) discuss the various dimensions of these intricate dynamics in their book *Women's Role in Sub-Saharan Africa*. As spiritual leaders, men usually lead rituals, especially in public spaces, but women were never far from the rituals. Women also engaged in rituals, but their involvement was confined to private spaces (Alolo, 2007). Women were usually found in shrines and places of worship serving as priestesses, shrine servants and preparers of ritual meals. In some cases, especially with transitional rituals for women, we find women officiating. Asamoah-Gyadu (2005:55-56) asserts that "in the traditional religions of Africa generally, women dominate the priesthood, a vocation acquired principally through possession by a deity". Hence, women are seen as people who usually and frequently experience the divine through spirit possession, thereby becoming mediums who bring the message of the spirit world. Yet it is men who actually hold institutional and political authority. Alolo (2007) notes that in ATRs ideas and practices reveal three basic social principles: the subordination of women to men, differences between females and males, and the complementarity of males and females.

The continuity and survival of society preoccupies Africans, hence the two elements that are the sources of survival and procreation, that is Earth and women, require special attention. There are many rituals to ensure that nature, which was sacramental as well as the very source of livelihood, continued to flourish and remained favourable to the needs of humankind. In the same way, women underwent many rituals to keep them mindful of their role of procreation and of their duty to fulfil that role. In the next section, I explore the interconnectivity between Earth and women, looking at the negotiation of the tension between reverence for nature and patriarchal undertones.

Women and Earth in traditional Africa: A mould from the same clay

In viewing the spaces of traditional African religion and culture, we come to appreciate the role played by nature as sacramental and revered. This is because of the belief that nature is possessed by spirit beings or gods who are in control of the various aspects of life such as rain, harvests and fruitfulness. Elements of nature like land, water and the forests were seen as being the custodians of life itself as they provided the necessities for the survival of the human race. Many rituals were thus performed in homage to these 'deities' to ensure that they continued to provide for human survival. Rituals would therefore appear to be an attempt to control the elements of nature by maintaining harmonious relationships with the deities involved. Boaten (1998:45), writing about Ghanaian indigenous culture, affirms that "Earth has a spiritual power and that it is her spirit that makes plants grow; besides, she has the power of fertility". Resources such as land, water and forests have enjoyed being the sites and objects of indigenous worship, because they are inhabited by spirits that are conduits to the Supreme Being known to the Akan of Ghana as *Nyankopon*. In the language of worship, we also find that these spirits are continually referred to, for example, in the pouring of libations.[2] *Nyankopon* is first mentioned and then *Asaase Yaa* (Mother Earth) is mentioned next, indicating the significance attached to reverence for Earth (Yankah, 1995). Names of other spirit forms, like river gods and forest gods, may also be mentioned alongside those of ancestors. Again, in terms of language, the reference to Earth as *Asaase Yaa*, implying "Mother", indicates the regard for Earth as provider and sustainer of life (Boaten, 1998). Akan spirituality perceives Earth as a life-giver, an entity that has the ability to reproduce. Earth, therefore, is a woman and her fertility is revered because it is the source of sustenance and reproduction. The spiritual connection between *Asaase Yaa* (Mother Earth) and women in Africa cannot be overemphasised. They are moulds from the same clay.

Traditionally, in Ghana, especially amongst the Akan, men assumed custodianship of land. Land and land resources are vested not in individuals but in clans or lineages, and these clans are headed by men. Men therefore hold custodianship on behalf of the community. In terms of the land, women had the right to use land resources because they were part of the community. Women, who are burdened as mothers with the responsibility of procreation, nurturing and caring for the community, are usually dedicated to Earth and its ability to play its role in the survival needs of the community. Women therefore ensured that the rituals for the wholeness of Earth were observed to safeguard community survival.

---

2   Libation is the offering of a drink, a pouring out of a small quantity of wine, water or other liquid in a ceremonial act. Culturally, it is a form of prayer, both individual and communal.

3

Oduyoye (2005), in addressing patriarchy's manifestation in African rituals, asserts that traditionally, the rituals for women are more than that for men, which may be evidence of the superior spiritual strength of women compared to men. The rituals for women appear to be intended to constrain the use of such strength in the favour of men. Edet (2005:26) also notes that "women's rituals in Africa fall under ritual ideology which aims at controlling, in a conservative way, the behaviour, the mood, the sentiment, and the values of women for the sake of the community as a whole". The menstrual blood of women was the object of great mystery as it was celebrated as evidence of womanhood or ability to reproduce. However, at the same time, it was also seen as dangerous, unclean and capable of weakening the male species (Adasi, 2016). When women did not submit to these rituals, this was seen as breaking the wholeness of community and especially bringing misfortune to the male species. For men to progress and find wholeness in community, they must ensure that the women were conforming to all the rituals that were designed to keep women under subjugation. Sometimes, in ensuring this, violence against the woman was legitimised. Baden, Green, Otoo-Oyortey and Peasgood (1994) have observed that there is evidence to show that women themselves feel that certain kinds of behaviours on their part, which did not conform to the expected submissive roles, could be expected to lead to domestic violence and were therefore unwilling to report such violations to the authorities. It may be these same expectations that women have and the burden to maintain community wholeness that may have led women to be burdened again with rituals for maintaining the wholeness of Earth itself. It is easier for women to appreciate that rituals for Mother Earth, when not performed, may in like manner lead to some form of brokenness in society. While these rituals purported to ensure the wholeness of community, the wholeness of the woman was sometimes not factored into the 'complex calculations' of the wholeness of community. The wholeness of the woman was irrelevant.

Rituals involved in the *Trokosi* system, popular amongst the Ewe tribe in Ghana and the Gambaga witch camp in northern Ghana, are examples of rituals that do violence to women in the name of maintaining community wholeness. The system of *Trokosi*, which literally means 'slaves/wives of the gods', is the practice where a family offers a young virgin girl to the fetish priests to serve for a number of years or for a lifetime because of a crime committed by a member of the family. Such girls help in rituals at the shrine, as well as service the home and bed of the fetish priests. This is to ward off any evil that may befall the family. Issues around the Gambaga witch camp and others like it are even more complicated. Women, usually elderly, are dragged there by family or flee to the camps after being accused of witchcraft in the event of particular misfortunes befalling the family. The camp priests at Gambaga would go through some rituals and declare these women truly witches as accused and the women would have to accept the verdict. In Badoe's (2012) article on the witches of Gambaga, men's perception of women is summarised as follows: "*Abukari* (a camp priest) intervened again: 'Women are by nature witches,' he explained patiently, 'while men are more likely to be thieves'*." Other ways that women are abused is through puberty and widowhood rituals. Community wholeness is usually the objective of all this violence. A woman who submits herself to these and does not resist is revered.

While Earth is a spirit and has transcendental value because of its ability to ensure the sustenance of life, the traditional Akan also ascribe motherhood to Earth. Women are highly valued for the essential role they play in the continuity of human life through reproduction. Religious rituals are observed for both Earth and women to maintain sustenance and continuity. Women feel a special bond to Earth in ensuring that such rituals are not broken. In the following sections, I examine colonial and postcolonial worship spaces and how they have embraced and rejected the sacramental places of Earth and women in indigenous African worship.

Colonial religion and impact on Earth and women

The history of colonialism in Africa, and in Ghana in particular, is also the history of Christian churches that were established by Western missionaries. Historic mission churches (HMCs), or mainstream churches, is the term used refer to those churches whose presence is a direct result of missionary activities during the period of colonisation. In Ghana, mention can be made of the Catholic Church, the Presbyterian Church of Ghana, the Methodist Church Ghana, and the Evangelical Presbyterian Church of Ghana, amongst others. The Western missions that founded these churches had beliefs and practices that demystified the taboos and norms that defined the culture of care for the environment. In this way, the fear that used to be attached to observing taboos and observing rituals related to Earth was lost. They also demonised many of the rituals that were performed to preserve the sanctity of Earth and hence the wholeness of community. Therefore, apart from the fear being lost, the new Ghanaian Christians began to see those rituals as evil and having no value in sustaining community wholeness. The missions introduced an eschatological religion that was more interested in life in heaven than the life on Earth, and hence did not place much emphasis on conserving nature.

For most of these aforementioned churches, women had their place in the worship service, but it was certainly not in the ordained ministry or in the hierarchies of leadership. Women have been involved in evangelism, Bible study, literacy programmes, teaching, nurturing the children's ministry, and financial support of the church (Adasi, 2016). Women were mainly schooled by other Western women, who were their colonisers, in how to make good supportive and submissive wives to their Christian husbands. This kind of education did not prepare women to take any kind of lead or administrative roles in church or worship. The double disempowerment of women in this situation is that they were also not prepared, with this kind of education, to take their place as co-owners of land, in community with African men, within the scope of the new ways in which land was administered and used in colonial Africa.[3] This was a far cry from the indigenous religions where women could lead rituals and become priestesses and mediums.

These points are not to suggest that all the churches' practices were negative towards women and Earth, but they indicate that the sacramental rituals that indigenous religion performed on account of women and Earth were minimised or completely rejected. Colonialism took away from the land, because it dispossessed it of its sacramental value. In the same way, it took away whatever sacramentalism was attributed to women in the religio-cultural indigenous environment by introducing religious systems in which there was no place for women in mainstream worship.

Postcolonial worship spaces and the place of women and Earth

The struggle for independence in Africa was a struggle to gain back control of the land from colonisers (Sackeyfio, 2012). It was no less a struggle for the freedom for an enslaved land as for an enslaved people. However, if women had traditionally been linked to the land, during the struggle for independence the people had clearly lost their memory, for the place of women was defined by a lack of reverence for and further subjugation to the male figure after independence (Klingshirn, 1973). Earth was liberated, but not along with its sacramentality as this was lost to colonial religious influence. Mainstream churches, although they had struggled for church autonomy during the independence struggle, retained a legacy of Western theologies, liturgy and practices in which there was no place for reverence of Earth. Such reverence was seen as unchristian. Members of mainstream churches who attempted to infuse indigenous culture into Christian worship were resisted to the point where they had to leave the churches or were excommunicated. Churches initiated by Africans were thus formed by some of these people as a way to resist the Western hold on Christian

---

3   In precolonial Ghana, land was not owned or managed by one person but by a clan or family head in a land tenure system. Members of the clan or family had access to the land use and were all communally responsible for keeping every ritual demand of the land. Strangers underwent necessary rituals to be accepted into the family before clan land was allocated to them. Colonial powers did not understand or appreciate this and brought their own modes of ownership and land use, which was usually based on economic value. They transplanted their Western ways of land ownership and management to Africa through land reforms where land ownership was individualised. Commodifying land was a way of disempowering Ghanaian women from ownership and use of land as they are economically disadvantaged (Boateng, 2017; Quansah, 2012).

worship. These churches, also known as African Initiated Churches (AICs), have been established as a way to resist the colonisation of religious spaces and reconnect with African spirituality. I will examine the AICs to discover the place of *Asaase Yaa*[4] and women. I will also subsequently examine the space of colonial religious practices in a postcolonial environment that had been influenced by the AICs with a view to discover how the place of women and Earth had evolved.

African Initiated Churches

African Initiated Churches, also called African Independent Churches or AICs, are churches that sprouted as a way of bridging the gap between mainstream churches and the African cultural world view. Oduro (2016:3) indicates that AICs are so called because

> [m]ost of them initially, clamoured for religious independence from the western mission-founded churches. Consequently, many leaders of the AICs either left western mission-founded churches in protest or were excommunicated by leaders of the western mission churches. The chief objective of their struggle for religious independence was to worship God and formulate theology in the context of their worldview, culture, environment and pre-Christian religious experiences.

In AICs, the emphasis is on Holy Spirit experiences and hence mysticism. This has led to their being given the name *Sunsum Sore* (Spiritual Churches) in Ghana. Examples of AICs include Church of the Lord (*Aladura*) of Nigeria, as well as the Musama Disco Christo Church, Church of the Twelve Apostles, Kristo Asafo (Christ Reformed Church), and Memeneda Gyidifo (The Saviour Church), all in Ghana. All of the churches listed above are breakaways from mainstream churches or Western mission-founded churches (Oduro, 2016). AICs blend the practices of African Indigenous Religion with Christian worship in an attempt to create an authentic African religion.

AICs believe in faith healing and therefore emphasise praying to God for healing instead of going to the hospital or using medicines. In their faith healing, we find the use of traditional methods and use of nature's resources, which means that nature is accorded some amount of transcendental value. For example, blessed rain became a source of curing influenza and bubonic plagues through the prophecy of Sophia Odunlami of the *aladura* faith (Oduro, 2016). Also, holy water, salt and spirit-directed herbs have been used in faith-healing processes (Oduro, 2018). These natural elements were seen as agencies of healing; that is, the Spirit, through prayer, uses these elements to heal. The practice of faith healing in this way mimics indigenous

---

4   I use *Asaase Yaa* here instead of the usual Earth to show that I mean Earth in the perception of Traditional African worship: Earth as revered, as life-giver and sustainer, and as a spiritual force.

3

cultural healing practices where nature's resources are used. AICs, however, cannot be said to hold the same reverence for nature as ATRs do. AICs preach and teach that people must break away from their indigenous gods.

However, because of their emphasis on the Holy Spirit, AICs are more spiritual in the way Africans are spiritual and this translates into prophesying under the power of the Spirit, extended and extempore prayers, fasting, speaking in tongues, drumming, and dancing. Many of these activities of AICs' spirituality included women. Even though male dominance in the forming of AICs can be seen with the likes of Wade Harris, Samson Oppong, John Swatson, William Egyanka Appiah, etc., mention is also made of women who were significantly involved in the development of AICs like Grace Tani, Christiana Abiodun Akinsowun, and Hannah Barnes (Novieto, 2013). As Asamoah-Gyadu (2005:59) notes, "[t]hrough the ministry of the Sunsum sore (Spiritual churches), women broke free of the auxiliary, marginal and subservient role fashioned for them in the various traditional Western mission denominations." In many of these churches, women are usually at liberty to use their gifts and graces as given by God without the traditional roles assigned becoming a hindrance. The efficacy of the ministry of women in such religious spaces is affirmed through the evident leadership roles women play, especially as prophetesses, mediating the divine to congregants. Yet in some AICs, notably the Church of the Lord (*Aladura*) in Ghana, women who are on their period have had to sit at the back of the church because they are regarded as unclean (Oduro, 2016). AICs are doing their bit in indigenising worship, but not necessarily with a view to building a sustainable relationship with Earth or liberating women.

Postcolonial mainstream churches' worship space

The success rates of the AICs in indigenising worship has led to increases in their attendance numbers and have given mainstream churches something to reflect on. Mainstream churches are therefore taking significant steps to put in place reforms to make their worship more suited to the culture of the people. Thus worship forms such as extempore prayer, praying in local languages, clapping, singing local choruses and dancing were adopted. We also find mainstream churches indulging indigenous culture by opening up more for practices of ATRs like creating space within their worship services to have the chiefs and people of a town to have a thanksgiving service with the church for a successful festival, as well as acknowledging chiefs by creating designated seats for them in their places of worship. Others have also created church liturgies for some traditional rituals. We can, for example, speak of widowhood rites that the churches have adopted into their liturgies.

Concerning women's participation, mainstream churches in the postcolonial period have battled with the inclusion of women in worship, even though women have taken up more important roles in their worship over the course of time. In the case of Presbyterian Church of Ghana (PCG), for example, it took over twenty years to take a decision to ordain women (Opare-Kwakye, 2018) and even after such a decision was finally taken in 1976, the ratio of women to men in the ordained ministry leaves much to be desired. One of the reasons for the lag in taking the decision, according to Adasi (2016), was that women were believed to be unclean and capable of making everything else unclean if allowed to minister. The situation of the PCG is not much different from the other mainstream churches in Ghana, which currently ordain women. An important point to note is the traditional roles that ordained women have played in the church. For example, ordained women are expected to be silent[5] associate ministers, or to take up chaplaincy roles in hospitals and schools, and attend to issues affecting women. But the situation keeps improving, although slowly.

The attempts of AICs to build an African-oriented worship and the adjustments being made by mainstream churches to bridge the gap between their Western heritage and authentic African worship are commendable and moving in the right direction. This is even more so in a world where climate change and an imminent irreversible disaster for humankind unfolds ever so rapidly and urgent calls are being made for mitigation measures. Progress made in development is damaging indigenous spiritual systems; Westernisation has dampened African sensitivity to nature and is still present in neocolonialism. Thus, Christians must turn to the scriptures to find resources within it that teach us to develop our sensitivity to the environment that sustains us. Therefore, to lend even more impetus to the need for Christian religious spaces in Africa, notably Ghana, to continue to explore safer and more liberating practices towards women and Earth, this chapter hopes to add to already existing theologies (Kebaneilwe, 2015; Dube, 2015; Masenya, 2003) by offering an ecowomanist reading of the resurrection story of John 20:11-18.

An ecowomanist reflection on John 20:11-18

The book of John is a fascinating book by many standards; however, this researcher's fascination with it is based on the book's copious use of ecological terminology. For example, in the seven 'I Am' sayings alone, five of them employ ecological terminology: bread, light, shepherd, vine and life. The incarnation also offers its own ecological inference by suggesting that the divine became a part of Earth community. Imagery such as garden, water, bread, sheep and others engage ecology in ways that

---

5   Adasi (2016:99) records the words spoken to Reverend Dora Ofori Owusu, the first ordained female missionary of the PCG at her ordination as "[r]emember you are a woman and you would better keep silent".

cannot be missed. In line with African spirituality, the place and events of Jesus's resurrection from the dead are worthy of being accorded a sacred space.

In the resurrection account in John 20:11-18, three things of interest come together: the resurrected Jesus, the garden where he first appeared, and the person to whom he first appeared and who first worshipped him – a woman. Using a reverse hermeneutical approach,[6] we read Black indigenous African culture into the texts and propose that African Christian Worship revisits an Earth-centred worship and takes a liberating stand for women in spaces of worship.

John 20:11-18 is the account of Mary Magdalene's return to the tomb after she had gone to report the Lord's disappearance to Simon and the other disciple, and they had come to look and left the scene. In the passage, we note some important points. Mary persisted at the scene and was unafraid to show her emotions (John 20:11). Mary had a keener sense to perceive the angelic presence and also communicate with them (John 20:12-13). Jesus's first post-resurrection appearance was to a woman (John 20:14). Jesus was taken for the gardener by Mary (John 20:15). A woman was the first to worship the risen Jesus by calling him 'Teacher' not 'Master' (John 20:16). And the first person to be commissioned to spread the message of the gospel was a woman and she was commissioned by Jesus (John 20:17).

That Mary Magdalene stayed behind and wept displays a marked trait of women as more 'heart than head', a trait that has been frowned upon by a male-dominated world as illogical and weak. Yet, it is such a 'weak' moment that Jesus chooses to honour. Mary Magdalene's persistence in searching for the body of Jesus is striking, especially in relation to the two disciples who had gone home after finding Jesus's body missing (Varghese, 2009). Some commentaries, as in *The preacher's outline and sermon Bible* (Leadership Ministries Worldwide, 2000), tell us that Mary saw the angels in the tomb, while the two disciples who had came earlier did not (John 20:1-10), because the angels came in later. But I choose to argue that Mary was more tuned in to the spiritual, which is why she saw the angels and the two disciples did not. This is consistent with how Africans have traditionally seen women as more open to the divine and, therefore, have served more in the role of diviners and priestesses. It is curious then that Mary, with that heightened sense of awareness, still supposes Jesus to be the gardener, whereas she had not thought of the two angels as gardeners. I submit that Jesus's posture could only have been one of tender care towards the garden in which they were standing for Mary to make such an assumption. The controversial chapter by Audlin (2016) points out that the text

---

6   For the purposes of this chapter, we will explain a reverse hermeneutical approach as reading the text, not particularly to determine what the author meant, but with a contextual approach from an ecological perspective but that will also read Black African indigenous culture into the text.

makes no reference to a mistake having been made on the part of Mary in thinking Jesus was the gardener, but that this had been read into the text by interpreters. The fact that Jesus did not correct her but only called her by name leads us to this conclusion. Also, Mary's response was not 'Lord' or 'Master' but 'Teacher', which shows us that at that point Mary recognised the risen Lord as someone who was instructing her. Can we therefore learn from the Teacher who attends to the garden as first priority after resurrection? Perhaps women's concern for land and land rituals in the African cultural milieu may be explained with this lesson that Jesus taught the woman on such an august occasion! Referring to Jesus as Teacher also ensures that we do not miss the point that Mary was a disciple of Jesus. Finally, Jesus commissions her to go carry the good news to the disciples; she was the apostle to the apostles.

There is no denying that Jesus had acted in a contrary manner in doing the things that he did. First, tending to the garden upon his resurrection, while telling humanity not to cling to him as he had to go to the Father (John 20:17); humans always believe we are more important in the hierarchy of things than the rest of creation. Second, Jesus did not resent staying at the tomb and receiving his first act of worship there in such an unlikely place. Jesus could have chosen to go to the temple, but instead he chose the garden. In his lifetime, he has always occupied such unlikely places: at his birth, he was found in the stall of animals; at his arrest, in the garden; at his transfiguration, on the mountaintop; in his prayer times, in the garden and in hills. Perhaps Christians will have to think again about the way we have looked upon indigenous sacred places of worship as evil. Perhaps we could employ a botanically inspired theological hermeneutic to decode indigenous practices and stories to discover their environmental value, as Pu (2017) suggested, to reclaim the knowledge of sacred sites of indigenous religions.

Jesus also commissions a woman to share such weighty news without expecting her to be different from what women are expected to be – that is weepy, persistent, afraid and excited. Who women are does not make them the weaker sex or inferior. The world today has no time for who women are, and many women who excel and find themselves in places traditionally reserved for men sometimes have been forced to reject their true nature and act like men. In the midst of the patriarchy of Israel at that time, Jesus chose the women, showing that women are not intrinsically weak or inferior, or the bane of the male species. The story of the fall of humanity has often been referred to in justifying the need to curtail the strength of women. But this researcher maintains that, if Eve introduced Adam to the apple, Mary Magdalene and the other women (in the other resurrection narratives in Matthew, Mark and Luke) introduced the new Adam to men. If men, since the fall, have feared women and therefore sought to subjugate and tame them, men, after the resurrection, should celebrate women and encourage their strengths and potential.

The call of Jesus at the resurrection is a call to an Earth-centred worship, one that not only reveres Earth for what it can give to the human race but for Earth's sake, for being a creation of God for which God also cares; not revered for its fertility only, but seen in terms of being a part of all that the love of God has redeemed. The redeemed person must therefore be seen to celebrate their redemption alongside Earth. Women's productivity and sexuality are also to be celebrated and not something to be feared. They have to be given every opportunity to be all that they can be spiritually, emotionally, intellectually and physically as this is what brings about wholeness in a broken community. To proclaim Jesus as Lord would then mean to give the space to women to assume their full potential; it means to recognise that Earth-care is not about taming Earth but about existing in community with Earth.

Conclusion

This chapter has attempted to trace the changing place of Earth and women in African worship spaces, beginning with an exploration of the worship spaces of indigenous African worship and then considering postcolonial African Christian worship spaces in the particular case of Ghana. I have discovered that indigenous religions in Africa had a healthy reverence for, and assigned sacramental value to, Earth and women because of their ability to ensure survival and fulfil procreative needs as well as their close connection to Earth. Patriarchal undertones in indigenous culture, however, ensured that women were subjugated to the male figure through various rituals, taboos and religious injunctions, and they suffered violence as a result. Colonialism further entrenched the subjugation of women by stripping away any reverence they may have enjoyed and also took away the sacramentality of Earth in the culture of the people. Hence, postcolonial worship spaces have tendencies towards anthropocentrism and patriarchy. I have proposed, through an ecowomanist reflection on John 20:11-18, that African Christian worship should revisit an Earth-centred worship and embrace liberating perspectives for women as Jesus teaches us in the gospel narrative.

References

Acheampong, E. 2010. The role of Ghanaian culture and tradition in environmental stability. *Modern Ghana*. https://bit.ly/30rThE9 [Accessed 24 July 2019].

Adasi, G.S. 2016. *Gender and change: Roles and challenges of ordained women ministers of the Presbyterian Church of Ghana*. Accra: Gavoss Educational PLC.

Afisi, O.T. 2010. Power and womanhood in Africa: An introductory evaluation. *The Journal of Pan African Studies*, 3(6):229-238.

Akyeampong, E. & Obeng, P. 1995. Spirituality, gender and power in Asante history. *The International Journal of African Historical Studies*, 28(3):481-508. https://doi.org/10.2307/221171

Alolo, N.A. 2007. African Traditional Religions and concepts of development: A background paper. *Religions and Development Research Program*. http://epapers.bham.ac.uk/1498/1/Alolo_2007.pdf [Accessed 29 July 2019].

Amoah-Boampong, C. & Agyeiwaa, C. 2019. Women in pre-colonial Africa: West Africa. In: O. Yacob-Haliso & T. Falola (eds), *The Palgrave Handbook of African Women's Studies*. Cham: Palgrave Macmillan. https://doi.org/10.1007/978-3-319-77030-7_126-1

Asamoah-Gyadu, J.K. 2005. *African charismatics: Current developments within independent indigenous Pentecostalism in Ghana*. Leiden: Brill.

Audlin, J.D. 2016. No mistake: Mary was right to think Jesus was the gardener. In: V. Baru (ed), *The Gospel of John: The original version restored and translated*. https://bit.ly/3fKgjgb

Baden, S., Green, C., Otoo-Oyortey, N. & Peasgood, T. 1994. Background paper on gender issues in Ghana: Report prepared for the West and North Africa Department, Department of Overseas Development (DFID), UK. *BRIDGE (development – gender), Report 19*. Brighton: Institute of Development Studies, University of Sussex. https://bit.ly/3hgcUGd [Accessed 5 August 2019].

Badoe, Y. 2012. Representing witches in contemporary Ghana: Challenges and reflections on making 'The Witches of Gambaga'. *Feminist Africa*, 16:82-97.

Boaten, B.A. 1998. Traditional conservation practices: Ghana's example. *Research Review (NS)*, 14(1):42-51.

Boateng, P.K. 2017. Land access, agricultural land use changes and narratives about land degradation in the Savannahs of North-east Ghana during the pre-colonial and colonial periods. *Social Sciences*, 6(35):1-26. https://doi.org/10.3390/socsci6010035

Dube, M.W. 2015. "And God saw that it was very good": An earth-friendly theatrical reading of Genesis. *Black Theology*, 13(3):230-246. https://doi.org/10.1179/1476994815Z.00000000060

Edet, R. 2005. Christianity and African women's rituals. In: M. Kanyoro & M.A. Oduyoye (eds), *The will to arise: Women, tradition and the church in Africa*. Eugene, OR: Wipf and Stock. 25-39.

Falola, T. & Amponsah, N.A. 2012. *Women's roles in Sub-Saharan Africa*. Santa Barbara, CA: Greenwood ABC CLIO.

Harris, M.L. 2017. Ecowomanism: Black women, religion, and the environment. *The Black Scholar*, 46(3):27-39. https://doi.org/10.1080/00064246.2016.1188354

John. 2001. *The Holy Bible: English Standard Version*. Wheaton, IL: Crossway.

Kanyoro, M.R.A. & Oduyoye, M.A. 2005. *The will to arise: Women, tradition and the church in Africa.* Eugene, OR: Wipf and Stock.

Kebaneilwe, M.D. 2015. The good creation: An eco-womanist reading of Genesis 1-2. *Old Testament Essays*, 28(3):694-703. https://doi.org/10.17159/2312-3621/2015/v28n3a8

Kilson, M. 1976. Women in African traditional religions. *Journal of Religion in Africa*, 8(2):133-143. https://doi.org/10.2307/1594783

Klingshirn, A. 1973. The social position of women in Ghana. *Law and Politics in Africa, Asia and Latin America*, 6(3):289-297. https://doi.org/10.5771/0506-7286-1973-3-289

Leadership Ministries Worldwide. 2000. *The Preacher's Outline and Sermon Bible.* Vol. 1. Chattanooga, TN: Leadership Ministries Worldwide.

Masenya, M. 2003. A *bosadi* (womanhood) reading of Proverbs 31:10-31. In: M. Dube (ed), *Other ways to read the Bible: African women and the Bible.* Geneva: WCC. 145-157.

Mbiti, J.S. 1969. *African religions and philosophy.* Oxford: Heinemann.

Novieto, E.E. 2013. Women leaders in Ghanaian Pentecostal / Charismatic Churches. PhD thesis, University of Ghana, Legon.

Oduro, T.A. 2016. *Church of the Lord (Brotherhood): History, challenges and growth.* Accra: SonLife.

Oduro, T.A. 2018. The African Independent Churches in Ghana. In: J.K. Asamoah-Gyadu (ed), *Christianity in Ghana: A postcolonial history.* Accra: Sub-Saharan Publishers.

Oduyoye, M.A. 2000. *Hearing and knowing: Theological reflections on Christianity in Africa.* Accra: Sam-Woode.

Oduyoye, M.A. 2005. Women and ritual in Africa. In: M. Kanyoro & M.A. Oduyoye (eds), *The will to arise: Women, tradition and the church in Africa.* Eugene, OR: Wipf and Stock. 9-24.

Okeke, C.O., Ibenwa, C.N. & Okeke, G.T. 2017. Conflicts between African Traditional Religion and Christianity in Eastern Nigeria: The Igbo example. *SAGE Open Journal*, April-June:1-10. https://doi.org/10.1177/2158244017709322

Opare-Kwakye, N. 2018. Presbyterian Church of Ghana. In: J.K. Asamoah-Gyadu (ed), *Christianity in Ghana: A postcolonial history.* Accra: Sub-Saharan Publishers.

Pu, X. 2017. Turning weapons into flowers: Ecospiritual poetics and politics of Bön and ecowomanism. In: M. Harris (ed.), *Ecowomanism, religion and ecology.* Leiden: Brill. https://doi.org/10.1163/9789004352650_005

Quansah, E.S.T. 2012. Land tenure system: Women's access to land in a cosmopolitan context. *OGIRISI: A New Journal of African Studies*, 9:141-161. https://doi.org/10.4314/og.v9i1.8

Sackeyfio, N. 2012. The politics of land and urban space in colonial Africa. *History in Africa*, 39:293-329. https://doi.org/10.1353/hia.2012.0005

Varghese, J. 2009. *The imagery of love in the Gospel of John.* Rome: Gregorian and Biblical Press.

Yankah, K. 1995. *Speaking for the Chief: Okyeame and the politics of Akan royal oratory.* Indianapolis, IN: Indiana University Press.

4

THE ROLE OF RAINMAKERS IN AWAKENING ENVIRONMENTAL CONSCIOUSNESS

A postcolonial ecocritical analysis

Kenosi Molato[1]

Abstract

The most stressful periods in Setswana cultural history are mostly those that were dominated by extended drought. The cosmological interpretation of the cause of droughts is that the ancestors were displeased with the condition of the land and the harm inflicted on it had to be atoned for. In Setswana cosmology, the only person who could perform this act was the rainmaker. His/her role involved appeasing the ancestors and educating the people on the importance of ensuring harmony between nature and the ancestors. Under the direction of the rainmaker, the ceremonies and associated dances were practised and executed at specific times in the natural cycle, thereby expressing the community's gratitude for the roles of the environment and the ancestors, as well as promoting the understanding of cosmological interconnectedness. Following their mid-nineteenth century arrival in the Batswana tribal territories that constitute modern-day Botswana, the missionaries abolished the rainmaker leadership role, replaced it with Christian prayer meetings, and initiated environmental injustice in the land. This chapter utilises postcolonial and ecocritical theories to examine the cultural and environmental impact of this abolition and the waning of environmental ethics in Botswana.

Introduction

Our current global environmental crises are dynamic, demanding diverse approaches to conservation and sustainable solutions that differ from one region to another. Thus, ecological solutions employed in one country may differ from those applied in another country. However, contemporary ecological solutions to environmental conditions are mostly Western in conception and argue that traditional African ecological solutions, as utilised by indigenous cultural groups in order to reduce

---

1   Mr Kenosi Molato is an ecotheologian and he works as a researcher at SHINE Africa Project in Gaborone, Botswana. [Email: kenosimolato@gmail.com]

the impact of environmental crisis, are inadequate to address our current African ecological crises. Moreover, some have even suggested that African religions have nothing to offer in the domain of solutions to environmental degradation. In consequence, this has led Africans to neglect the preserved wisdom of practices, which their forefathers imparted from generation to generation to reduce the negative environmental impact of routine procedures on their societies. This chapter seeks to demonstrate that in the precolonial era that preceded the Bechuanaland Protectorate and independent Botswana, it was acknowledged by the people that there was one person entrusted with the responsibility of taking care of the environment – for the purpose of this chapter this person is defined as the man or the woman of nature, referred to as the rainmaker. Furthermore, the rainmaker's role was not only limited to the nominal rainmaking, but covered a range of environmental functions that included: atoning for the land when the environment was harmed, raising ecological awareness amongst the people, and promoting a general preoccupation with harmonising society and nature "lest the land would vomit them out from the earth". Be that as it may, the missionary agenda in Setswana communities as outlined by John and Jean Comaroff (1991:190) was "seizing the hearts and minds of its wild inhabitants, rousing them from a state of nature by cultivating their self-consciousness". The description carries several ironies. Here were the missionaries rejecting the rainmaker's role of introducing to his/her people an awareness of their oneness with nature and categorising this awareness of the existing order of the Setswana world as primitive. As Comaroff and Comaroff (1991:190) suggest, the missionaries interfered with the Setswana sense of oneness with nature by promoting a state of self-consciousness that the ecological techniques of the rainmaker and the unity of the Setswana community with nature were uncivilised. From a modern perspective, there is the additional irony in that back in England industrialisation had unleashed a massive negative force on the environment and destroyed the agrarian existence of a large part of the population. In consequence, the transformative Christianity of the missionaries sowed the seeds of environmental degradation and immorality in Batswana society. This chapter uses a postcolonial ecocritical analysis to examine the historical encounter between the traditional role of the rainmaker in Setswana cosmology and the historical impact of the dismissive view of that role in the Western world view imposed by the missionaries in relation to the environment and the subsequent colonisation of indigenous ecological knowledge.

Postcolonial ecocritical analysis

The African colonisers were interested in replicating their own image in the nations they conquered and subdued. This implies that they represented and carried their cultural ideas and aimed to instil them into the people whom they had subjugated and triumphed over. Moreover, their world view was generally different from the African world view, including what the relationship between humans and the natural environment was. This led not only to the colonisation African nations but the colonisation of African environmental thinking. This interdisciplinary chapter consequently draws on postcolonial and ecocritical theories. These theories show the unavoidable link between humanity and the environment, and that the influences that have harmed the people are fundamentally linked to those that have harmed the environment (Mason, Jones & Steenkamp, 2014:2). The correlation between nature and people in the African world view implies that colonisation affected both the environment and African people. This presupposes that an African environmental consciousness preceded colonisation and was eroded by Western philosophies concerning nature and man in nature. Postcolonial theory is concerned with "excavating or reimagining the marginalised past: history from below and along borders, such as transnational axes of migrant memory" (Mason et al., 2014:2). Furthermore, postcolonial theory investigates the reverberation of colonial themes and their re-emergence in the "post"-colonial era. In effect, colonialism cannot be archived simply as a record of the past, because it continues to reverberate in the inextricability of the past and present (Dube, 2012:3). Ecocriticism, according to Mason et al. (2014:2), is concerned with "examining the relationship between the biophysical environment and the texts such as climate change, soil and water through the lens of environmental theory". Ecocriticism studies ecological knowledge and the experiences of the people relating to nature in order to examine the ethical issues inherent in our concept of the environment. Ecocriticism may be distinguished from postcolonial theory in its concern with humanity as a component of the biophysical environment. Thus, in this chapter postcolonial theory is used as a historical tool to evaluate the impact of the missionary movement on the Batswana, while ecocriticism is used to investigate the precolonisation relationship between the Batswana people and nature.

Setswana community in harmony with nature

In Setswana cosmology, nature encapsulates the entire world and includes both living and nonliving things, visible and invisible powers, the natural phenomena, land, rivers, bushes, forests, animals, birds, insects, minerals and whatever they perceived was not of human origination, but created by God (*Modimo*) to whom they owed allegiance. Batswana were surrounded by nature, lived in nature and were defined by nature. Consequently, they perceived the natural world as an immense womb that they relied on for food, shelter and medicine. As Edward Kanyeki (2018:1) notes, "nature to Africans was a womb, warm and pulsating with life and reality."

4

The Setswana cultural concept of the harmony of nature and humanity cannot be overemphasised, for it is through this that the community perceived their entitlement to benefit and enjoy the goods derived or sourced from the environment. True communal spirituality in Setswana culture entailed being in tune with one's surroundings. The ecotheologian, Sallie McFague (2013:35) defined the term 'communal spirituality' as "recognizing that all life is interrelated and interdependent". This term also refers to the spiritual union that exists between nature and humanity at large. Therefore, a 'spiritual connectedness' is created when this communion is harnessed in the society. The ultimate goal of the community in Setswana cosmology is to be in tune with nature or of continuously being at one with nature. This harmonious relationship between nature and the community is perceived to constitute a blessing upon the community and nature at large. The concept of being in tune and at one with nature is encapsulated in totems and phrases such as "I'm an elephant" or "I'm a monkey", which are used by individuals to introduce themselves to another and exemplify a society which strives to be continuously in harmony with nature. This state of being in tune ensured mutual respect in engaging with other clans to which they verbalised their interconnectedness being in harmony with nature. It is this 'interconnectedness' to which the Comaroffs (1991:194) point in stating that the Tswana people were in a state of nature before the missionary influence was initiated. The implication is that the people could not be separated from nature, and it was nature that defined them and gave them an identity. Gabriel Setiloane (1985:4) notes that the Bantu phrase "I'm the son of the soil" deserves a literal interpretation and that in the uncontaminated African world view, human beings constituted a part of the soil in body, soul and mind.

Three factors are intertwined in the importance of being in harmony with nature in Setswana cosmology: (i) the scarcity of rain, (ii) interconnectedness with the ancestors, and (iii) spiritual communion.

The scarcity of rain

Rain in rural Botswana is critical for survival and constitutes a sign that the ancestors and nature are satisfied and happy with the people. However, it should be borne in mind that in the Botswana ecological system rain is scarce (Landau, 1993:1). Paul Landau points out that a good harvest requires approximately 250 mm of rain during the agricultural season and that for fifty years this level has not been received in the village of Molepolole (1993:1). The natural shortage of rain enhanced the desire to live in harmony with nature as the belief structure conveyed the conception that rain was provided by the ancestors and God (Modimo). Therefore, the community is supposed to respect and honour the taboos of the ecological traditions that maintain the society in a condition that is favourable to the ancestors and environment.

Failure to do this has an inherent implication that the society is morally degenerate, resulting in drought and famine in the land. For example, in 2000 Botswana was blessed with extensive rains. Towards the end of that year, the nation welcomed home the physical remains of El Negro, a Tswana man of unknown tribal origin who had died c.1825 and whose bones had been exhumed and displayed in parts of Europe. The arrival of El Negro's bones was followed by a drought which began in 2001, the cause of which was interpreted in several ways by the Batswana. Jan-Bart Gewald (2002:38) noted four interpretations, which included one that reasoned that El Negro had been a man whose burial had either angered the ancestors or that he, personally, was angry. This disrespect had interrupted the social harmony with nature. In general, the natural scarcity of rainfall encourages Setswana communities to be alert and vigilantly to examine their relationship with their environment.

The interconnectedness with the ancestors

James Amanze notes that in Setswana culture the ancestors are buried in the ground (2002:68). They are not perceived as 'dead', but their state is alluded to in phrases such as "those who have left us" and "those who are no longer with us" (2002:68). The ancestors are concerned with the fabric of their society and its productivity. Amanze (2002:68) writes: "The ancestral spirits are also concerned with the fertility of their descendants, the fertility of the soil, and the availability of food, upon which the other two are dependent." Thus, the ancestors are interconnected with nature because of their final resting place in the soil, and hence society must be in tune with nature to maintain harmony with the ancestors. To be in harmony with the ancestors is to be in tune with nature and tampering with nature implies tampering with the environmental ethics granted at the behest of the ancestors. Environmental malpractice may cause misfortune to come upon a man's family in the form of miscarriages, livestock reproductivity of only male calves, and crop failures. Furthermore, some Setswana communities such as the Babirwa believe that the ancestors inhabit and surround the places where they live. Paul Landau (1993:8) writes: "They also believe the ancestors traverse the Tswapong Hills and police the use of the natural resources of the district. Consequently, placating the ancestors refreshed the Pedi's relationship with the land, by mapping the contentment of the human community in natural and geographic terms." The ancestors are the true owners of nature, which entails that those who are alive are to be good stewards of the environment. Failure to adhere to these ethics implies that the living are living in disobedience to the indigenous ecological ethics which govern the community. Consequently, this can harm the environment.

Spiritual communion

Nature in Setswana cosmology is synonymous with spirituality and is not perceived in the Western abstract form, but as it manifests in material form. It is believed that nature is the abode of spirituality; hence, the ancestors and ancestresses engulf the environment in sacred places such as rivers, hills and trees. Therefore, the environment is the place of worship and worshippers may enhance their spirituality by visiting these sacred places to commune with the living dead. This spiritual communion is central to the survival of an individual in a collective group because one's spirituality connects one with the guardians of the community, namely the ancestors.

One of the requirements of the person who has been called by the ancestors to be a traditional healer is being able to live in nature for many weeks without the assistance of or interference by others. The apprentice is tested on whether he is able to gain experiential knowledge by being intimate with nature. Thus, the traditional healer's role is to guide those who seek spiritual intimacy with nature, a calling that demands that the practitioner of traditional medicine must be capable of seeking spiritual guidance from nature. The indigenous worshippers' insights into the future through nature and the signs depicted require interpretation by a skilled traditional healer trained to read these signs (Kanyike, 2018:1). Hence, nature is an ally or colleague in this world, assisting the people in the avoidance of bad luck and death.

Since Setswana culture relies on nature for survival, it adheres to environmental ethics such as controls on overgrazing and the exploitation of forests and rivers. These indigenous environmental ethics were fundamental in maintaining the biodiversity central to preserving ecological systems and functioning (Kanyeki, 2018:1).

The role of rainmakers in the Setswana community

John Mbiti (1989:174) observed that rainmakers are regarded as having major status in almost all African societies. There are described by various names that translate as, for example, the shepherds of heaven, implying that they shepherd men, cattle and the society for God. In Setswana communities, where the rain is the most desperately needed commodity for survival, rainmakers are consequently central to the survival of the community (Mwakakigile, 2009:199). The underlying concept is that rainmakers shepherd the society into a harmonious relationship with nature. Hence, rainmakers are men of nature required to be in tune with nature if the society is to remain in tune with nature. They are the compass which determines whether the society is retracting from its unity with nature and they provide the ecological ethics to which the society must adhere in order to receive the abundance of the blessing of the land. According to John S. Mbiti (1989:176): "Those who are engaged in the art of rainmaking are well versed in weather matters and may spend long period acquiring their knowledge. This they obtain from observing the sky, from studying the habits of tress, insects and animals, from studying astronomy and the use of common sense." This would appear to indicate that natural science was vital for their craft. They spend hours studying environmental behaviour and teaching the traditional ecological ethics to their communities. Furthermore, they observed the behaviours of their communities that they might give wise counsel in how the land should be treated and also prescribe the necessary ingredients that can heal the environment when it has been harmed by misuse.

The rainmakers did not only teach the society on how to live with nature. James Amanze (2002:116) points out: "One who was chosen to be a rainmaker was supposed to lead an exemplary life. For example, he or she is expected to be self-respectful, not drunkard, not violence and not to do anything which can bring shame to the community." This points to the fact that correct social behaviour and the people's relationship to the environment have always been at the core of environmental preservation in Setswana cosmology. Moreover, the rainmaker was supposed to exemplify this to the community in his/her personal conduct.

The rainmaking ritual

Several studies have focused on the rainmaking ritual. This chapter seeks to analyse and demonstrate from an ecological perspective that the ritual is essentially an ecological technique that lifts the community to the state of being in harmony with nature (Landau, 1993:3). By restoring the rainmaker to his/her practice, it may be proven that rainmaking is an ecological technique, which was utilised not only for bringing the rain but also to respond to ecological crises experienced by the community (Landau, 1993:3). Furthermore, rainmaking has also been depicted and perceived as a form of environmental religion, and so using this term to refer to the rainmaking ritual implies the connecting of the community to the environment (Landau, 1993:6). The major cause of shortage of rainfall results from the community failure to adhere to the ecological ethics that guide the community's behaviour towards the environment. Therefore, it is the duty of the rainmaker to detect the transgressed taboos that the land might be cleansed. An example of unethical behaviour is the use of certain plants known to cause air pollution for firewood and thereby polluting or harming the land. The lack of rain indicates the result of the degrading of the environment.

This chapter argues that rainmaking should be regarded as an ecological technique in the sense that the rainmaker's responsibility is to ensure that the community is in tune with the environment (Landau, 1993:10). In Batswana cultural history, the rainmaking practitioner was additionally at one with nature and able to raise

4

an ecological consciousness in Setswana communities. Therefore, the process of rainmaking incorporated traditional dancing, which amongst the Batswana was primarily not performed merely for entertainment but in recognition of seasonal agricultural rites under the guidance and leadership of a rainmaker, fulfilling his overall environmental role.

Maele, performed mostly in Maphoka village, is a dance performed by women around the month of September to ask the ancestors for rain during the dry season. Another dance primarily associated with the environment is *Ndazula*, which expresses gratitude to the ancestors for a good harvest and is accompanied by beer drinking. Ceremonies associated with rainmaking such as these two are considered important in the Setswana world view, because it is during the pouring rains, ploughing and harvesting that the consciousness of the value of the Earth is heightened. If the environment is not kind to the Sotho-Tswana peoples, they will offer appeasement through rituals such as the rainmaking dances and the sacrificial slaughtering of sacred animals, which are kept for these ritual events (Masondo, 2014:85).

In Botswana, people observe agricultural rites such as *Letsema* (commencement of ploughing), *Molomo* (tasting of the first fruits) and *Dikgafela* (Thanksgiving festival for rain after harvest) (Nkomazana, Kealotswe & Amanze, 2010:123). Monkagadi Gaothobogwe (2009) states: "*Dikgafela* is a traditional harvest festival, [which] is meant to appease the skies or ancestors (*badimo*) to release the rains, well in time before the looming ploughing season beckons." For *dikgafela*, the women prepare beer, which is handed to the chief during the celebration. The chief takes a sip and pours the remainder onto the ground. Kenosi Molato and Musa Dube (2019:5) note: "The reasons for performing this act have various interpretations, one being that the chief recognizes the covenant which they have with the Earth and by doing so he acknowledges the interconnectedness between the Earth which has been given to them by God." Moreover, they point out that an alternative interpretation of the chief pouring traditional beer onto the ground is that the chief venerates the ancestors who have given them rain and indicates that they, therefore, deserve to test the first fruit from their land (Molato & Dube, 2019:5). Some argue that by pouring the beer onto the Earth, the Chief acknowledges that the ancestors are part and parcel of the Earth and feeds them.

At the heart of the role of the rainmaker and the rainmaking rituals is the relationship between the people and the environment. The rainmaker led this procession of environmental consciousness in the community. His removal from performing his craft left the community without a leader and environmental educator, and hence environmental degradation became inevitable.

Missionary enterprise

The missionary enterprises into Africa were characterised by three Cs, "namely by the introduction or the imposition of the so-called legitimate commerce and Christianity as a key to civilization and eventually colonization was seen by most abolitionists, humanitarians, philanthropists and missionaries as the only remedy" (Vilhanová, 2007:252). The underlying argument is that the missionary movement perceived Africans as trapped in ignorance, and as disorganised and superstitious; they were cannibals and barbarians who needed to be redeemed from debauchery and, consequently, in need of civilisation. Therefore, it is no surprise that some of the missionaries perceived some of African tribes as a link between rational and irrational creatures (Moffatt, 1842:6).

It should be noted that missionaries were men who came from and represented Western civilisation. Disciplines such as Western philosophy and science, which were used to bring civilisation, failed to unite the African continent with the 'civilised nations', and Robert Moffatt noted that the only hope of imparting civilisation in Africa would be attained through the gospel (Moffatt, 1842:iii). Hence the gospel became the sole instrument of the missionaries' goal to convert Africans to Christianity. Furthermore, in converting Africans, they built schools, which resembled those in the Western education model, as well as boarding schools, which provided a means of isolating children from the values of a "pagan" life, where they could impose on learners European values and Western thoughts. Comaroff and Comaroff (1991:xi), in their study of the colonisation of consciousness amongst the southern Tswana, argue that the main objective of the nonconformist missionaries was to change not only the hearts and minds, but also the signs and practices of the southern Tswana. This objective was described as "seizing the hearts and minds of its wild inhabitants, rousing them from a state of nature by cultivating their self-consciousness" or "to reconstruct them into their own image".

The missionary targeting of rainmakers

The first major compact of the missionary enterprise was the role of rainmakers. Jan Gewald (2002:3) says: "The central importance of access to and control over rain was an issue that soon became apparent to European missionaries who started working within Tswana society in the early nineteenth century." The missionaries observed that the rainmaker held a high status in Setswana cosmology. Robert Moffatt noted that the rainmakers "are our inveterate enemies, and uniformly oppose the introduction of Christianity amongst their countrymen to the utmost of their power". Missionaries described the rainmakers contemptuously as a "vile imposture" and "transparent deception" (Moffatt, 1842:6).

The core of the power struggle was the missionaries' desire to control the community and, thereby, to reconstruct the Batswana in their [the missionaries'] image. The nonconformist missionaries, representing English Protestant denominations and sects who did not conform to the doctrines and practices of the Church of England, realised that if they were to seize the Batswana consciousness and control their communities, it was necessary to eradicate the rainmaking rituals.

In the recorded debate between David Livingstone and the rainmaker of the Bakwena, David Livingstone referred to the rainmaker as 'doctor', which "implies an ironic conviction that the contest is being waged on equal ontological ground" (Comaroff & Comaroff, 1994:210). Thus, he allows his interlocutor to suggest a functional correspondence between Tswana material icons and European verbal signs, and to call into question the Christian distinction between sacred and secular activity.

The abolition of Bakwena rainmaking led to its replacement by the Christian prayer meeting, generally held in the homes of the missionaries. A similar transfer of community activity followed amongst the Babirwa and most other Botswana communities. The years 1821-1823,1845-1847 and 1862-1863 were characterised by serious droughts throughout southern Africa. In the land occupied by the Bakwena, the drought of 1845-1847 extended into 1848, the year of the Christian baptism the Bakwena chief, Sechele, by David Livingstone. Similarly, the abolition of rainmaking amongst the Babirwa was followed by drought. The question arises: What led to the extension of these droughts in specific territories? The logical conclusion of the researcher is that the natural order, under which the society had functioned, was disturbed by a permissive attitude that facilitated missionary intrusiveness. The indigenous ecological knowledge was targeted and colonised by Western religion, destroying the harmony between human beings and the environment. The long-term impact on environmental degradation caused by the missionaries' unilateral exploitation of Batswana communities and the scorn shown for indigenous ecological knowledge demands an interdisciplinary historical ecological and anthropological examination.

The implications of the abolition of rainmaking in Setswana communities

It was established that the rainmaker was the man/woman of nature who was in tune with nature and functioned as the compass of the society, directing it towards a harmonious union with the environment. The abolition of this leadership and educationalist role left a vacuum in the Setswana societal relationship with their environment. The environmental consciousness gradually dissipated, and the vacuum was filled by a Western environmental approach that became implemented in the culture. The indigenous people relinquished the conception of being one with nature and the environment became viewed as a resource that could be used for financial gain, as in the Western perspective.

Secondly, the objective of missionary enterprise was to destroy the Setswana community state of interconnectedness with nature and instil a state of self-consciousness. To achieve their goal, the missionaries realised that the removal of the nature man/woman was imperative. The consequence was that Batswana communities that had existed in tune with nature turned from their ecocentric state to individualism and the rise of consumerism. The environment was no longer viewed as community property and the individual could use it in any way, he desired without consulting the community. Sacred places that had been used for spiritual communion by the rainmakers became the property of individuals. The practices of overgrazing and deforestation have their historical roots in the seeds of individualism, sown in Batswana society by nonconformist missionary teachings.

Thirdly, while the land had been harmed or polluted, there was now no one capable of directing her cleansing, let alone to atone for the injury inflicted. Thus, the land continues to cry for help and will finally spew out humanity. Thus, the important role of cleansing remains unfulfilled as the rainmaker has not been replaced. Although the missionaries implemented the practice of praying for rain in church, this was by no means an equivalent to the cultural concept of the cleansing of nature from pollution. Praying for rain does not entail the incorporation of traditional environmental ethics, which was the foundation of Setswana systematic cosmology.

Fourthly, the new teaching of the missionaries disrupted the natural order in Setswana cosmology and promoted adherence to the Western view of the relationship between nature and the environment. One consequence was the implementation of irrigation systems, which disrupted streams and rivers. The natural movement of streams was diverted and channelled to water the fields. This may be seen as beneficial to the community, but it is ecologically wrong in the sense that nature is disturbed or disrupted. The nonconformist missionary objective of promoting individual self-consciousness resulted in the replacement of Batswana ecological traditions with a European perspective.

Fifthly, the abolition of the rainmaker also introduced a gender factor as rainmaking gave women a voice in a patriarchal society and served as an example showing that women could play a role in the direction of the community.

4

Conclusion

The chapter presented the theory of interconnectedness between the environment and the human-ancestral relationship in Setswana cosmology. It then covered environmental practices, focusing on the importance of environmental knowledge, and leadership by example, of the rainmaker in leading the community to experience the natural cycle through the symbolic celebratory and thanksgiving rituals and associated dances.

Thus, the rainmaker was established as the pivotal role in the cosmological inter-connectedness of humanity and environment at the time of the arrival of the non-conformist missionaries, who set about abolishing the role and replacing it with prayer meetings. This chapter then discussed the implications of the abolition of rainmaking in Setswana community.

The reverberations of the colonisers' misjudgement of the role of the rainmaker and environmental rituals can still be felt today through the reality of environmental degradation in Botswana, which is essentially linked to the missionary promotion of an individual consciousness and its potential to exploit, together with the disappearance of the concept that the environment and community were interconnected.

References

Amanze, J. 2002. *African Traditional Religions and culture in Botswana: A comprehensive textbook*. Gaborone: Pula Publishers.

Brown, T. 1926. *Among the Bantu nomads*. New York: Negro University Press.

Comaroff, J. & Comaroff, J. 1991. *Of revelation and revolution: Christianity, colonialism and consciousness in South Africa*. Chicago, IL: University of Chicago Press. https://doi.org/10.7208/chicago/9780226114477.001.0001

Dube, W. 2012. The scramble for Africa as the biblical scramble for Africa: Postcolonial perspectives. In: M. Dube, A. Mbuvi & D. Mbuwayesango (eds), *African Biblical Interpretation*. Atlanta, GA: Society of Biblical Literature. 1-25.

Gaothobogwe, M. 2009. Moshupa revives Dikgafela. *Mmegi Online*. https://bit.ly/2Cuw6RH

Gewald, J. 2002. El Negro, el Nino, witchcraft and the absence of rain. *Pula: Journal of African Studies*, 16(1):37-51. https://bit.ly/399l6VM

Kanyike, E. 2018. *African traditions and religion: The sacredness of nature*. South World News and Views from emerging Countries. London: Comboni House.

Landau, P. 1993. When rain falls: Rainmaking and community in a Tswana village, c.1870 to recent times. *The International Journal of African Historical Studies*, 26(1):3-30. https://doi.org/10.2307/219185

Mason, T., Jones, L. & Steenkamp, E. 2014. Introduction to postcolonial ecocriticism among settler-colonial nations. *Ariel: Review of English Literature*, 44(4):1-11. https://doi.org/10.1353/ari.2013.0037

Masondo, M.C. 2014. Sotho-Tswana mythic animals: Stratagem for environmental conservation. Paper presented at the Historical Association

of South Africa Biennial Conference, hosted by the History Education Programme, University of KwaZulu-Natal, Durban, 26-28 June.

Mbiti, J.S. 1989. *African Religions and Philosophy*. Portsmouth: Heinemann International Literature and Textbooks.

McFague, S. 2013. *Blessed are the Consumers – A Fortress Digital Review: Practicing Restraint in a Culture of Consumption*. https://bit.ly/2ZMCFYZ

Moffatt, R. 1842. *Missionary labours and scenes in Southern Africa*. New York: Cambridge University Press.

Molato, K. & Dube, M. 2019. Moral degradation and environmental degradation: Towards Setswana ecological Biblical interpretation. Paper presented at Boleswa conference, Swaziland, April.

Mwakakigile, G. 2009. *Botswana since independence*. Pretoria: New Africa Press.

Nkomazana, F., Kealotswe, O. & Amanze, J. 2010. *Biblical studies, theology, religion and philosophy: An introduction for African universities*. Kenya: Zapf Chancery Research Consultants and Publishers.

Setiloane, G. 1985. *African theology: An introduction*. Braamfontein: Skotaville.

Vilhanová, V. 2007. Christians missions in Africa and their role in the transformation of African societies. *Asians And African Studies*, 16(2):1-30. https://bit.ly/39cQeDY

5

THE SEDATED SACRED

A socioreligious analysis of Zimbabwe's land reform programme and environmental degradation

Molly Manyonganise[1] & Godfrey Museka[2]

Abstract

Traditionally, amongst the Shona of Zimbabwe environmental conservation was greatly tied to their religious beliefs. The use of taboos was meant to regulate the way natural resources were utilised. Academic scholars have noted how taboos played a crucial role not in only promoting environmental conservation but also in punishing those who would degrade the environment. Appealing to the sacred was a useful tool in ensuring adherence to the socioreligious beliefs that were meant to maintain sustainability within the environment. That colonialism tampered to a certain extent with these beliefs is well documented. Within the Zimbabwean context, the Fast Track Land Reform Programme (FTLRP) of 2000 seems to have had a negative impact on what was left of the taboos amongst the various Shona ethnic groups. It is the contention of this chapter that the FTLRP has had the effect of 'sedating' the sacred, as people have violated the taboos related to the environment with impunity. The focus of this chapter is to find out if a process of reawakening the sacred amongst the Shona would help in promoting the kind of land ownership that is closely linked to environmental conservation, which would in turn eventually lead to sustainable development for Zimbabwean communities. In this endeavour, the critical role of women in environmental conservation needs some interrogation. The chapter is a desktop study, hence it draws largely on secondary sources. Ecowomanism will be used as the theoretical framework informing this study.

Introduction

The nexus between religion and the environment is indisputable and "it is not new" (Simkins, 2008:1). The contemporary world at large is facing an environmental crisis. It is beyond doubt that human beings are at the centre of this crisis. As such,

---

1   Dr Molly Manyonganise is a senior lecturer at the Zimbabwe Open University, Faculty of Arts, Culture and Heritage Studies, Department of Religious Studies and Philosophy. [Email: mollymanyonganise@yahoo.com]

2   Dr Godfrey Museka is a senior lecturer at the University of Zimbabwe, Faculty of Education, Department of Curriculum and Arts. [Email: godiemuseka@gmail.com]

the environmental crisis that Africa, in general, and Zimbabwe, in particular, face brings to the fore not only questions about how religions have contributed to the crisis, but also how they can offer a solution to this predicament. This chapter seeks to make a socioreligious analysis of the impact of the Zimbabwe Fast Track Land Reform Programme (FTLRP) on the environment. Our major argument is that the sedation of the sacred that occurred through, amongst other things, the silencing of women, the incapacitation of traditional leaders, and the perceived inaction of the spiritual entities has led to the exploitation of the natural environment both for the rural and resettlement areas in Zimbabwe. The chapter relied heavily on secondary sources, since it is largely a desktop study. In terms of theory, the chapter is informed by the African ecowomanist theory. According to Harris (2017), ecowomanism is a theoretical framework that features race, class and gender, as well as intersectional analysis, to examine environmental injustice on the planet. In her explanation, Harris (2017) says that ecowomanism builds upon an environmental justice paradigm that links social justice to environmental justice. As such, it highlights the necessity for race-class-gender intersectional analysis when examining the logic of domination and unjust public policies that result in environmental exploitation (Harris, 2017). Critical to this chapter is how the theory is shaped by religious world views reflective of African cosmologies that uphold a moral imperative for Earth justice (Harris, 2017). From an African ecowomanist perspective, we seek to analyse the environmental injustice that was unleashed by the FTLRP in Zimbabwe. By employing the ecowomanist theoretical framework, we seek to show that the reawakening of the sacred amongst the Shona requires the recognition of Shona women's knowledge of environmental management and protection.

Clarification of key terms

The term 'sacred' is etymologically derived from the Latin word *sacer* meaning holy. Defining the term can be done using substantial and situational approaches. In the former, the sacred is seen as the mysterious and powerful manifestation of reality, and emphasises the ultimacy of the supernatural significance. In the latter, nothing is seen as inherently sacred and the meaning of sacred is open to any interpretation (Chidester & Linenthal, cited in Mu, 2015). The two approaches are relevant for our conceptualisation of the sacred in this chapter. In our analysis, the 'sacred' is conceptualised at three levels. We conceptualise it first at the level of what Rudolf Otto (1869-1937) calls the 'Holy', meaning the *numinous*, and as that which is central to religious life. At the second level are the traditional leaders who are referred to as sacred practitioners and are seen as the custodians of the land (the environment included). The third level is that of the Shona women who, through an ecowomanist lens, are seen as the feminine divine and whose role within the environment cannot be overlooked. On the other hand, the term 'sedation' is rooted in the medical field, where anaesthetics are used in order to make one unconscious of the pain in their body. In this chapter, we wish to show how the FTLRP has had the effect of silencing and disempowering the sacred, as conceptualised according to the aforementioned levels, to such an extent that environmental degradation goes on unabated. The application of 'sedation' in relation to religion was first used by Karl Marx, when he implied that the sacred is a narcotic which, while it may be utilised to alleviate pain, remains an illusory amelioration in a situation of despair (Luchte, 2009). In this chapter, we are not looking at the sacred as a sedative, but as an object that has been sedated. We apply the term sedation not in its literal sense, but as a metaphor for inaction, incapacitation, disempowerment and/or silencing of those who are usually expected to act in the interest of the environment. In the next section, we analyse environmental conservation in precolonial Shona society.

Environmental conservation in traditional Shona society: Bringing women to the centre

The environmental catastrophe that Africa faces today requires an exploration of the potential role that African Traditional Religions can play in mitigating the crisis. What this implies is that African indigenous ecological knowledge can offer a solution to the crisis. A reading of Mbiti (1969) has shown that is very difficult to extricate the religiosity of Africans from their day-to-day lives, including their engagement with the environment. African Traditional Religions are closely linked to the environment. Nana (2016:164) highlights that "it is impossible to separate African Traditional Religion from ecological system and all that are in its trees, oceans, rivers and seas, mountains, stones which serve as mediums through which Africans worship the Supreme Being". A number of scholars agree that African Traditional Religions have inherent mechanisms that acted as a resource for environmental conservation and management principles (Daneel, 1999; Nana, 2016; Tarusarira, 2017).

The traditional[3] Shona world view is consistent with the general traditional African world view (Taringa, 2014). Basically, Shona cosmology is tripartite in nature comprising the underworld, the physical world and the spirit world. Though divided into three discrete entities, these three worlds are closely interconnected. The spirit world is where the Supreme Being (*Mwari*) resides. *Mwari* produces the rain that fertilises the Earth. Very close to the Supreme Being are spirits, that is, ancestral and nature spirits. Moving from the spirit world, there is the physical world. People occupy the physical world. However, *Mwari* is also found in caves and mountains, for example, the Domboshava caves. The implication is that for the Shona, *Mwari* is

---

3   The word 'traditional' is used to denote precolonial society as well as the world view, cosmology and
     culture that have evolved from the personal experiences of indigenous African peoples.

both transcendent and immanent. Other things found in the human world are hills, mountains, trees, grass, animals, creatures and reptiles, caves, and birds. All these animate and inanimate objects are important because *Mwari* and spirits can reside in them, so to some extent they are sacred. Finally, there is the underworld. The underworld is the abode of the ancestors; they are buried in the graves. The dead are perceived not as dead, but as asleep. Once in the grave, the human being takes on a spiritual form. Water is also found in the underworld and can be the abode of mermaids. Eneji and Ntamu (2012) aver that despite humanity, nature and the gods being distinct concepts, they belong to some ontological categories that are interrelated and interdependent. Gwaravanda (2016) concurs with this view when he explains that African environmental philosophy through *ubuntu* emphasises cosmic interconnectedness, relationality and coexistence. As such, the Shona were able to use natural resources constructively in ways that ensured that they were not depleted. To this end, Shona practices ensured that the equilibrium within the ecosystem was maintained.

Makaudze and Shoko (2015) posit that traditional Shona society jealously guarded against the devastation of the environment and other natural resources, since the focus was not only on exploring and utilising the environment, but also devoting equal attention to safeguarding it against extinction or pollution. In Makaudze and Shoko's analysis, this was crucial as it aided in curbing problems such as erratic rainfall patterns, desertification, siltation, etc. Other scholars writing on Africa concur with this view. In their study of Ghana, Alexander, Agyekumhene and Allman (2017) note that before the introduction of Western conservation methods to Africa, many communities had already established resource management systems based on complex religious and cultural belief systems that incorporated myths, taboos, totems and social norms. In the same way, the Shona had environmental taboos that played the moral role of sustaining the ontological well-being of both the people and the environment (Chemhuru & Masaka, 2010). Taboos, like other African oral art forms, are based on the immediate environment and are passed from one generation to the other (Makaudze & Shoko, 2015). For example, in order to protect the habitat in the mountains, there were prohibitions and restrictions through taboos that governed access. For the record, certain mountains amongst the Shona are considered to be sacred because chiefs are buried in caves in the mountains. A case in point is the Chikapakapa Mountain in the Kadoma district (Mashonaland, West Province). Traditionally, this mountain was believed to be home to the ancestors of the Mushava clan. Going by its name, Chikapakapa has sexual connotations. The term '*chikapa*' refers to the rhythmic sexual movements that are performed for the man by a woman during sexual intercourse. What this implied was that Chikapakapa was the mountain of creation. Reduplicating the noun showed that it was not only the mountain of creation but of recreation as well (the woman is central to this creation and recreation). Tales are often told of how cries of young babies were heard on particular days from the mountain. The spirit medium of the Mushava clan resided close to this mountain and the rainmaking rituals were performed there. There is a point at which this mountain is split into two by the Manhize[4] River. At the point of the split is where the river's source is situated and just below it is a sacred pool.[5] People would observe taboos associated with both the mountain and the pool. For example, permission had to be sought if people wanted to go to the mountain to gather wild fruit and they were instructed never to complain if they found rotten fruit. The other taboo was never to throw stones as a way of getting the fruit from the trees. Only fruit that had fallen from the tree could be gathered. If one got thirsty and wanted drinking water from the pool, one was expected to use the shell of Mutamba fruit. The whole idea was that, if the shell accidentally falls into the pool, it would float and could easily be taken out of the water, thereby ensuring that the water remained clean. Such taboos apply in other areas such as natural vegetation and wildlife as well.

Through totemism, the Shona were able to maintain a balanced ecosystem. Mandillah and Ekose (2018) explain that a totem is any natural or mythical animal, plant, bird or insect that serves as a symbol of a family or clan whose members feel a close connection during their lives and these members do not eat, kill or trap such totemic animals, birds or fish. From Mandillah and Ekose's (2018) point of view, totems have been used for the primary purpose of preserving humanity, in that they have in many ways culminated in the preservation of other life forms bequeathed to humankind on whom one is dependent such as sacred forests, rocks, mountains and rivers. The belief in totemism needs to be understood as a way of trying to manage how these resources were used by the Shona. The chief and other sacred practitioners, such as spirit mediums, played important roles in this regard.

In terms of cultivation, the Shona had high regard for the land. Taringa (2014) points out that the sacredness of the land lies in the fact that the Shona believe that it is the back (*musana*) of the ancestors on which nature and humanity are carried. As such, it is in the land that one's *rukuvhute* (umbilical cord) is buried. This is the reason why there is a common phrase uttered by the Shona about themselves: '*mwana wevhu*' (a child of the soil). This is a clear indication of how the Shona understand their connection to the land, which clearly shows that a baby is not only a part of the family but of the whole community. The umbilical cord was also

---

4   Manhize is a name given to one of the ancestors of the Mushava clan, meaning that the river itself is sacred.

5   The sacred pools were dotted along the river until the point it met with Mungezi River.

regarded as a symbolic connection with one's ancestors. Women become crucial in this regard, because it is they who mediate the child's connection to the land by burying the umbilical cord in the soil. This is the reason why in precolonial Africa women often played a key role in indigenous systems of environmental protection, because for them the environment guaranteed the existence of future generations. As such, women were transmitters of key environmental knowledge to younger generations. In traditional Shona society, women played pivotal roles especially in the socialisation of the child. First, through the art of mothering, Shona women were able to transmit knowledge about the environment to their children. It is the mother who would teach the child the expectations of society, including how the child would relate to nature. It is therefore not surprising that the majority of storytellers amongst the Shona were women. Folk tales were told by women to children around a fire.

Women in traditional societies also had a close relationship with the environment, because they were the ones who gathered fruit and firewood, and collected water from the water sources. It is women who, on a daily basis, were confronted with the need to observe taboos associated with the environment. Thus, Mazarire (2003:41) notes that "though women were subordinate to men in pre-colonial societies, they were viewed as important in the roles of managing the environment". This is evidenced in that female symbolism is typical of Shona cosmology. In his study of Chivi society in Zimbabwe, Mazarire (2003) concludes that the importance of women and their role in utilising and conserving the environment was acknowledged.

Generally, in traditional Shona society women were tillers of the land. Precolonial Africa was dependent on agriculture, and women and children did much of the work. This is the reason why polygamy was acceptable, as men were looking for more people to work the land. In this regard, women were careful in the way that they treated the land, because they understood that their livelihood depended on the land. The Shona were to a very large extent not shifting cultivators,[6] but had other ways of preserving the fertility of the soil. For example, practices such as crop rotation and intercropping were key. Since women were tillers of the land, they held the knowledge of how these activities were done. We make these assertions cognisant of the fact that Shona society was largely patriarchal and men would at times dictate what needed to be grown on which piece of land. However, women would always bring the knowledge of what was planted in the different pieces of land and what could be planted in each season, so that the fertility of the soil was not compromised. Women played pivotal roles during ritual performances that demanded a strict

6   A form of agriculture, used especially in tropical Africa, in which an area of ground is cleared of vegetation and cultivated for a few years and then abandoned for a new area until its fertility has been naturally restored.

adherence to specific regulations that had to do with the environment. For example, beer for rainmaking rituals was brewed by postmenstrual women.

Colonialism, the Shona and the natural environment: Pushing women from the centre

Ikuenobe (2014) notes that a significant difference between Africans and Europeans during colonisation was their moral attitudes towards nature. He further argues that activities that have raised environmental concerns in Africa did not exist prior to colonialism, because Africans adopted conservationist values, practices and ways of life. Although such a view tends to romanticise the African past, and are largely disputed by Taringa (2014), they do reflect the African attitude towards nature.

The land division through the Land Apportionment Act (1930), Land Husbandry Act (1951) and Land Tenure Act (1969) alienated the traditional African ecologists from the holy places situated on white farms because traditional land tenure had been badly disrupted (Daneel, 1999). The laws apportioned the land area equally between whites and blacks, with 50.8% of good-weathered fertile soils for the white minority and the rest for Africans and wild animals (Essof, 2013). Actually, Africans were given 30% of the low-rainfall areas with poor soils (Masengwe, 2011; Christopher, 1971). Manley (1995) argues that the Land Husbandry Act completely ignored the customary basis of African land tenure by introducing the principle of individual and negotiable rights to strictly demarcated registered holdings.

The colonialists brought with them their flora and fauna, which disrupted the ecological landscapes of most Shona societies. The Shona did not have any knowledge of how to manage these or their effect on the natural environment. Carruthers (2004) has highlighted the importance of the indigenous versus introduced or exotic animals and plants. The other danger was that colonial powers introduced to Africa the commodification of land.

Apart from this, there was a clash of religions: that is, African Indigenous Religions versus Christianity. To a large extent, African Indigenous Religions were demonised. Africans' reverence for nature was misconstrued as animism and therefore heathen. Africans were made to hate their traditional forms of knowing and ways of acquiring knowledge (Ndlovu-Gatsheni, 2018). Christianity presented the Earth as an object to be subdued (Chidester, 1987). Human beings were to have dominion over the Earth. This was in sharp contrast to the traditional view that encouraged people to be responsible and accountable in their dealings with the environment. Ndlovu-Gatsheni (2018) has argued that Christianisation constituted a form of education and an epistemicide implying that it killed the African epistemologies. White (1967) blames Western traditions of technology and science for this ecological crisis.

5

She castigates Christianity for establishing the dualism of humanity and nature, while at the same time insisting that it is God's will that humans exploit nature for their proper ends. Boersema, Blowers and Martin (2008:218) have called this the "desacralisation" of nature. White (1967) further argues that by destroying 'pagan animism', Christianity made it possible to exploit nature with indifference to the imperatives of natural objects. This has been due to the fact that the whole concept of sacred groves is alien to Christianity, as well as to much of the philosophy of the West, which has resulted in missionaries destroying sacred groves that, from their point of view, were idolatrous because they assume the immanence of spirits in nature (Daneel, 1999). The sacred practitioners overseeing these groves were stigmatised as idol worshippers. Zimbabwe is currently faced with the dangers of Pentecostalism and its theology of prosperity that calls for domineering the Earth. The literalistic reading of biblical texts is dangerous for the environment, because it does not pay attention to the effects of resource depletion or environmental degradation.

From a gender perspective, it is imperative to engage with the history of colonialism and its impact on natural environmental conservation. From the onset, as alluded to above, traditional land tenure practices were greatly altered by colonial officials. Colonialism introduced a cash economy that prioritised male labour over female labour. As a result, men migrated to either the white farms or the urban areas to get formal employment and women were left to work on the land in the rural areas. However, Tiondi (2000:16-18) argues that "even when women became the primary breadwinners of families because of male migration, for instance, they continued to be defined in colonial practice largely as dependent housewives and mothers" and "under colonial law … women were declared legal minors and often lost their customary rights to land". Colonial administrators failed to appreciate the significance of indigenous land-tenure practices based upon principles of obligation and responsibility that guaranteed women access to land and control over certain crops (Tiondi, 2000:18). In such cases, the knowledge that women had in terms of environmental conservation was often not recognised. Yet when Western farming technologies were introduced, it was the women in the rural areas who continued using traditional methods that ensured environmental protection. However, in postcolonial Zimbabwe, this knowledge has been overlooked, because the post-colonial state has assumed the governance structures of the colonial power. The trivialisation of women's knowledge has been very evident from the environmental effects of the FTLRP in Zimbabwe.

The Fast Track Land Reform Programme

An overview

Land ownership has been a central issue in Zimbabwe since 1890 when the Pioneer Column set foot in Zimbabwe. The 1890 invasions by the Pioneer Column, led by Cecil John Rhodes, disenfranchised Africans and negated their land rights, amongst other things. They took away from the kings and their representatives the custodianship of the land (Bakare, 1993). This ultimately led to the war of liberation.

After independence, the government engaged itself in the first phase of land reform and resettlement, which was meant to decongest the 'reserves' that had been created in the pre-independence period and also to enable rural people to access arable land. Unfortunately, the government's plans could not materialise rapidly enough because of a number of issues, some of which were economic. The policy of willing seller/willing buyer also became an impediment to the government. Masiiwa and Chipungu (2004) have dealt with this issue at great length. In order to deal with the economic challenges, the government convened a donor's conference in 1998, which was aimed at soliciting external financial support for the second phase of the land reform and resettlement programme. Donors who pledged funding for this exercise made it clear that the government should first come up with a clear land policy and should establish transparent and accountable mechanisms for land acquisition and redistribution. From Essof's point of view, "the donor conference held in 1998 forced the government to concede that any land taken would be paid for up front" (2013:25). All this happened in the face of growing opposition from civil society, trade unions and the general public. In 1999, the Movement for Democratic Change, which later became a strong opposition party, was formed. It was at the same time that the government embarked on a process of replacing the Lancaster House Constitution. A referendum to adopt the draft constitutional document was held in February 2000 and Zimbabweans overwhelmingly voted against it. As a result, when the 2000 draft constitution was rejected, it provided the government with an opportunity to take the land forcefully. Various explanations have been given as to why, at this particular point, the government of Zimbabwe chose to take away land forcefully from the whites. Chan (cited in Sachikonye, 2003) views the land invasions as serving two purposes. First, it was meant to seize land and thus punish the white farmers for their political stance and, second, it was meant to close off the commercial farming areas to campaigning by opposition parties. In the following section, we look at how the land reform was conducted as well as its effect on the environment.

Its operationalisation and the sedation of the sacred

The land reform of 2000 was officially termed the 'Fast Track Land Reform Programme' (FTLRP) or Third *Chimurenga*. In some circles, it has been viewed as 'land invasions' or 'land occupations' and unofficially it has been called *jambanja*. Shoko (cited in Taringa & Sipeyiye, 2014) explains that *jambanja* is an informal Shona euphemism for violence. In this case, it denotes the violent nature with which land was taken. Sibanda and Maposa (2014:132) posit that "the *jambanja* was characterised by the use of unprecedented force leading to unprecedented loss of blood". In the same vein, Saunders (2011:124) argues that *jambanja* marked the "reintroduction of systematic political violence under the patronage of the state". Sachikonye (2003) is of the view that the overall image that the invasions conveyed was one of degeneration into lawlessness and violence. This is clearly evidenced by the way white farmers and their workers were displaced from the farms, with a lot of other abuses taking place in the process. Ganiel and Tarusarira (2014) observe that the farm invasions were accompanied by a wave of anti-white rhetoric and violence, which the security forces largely ignored. Chitando (2011) concludes that the philosophy of *jambanja* (militancy) that had emerged during the FTLRP implied that the rule of law could no longer be guaranteed. As such, the FTLRP is viewed in Zimbabwe as the starting point and/or the exacerbation of the Zimbabwean crises in the new millennium. In this case, the FTLRP can be viewed as aggravating the environmental crisis that Zimbabwe faces today. In this regard, we agree with Hentze and Menz's (2015) contention that the success of the land reform in Zimbabwe can be measured according to its impact on fighting environmental degradation in transferred farmlands and former communal areas.

The FTLRP led to a haphazard movement of people, with some settling in unfamiliar places. In most cases, the people resettled on lands that were farms or game parks. In addition, due to the fact that the traditional leaders were not fully engaged from the outset of this programme, taboos pertaining to sacred places within the resettled areas were not observed. As a result, the sacred places were desecrated. A good example is the Chikapakapa Mountain, alluded to above, where people from Buhera and Chikomba districts were resettled. The resettled people engaged in activities that desacralised the mountain. Once settled close to the mountain, the people wantonly cut down trees, including the fruit trees, so that they could sell firewood for profit. The sacred pool was desecrated and polluted to the extent that the water is no longer fit for human consumption. As noted by Chigumira (cited in Hentze & Menz, 2015), much of the environmental degradation is the consequence of human activity rather than climate change.

In other areas, the resettled people engaged in excessive hunting of wild animals. While on these hunting escapades, they usually started veld fires that destroyed large tracts of land, while at the same time affecting the ecosystem. Dube (2015) notes that the increase in the incidence of veld fires can be attributed to the resettled smallholder farmers. These fires have also destroyed those places and objects that the traditional Shona people have considered to be sacred.

Yet in other areas the resettled peoples have abandoned farming and have resorted to gold panning and gold mining. Gold panning is taking place unsustainably and unsystematically, usually in riverbeds, banks and flood plains, with no concern for the environment (Kori, 2013). Gold panning has affected the smooth flow of water in the rivers and this has been the major cause of floods. Gold mining is being carried out in the fields within which farming is expected to be taking place. In a study carried out in three resettlement areas in Kadoma (Fox, Chigumira & Rowntree, 2007), it was found that apart from the gold panning and mining, sand was being taken from absentee landlords' plots with or without the owner's knowledge. Furthermore, there was clearing of woodland, bushland and grassland for settlement and cultivation. Kori (2013) has accordingly concluded that environmental management is poor in resettled areas. What compounds the situation is that resettlement areas are government-controlled areas. A research participant interviewed by Manley (1995) highlighted that in the resettlement areas the traditional taboos do not apply.

Research carried out by other scholars has shown that the majority of black farm workers were of foreign origin (that is, non-Zimbabwean Black farmers) and they were also displaced together with their white employees. Sachikonye (2003) highlighted that it has been very difficult to account for these displaced Black non-Zimbabwean farmworkers. However, some of the workers were Zimbabweans who had sought employment on the farms. These displaced Zimbabwean farm workers came back to the rural areas, which the government had said it wanted to decongest, thus leading once again to overpopulation. The natural environment could not sustain the large numbers of people. The obvious result was that people ended up settling in areas that were meant for livestock grazing. This, to a large extent, altered the landscape of a number of rural areas, with some even settling on wetlands. In 1995, Manley noted how the rural areas were acutely congested, leading to a drastic reduction of grazing land to accommodate the excess population. He noted then that the result was severe overgrazing and land degradation. In his analysis, the major contributor to this was the limitation of the chiefs' powers in dealing with environmental issues, amongst others.

Tracing the place of women in the midst of this environmental degradation stemming from the FTLRP is important. Moyo (2013) is of the view that the FTLRP increased women's access to land ownership, although a number of women scholars dispute this view. From his statistics, 12-18% of women now own land.

He does acknowledge, however, that the women who own land do not come from vulnerable groups such as the poor, widows and divorcees. In resettlement areas that were given to the general (that is the non-elite) public, commonly known as A1 farms, the land permits were recorded using names of male spouses only. In other words, women were reduced to spectators of the whole land reform process. Chiweshe (2015) has highlighted the gendered nature of the post-fast track farms and blamed this on the patriarchal values that ascribe particular roles to men and women resulting in the determination of where women are located within social systems. In African social systems, a good woman is one who learns from and observes without challenging patriarchal power. In this regard, the FTLRP is no exception. Hence, women are practically silenced on what happens on the land, increasing environmental degradation through government's failure to enable women to either own or co-own land. What boggles the mind is why the violators of the taboos have not met with the punishment that the elders would always say the ancestors would impose? Observing the culture change in Zimbabwe, Bourdillon (1993) asked a pertinent question: Where are the ancestors? While this question still needs answering, we further ask whether the sacred can be reawakened to ameliorate the current environmental crisis? The next section looks at how Zimbabwean society can redeem itself from the environmental crisis.

Reawakening the sacred: Towards re-mothering the environment

The environmental crisis that Zimbabwe faces requires the reawakening of the sacred. In this study, we strongly put forward our claim that in order for this to happen there is a need to restore women's place in environmental conservation amongst the Shona people. In the colonial and postcolonial periods, environmental discourses have tended to marginalise women. Nnaemeka (1997:2) urges us to rethink marginality by insisting that we listen carefully to "marginal discourses" as manifested by the silences and other patterns of articulation of the marginalised. In dealing with the environmental crisis in Zimbabwe, there is a need to bring women from the margins to the centre. Madongonda (2017) notes that the role of women, especially in contemporary society, has often been ignored in the environmental discourse and they are often portrayed as the victims of land degradation and not key players in its protection. It is critical for Shona society in particular to take particular notice of the fact that their sacred has existed through the agency of women. It is unfortunate that colonialism, through industrialisation and urbanisation, tried to diminish the woman's role of mothering that ended up, to a large extent, creating a distance between women and their children, as well as destroying the social and religious spaces that were useful in the transmission of the much needed indigenous knowledge systems (IKSs) about nature. We are therefore indebted to academic scholars and gender activists from Africa and beyond who challenged the reductionist notions of motherhood. For example, Hudson-Weems, the Africana womanist (1997), sees mothering not as a weakness but a strength of the African woman.

As alluded to above, traditional society had interventions in place to deal with environmental conservation and interventions that targeted young audiences. The reawakening of the sacred requires that we restore the role of women as environmental conservationist teachers. The fireplace in the round hut needs to be reinvented, because it offers that sacred space where the woman would tap into cultural memory to impart knowledge about the environment to the children. From Nnaemeka's analysis:

> Story-telling registers survival on two scores – the survival of the story teller and that of his listeners. The story teller survives to tell the story and his/her listeners survive because they learned from the story. Those that fail to learn do so at their own peril.   (1997:2)

We do understand that in contemporary Shona society it is no longer possible to gather children around someone in the villages to tell them stories in whatever form, because of the major changes that were brought about by Western civilisation. The introduction of formal education through schools has made this a daunting task. Ndlovu-Gatsheni (2018) has called for epistemic freedom as he highlights that colonialism did not only destroy African Indigenous Knowledges (AIKs) but planted European memory as well. In concurrence, Chigidi (2009:183) observes that "the school encourages divergent thinking, creativity and individualism which tend to undermine the traditional mode of doing things and the basis for the implementation of the taboo system". Today's children, according to Chigidi (2009:184), may laugh off the perceived "lies" that are contained in the taboos. We, therefore, propose to make use of the schools as spaces for storytelling. There has been within Zimbabwe's urban primary schools an introduction of the concept of culture huts. These are round huts that are being constructed to educate the young children about our culture. We have noted with interest that the culture huts are being supervised by elderly retired female teachers. It is our conviction that this testifies to the important role that women play in educating young children about African cultural values and practices. It is only through this that children in contemporary Shona society can learn to value our indigenous culture. The ancestors and the traditional leaders will only gain respect when women within the culture huts at the schools play their important role of transmitting the knowledge about the environment and about key stakeholders in environmental protection. We do understand that the traditional taboos have been overtaken by new information technologies and have been rendered 'useless' by Western education. We, therefore, concur with Chigidi's (2009) submission that the taboo system needs to be modified and improved, so that it moves with the times. Instead of using taboos to create fear in children because they do not want to be punished, it would be wise to create new taboos that promise rewards to the children if they act positively towards the environment. Consequences of one's action need to be presented in the affirmative. For example, children could be told that if they desist from panning for gold in the river, the rivers would not be affected by siltation. This would be very effective, because children are able to see the detrimental effects of gold panning and mining within their various communities. These culture huts need not be a feature of urban primary schools only, but should be constructed in the rural as well as the resettlement areas. In doing this, there is a need to situate the new taboos within the socioreligious context of the Shona people. White (1967:1206) made the point aptly when she argued that "more science and more technology are not going to get us out of the present ecological crisis until we find a new religion, or rethink our old one". The second option is more appealing to us, because the African indigenous religious perspective allows Shona society to introspect and see where we have gone wrong. There is a need to rethink how Shona society has treated the ancestors, the sacred practitioners and women in the whole discourse about the environment. The following questions could act as a guide in this introspection:

1. Has society's total disregard of the ancestors been helpful in the light of the environmental challenges that are so glaring in rural and resettlement areas?

2. What has been the effect of disempowering and incapacitating chiefs and other sacred practitioners on the environment?

3. Can Shona society continue to marginalise and silence women if it wants to successfully solve the environmental crisis that has resulted from the FTLRP?

Conclusion

The aim of this chapter was to undertake a socioreligious analysis of the impact of the FTLRP in Zimbabwe on the environment. The intention was to see whether the FTLRP in some way 'sedated' the perceived 'sacred' within Shona society, especially considering the environmental degradation that is taking place both in rural and resettlement areas. The chapter, in its focus on precolonial, colonial and post-colonial Zimbabwe, and its discussion on the role of key indigenous stakeholders in environmental conservation, sheds light on the fundamental dynamic changes that have resulted, especially the marginalisation of women. This, in turn, has led to inaction from the ancestors and the disempowerment of the traditional leaders who, in Shona religious cosmology, are seen as sacred. In this case, the chapter has shown the simultaneous construction and influence of gender, religion and the environment, with an emphasis on women's roles and perceptions as well as the disempowerment of traditional leaders. This was shown to have resulted in people not fearing the consequences. In the final analysis, the chapter acknowledges that the very act of sedation is not permanent, as the sedated will come to a point of reawakening. As such, the chapter hinges the reawakening of the sacred on the restoration of women as transmitters of key environmental knowledge and has suggested that this be done within the culture huts that are being constructed at schools.

5

References

Alexander, L., Agyekumhene, A. & Allman, P. 2017. The role of taboos in the protection and recovery of sea turtles. *Frontiers in Marine Science,* 4(1):1-9. https://doi.org/10.3389/fmars.2017.00237

Bakare, S. 1993. *My right to land, in the Bible and in Zimbabwe: A theology of land for Zimbabwe*. Harare: Zimbabwe Council of Churches.

Boersema, J., Blowers, A. & Martin, A. 2008. Editorial: The religion-environment connection. *Environmental Sciences,* 5(4):217-221. https://doi.org/10.1080/15693430802542257

Bourdillon, M.F.C. 1993. *Where are the ancestors? Changing culture in Zimbabwe*. Harare: University of Zimbabwe Publications.

Carruthers, J. 2004. Africa: Histories, ecologies and societies. *Environment and History,* 10(4):379-406. https://doi.org/10.3197/0967340042772649

Chemhuru, M. & Masaka, D. 2010. Taboos as sources of Shona people's environmental ethics. *Journal of Sustainable Development in Africa,* 12(7):121-133.

Chidester, D. 1987. *Patterns of action: Religion and ethics in a comparative perspective*. Belmont, CA: Wadsworth Publishing Company.

Chigidi, W.L. 2009. Shona taboos: The language of manufacturing fears for sustainable development. *The Journal of Pan-African Studies,* 3(1):174-188.

Chitando, E. 2011. Prayers, politics and peace: The church's role in Zimbabwe's crisis. *Open Space,* 1:43-49.

Chiweshe, M.K. 2015. Women and the emergence of grassroots institutions on post-fast track farms. *Journal of Gender, Agriculture and Food Security,* 1(1):40-53.

Christopher, A.J. 1971. Land tenure in Rhodesia. *South African Geographical Journal,* 53(1):39-52. https://doi.org/10.1080/03736245.1971.10559483

Daneel, M.L. 1999. *African earthkeepers: Environmental mission and liberation in Christian perspective*. Pretoria: Unisa Press.

Dube, E. 2015. Environmental challenges posed by veld fires in fragile regions: The case of the Bulilima and Mangwe districts in Southern Zimbabwe. *Jamba: Journal of Disaster Risk Studies,* 7(1):1-8. https://doi.org/10.4102/jamba.v7i1.224

Eneji, C.O. & Ntamu, G. 2012. Traditional African Religion in natural resources conservation and management in Cross River State, Nigeria. *Environment and Natural Resources Research,* 2(4):44-54. https://doi.org/10.5539/enrr.v2n4p45

Essof, S. 2013. *Shemurenga: The Zimbabwean Women's Movement, 1995-2000*. Harare: Weaver Press.

Fox, R.C., Chigumira, E. & Rowntree, K.M. 2007. On the fast track to land degradation? A case study of the impact of the Fast Track Land Reform Programme in Kadoma District, Zimbabwe. *Geography,* 92(3):208-220.

Ganiel, G. & Tarusarira, J. 2014. Reconciliation and reconstruction among churches and faith-based organisations in Zimbabwe. In: M. Leiner, M. Palme & P. Stockner (eds), *Societies in transition: Sub-Saharan Africa between conflict and reconciliation*. Gottingen: Vandenhoeck & Ruprecht. 55-78. https://doi.org/10.13109/9783666560187.55

Gwaravanda, E.T. 2016. A critical analysis of the contribution of selected Shona proverbs to applied philosophy. Doctoral dissertation, Unisa, Pretoria.

Harris, M.L. 2017. Introduction. In: M.L. Harris (ed), *Ecowomanism, religion and ecology*. Leiden: Brill. https://doi.org/10.1163/97890 04352650

Hentze, K. & Menz, G. 2015. "Bring back the land" – A call to refocus on the spatial dimension of Zimbabwe's land reform. *Land*, 4(2):355-377. https://doi.org/10.3390/land4020355

Hudson-Weems, C. 1997. Africana womanism and the critical need for Africana theory and thought. *The Western Journal of Black Studies*, 21(2):79-84.

Ikuenobe, P.A. 2014. Traditional African environmental ethics and colonial legacy. *International Journal of Philosophy and Theology*, 2(4):1-21. https://doi.org/10.15640/ijpt.v2n4a1

Kori, E. 2013. From order to (dis)order in the Land Reform Programme of Zimbabwe: Was environmental sustainability retained? *Sustainable Development and Planning*, 173:101-110. https://doi.org/ 10.2495/SDP130091

Luchte, J. 2009. Marx and the sacred. *Journal of Church and State*, 51(3):413-437. https://doi.org/ 10.1093/jcs/csp095

Madongonda, A.M. 2017. Nurturing mother nature: Exploring the Zimbabwean woman's role in environmental conservation through storytelling. *African Journal of Children's Literature*, 1(2):86-98.

Makaudze, G. & Shoko, P.H. 2015. The re-conceptualization of Shona and Venda taboos: Towards an Afrocentric discourse. *Journal of Pan-African Studies*, 8(2):261-275.

Mandillah, K.L.L. & Ekose, G.V. 2018. African totems: Cultural heritage for sustainable environmental conservation. *Conservation Science in Cultural Heritage*, 18:201-218.

Manley, M. 1995. Land and soil: A European commodity in Shona traditional perspective. *Journal for the Study of Religion*, 8(1):27-54.

Masengwe, G. 2008. The church's role in social healing and reconciliation in Zimbabwe: An analysis of reconciliation in the National Vision Discussion Document of the Churches of Zimbabwe. Master's thesis, University of KwaZulu-Natal, Durban.

Masiiwa, M & Chipungu, L. 2004. Land reform programme in Zimbabwe: Disparity between policy design and implementation. In: M. Masiiwa (ed), *Post-Independence land reform in Zimbabwe: Controversies and impact on the economy*. Harare: FES and IDS University of Zimbabwe. 1-24.

Mazarire, G.C. 2003. The politics of the womb: Women, politics and the environment in pre-colonial Chivi, Southern Zimbabwe c.1840 to 1900. *Zambezia*, 30(1):35-50. https://doi. org/10.4314/zjh.v30i1.6739

Mbiti, J.S. 1969. *African religions and philosophy*. Oxford: Heinemann.

Moyo, S. 2013. Land reform and redistribution in Zimbabwe since 1980. In: S. Moyo & W. Chambati (eds), *Land and agrarian reform in Zimbabwe: Beyond white settler capitalism*. Dakar: CODESRIA. 29-78. https://doi.org/10.2307/j.ctvk3gnsn.8

Mu, Y. 2015. Local Perspectives of sacred landscapes and tourism: Exploring the linkages in Sagarmatha (Mt. Everest) National park, Nepal. Unpublished Master of Environment Studies thesis, University of Waterloo, Ontario, Canada.

Nana, A.E. 2016. The impact of ecology in African Traditional Religion. *International Journal of Theology and Reformed Tradition*, (8):164-174.

Ndlovu-Gatsheni, S.J. 2018. The dynamics of epistemological decolonisation in the 21st century: Towards epistemic freedom. *Strategic Review for Southern Africa*, 40(1):16-45.

Nnaemeka, O. 1997. *The politics of (m)othering: Womanhood, identity and resistance in African literature*. London: Routledge.

Sachikonye, L.M. 2003. The situation of commercial farm workers after land reform in Zimbabwe: A report prepared for the Farm Community Trust of Zimbabwe. https://bit.ly/39cUhAa [Accessed 24 June 2019].

Saunders, R. 2011. Questionable associations: The role of forgiveness in transitional justice. *The International Journal of Transitional Justice*, 5:19-141. https://doi.org/10.1093/ijtj/ijr003

Sibanda, F. & Maposa, R.S. 2014. Beyond the third *Chimurenga*? Theological reflections on the Land Reform Programme in Zimbabwe, 2000-2010. *The Journal of Pan African Studies*, 6(8):54-74.

Simkins, R.A. 2008. Religion and the environment. *Journal of Religion and Society*, 3:1-4.

Taringa, N.T. 2014. *Towards an African-Christian environmental ethic*. Bamberg: University of Bamberg Press.

Taringa, N.T. & Sipeyiye, M. 2013. Zimbabwean indigenous religions and political drama: The fast-track land reform and the fast-track change of attitudes to nature, 2000-2008. In: E. Chitando (ed), *Prayers and players: Religion and politics in Zimbabwe*. Harare: SAPES Books. 51-61.

White, L. 1967. The historical roots of our ecological crisis. *Science*, 155(3767):1203-1207. https://doi.org/10.1126/science.155.3767.1203

6

RETHINKING ENVIRONMENTAL SUSTAINABILITY THROUGH THE NDAU NOTION OF COMMUNAL EXISTENCE

Macloud Sipeyiye[1]

Abstract

The twenty-first century faces a life-threatening environmental crisis of unprecedented magnitude. Scientists posit that the balance of life on the planet Earth is in danger as a result of human activities. Religions have not been seriously considered as potential partners in providing solutions to the crisis, but are in fact often blamed for causing it. This can be explained by the misleading disenchantment theory that holds that religions expose nature to exploitation by humans, as they teach that humans are distinct from nature and have a divinely sanctioned right to exploit it. A rethinking of religion in environmental discourse proves otherwise. African Indigenous Religions, for instance, are biocentric as they see all living beings as elements of one interdependent spiritual community. In this chapter, I use the Ndau notion of communal existence to pursue themes of interconnectedness, reverence, embeddedness and reciprocity with nature that can advance the agenda for environmental sustainability. The chapter begins with a brief discussion of the identity of the Ndau and a description of their religio-cultural value system, and finally unpacks the notion of communal existence in the Ndau religious world view, finding synergies with the wider environmental protection agenda. The approach in the chapter is qualitative for it seeks to access the meaning embedded in the rich religious and or spiritual life of the Ndau in the context of the environmental crisis through in-depth interviews.

Introduction

The twenty-first century faces a life-threatening environmental crisis of unprecedented magnitude. Humanity worldwide faces a litany of serious threats to the environment that include, amongst other things, ozone depletion, emissions that produce the 'greenhouse effect' and global warming, pollution of the air, Earth and

---

1   Dr Macloud Sipeyiye is affiliated to the Department of Religious Studies, Midlands State University, Zimbabwe. He is also a research fellow at the Research Institute for Theology and Religion, Unisa, South Africa. [Email: macloudsipeyiye5@gmail.com]

water, deforestation of important tropical rain forests, and extinction of species due to habitat destruction and climate change (Young, 2013). Scientists posit that the balance of life on the planet Earth is in danger as a result of human activities. Recently, in March 2019, Malawi, Mozambique and Zimbabwe experienced the devastating effects of cyclone Idai. Many lives were lost and important infrastructure damaged, and the livelihoods of the survivors were affected drastically. Cyclones are one negative consequence of the 'greenhouse effect' and global warming as a result of climate change.

Religions have not been seriously considered as potential partners in providing solutions to the crisis, but in fact are often blamed for causing it. This can be explained by the misleading disenchantment theory which holds that religions, especially Western religions, expose nature to exploitation by humans as they teach that humans are distinct from nature and have a divinely sanctioned right to exploit it. As a result, this perspective has been applied to every religion. A rethinking of religion in environmental discourse proves otherwise. Religions hold great potential in managing the environmental crisis. African Indigenous Religions, for instance, are biocentric as they see all living beings as elements of one interdependent spiritual community.

In this chapter, I employ a socioreligious and cultural analysis of the Ndau notion of communal existence to pursue themes of interconnectedness, reverence, embeddedness and reciprocity with nature that can advance the wider agenda for environmental sustainability. I settled on a specific group of people, the Ndau in Zimbabwe a society that is characterised by diversity, ethnically and historically. The chapter begins with a brief discussion of the identity of the Ndau and a description of their religious and cultural value system, and it finally unpacks the notion of communal existence in the Ndau religious world view, finding synergies with the environmental protection agenda.

Methodological concerns

The approach in the chapter is qualitative for it is informed by a constructivist paradigm that seeks to access the meaning embedded in the rich religious and/or spiritual life of the Ndau in the context of the environmental crisis. Data were collected through interviews with purposively selected informants and accessing available secondary sources on the Ndau religion. Interviews required cultural familiarity as a key requirement to get the best from the target population. Mack, Woodsong, MacQueen, Guest and Namely (2005) state that in qualitative research scholars with a solid base of cultural awareness stand a better chance of gaining the confidence of the community under study, since they are more likely to get the informed consent of the potential informants. I am Ndau myself and my ethnic identity gives me some advantage because I am familiar with the culture of the researched community. However, I am also cognisant of the fact that familiarity with the researched community may lead to biases in the data gathered. In the light of this awareness, I commit myself faithfully to the phenomenology of religion's methodological principle of *epoché* (I hold back) that calls for the bracketing of preconceived ideas about the phenomena researched (Chitando, Mapuranga & Taringa, 2014).

Theoretical framework

The chapter employs the re-enchantment or re-imagination of nature theory as a lens in rethinking environmental sustainability through the Ndau notion of communal existence. The theory counters the disenchantment theory that accuses religion of complicity in the degradation of the environment (Watling, 2009). The disenchantment of nature theory has been driven by the modern Western world view that reduces nature to 'material' without life or spirit. Premodern ways of perceiving it as alive, interdependent and sacred are replaced with a mechanical understanding, seeing it as a secular repository of resources to be exploited (Watling, 2009). The re-enchantment or re-imagination theory holds that positive or negative attitudes for or against the environment are a result of a way of conceptualising the world that stimulates either constructive or destructive actions towards it. Re-enchantment theory revalues nature and disenchants humanity and the modern world view, creating human moral and spiritual reorientation in relation to it and re-roots humanity in and revaluing nature, evoking a wider environmental identity. The theory emphasises the need for new imaginations about nature that give it meaning, subjectivity and sacredness. One noted limitation of the theory is that it has the propensity to essentialise the sacredness of nature to the extent that it overshadows its utilitarian value, forgetting that although nature has an equal need to survive, humans need food, shelter and energy. Its focus, however, has to be understood in terms of a give-and-take relationship between people and nature: "We take care of the land and the earth also takes care of us" (Merchant, 2005:85).

Literature review

In this section, I review some available literature on African Indigenous Religions and the environment in sub-Saharan Africa in general, and in Zimbabwe in particular, in order to get the necessary background information on environmental sustainability through the said religions. I am doing this to widen the appreciation of the interface of Ndau indigenous religion and environmental sustainability. This

6

is in line with Michael and Isaac (2000), who posit that a literature review helps the researcher to articulate the research problem more precisely. A literature review also helps the researcher to make the right decisions about the methodology to be used in light of the success and failure of other methodologies used in an area of interest (Peter, 1994). Some of the relevant works from sub-Saharan Africa are reviewed below.

Okyere-Manu (2018) posits that ecological degradation is on the increase and the most vulnerable communities, particularly in Africa, are suffering the consequences; this includes ravaged farmlands, polluted river bodies, climate change, low food production, and many others. Okyere-Manu (2018) strongly stresses that the search for effective sustainable ecological conservation strategies can never be more relevant than now. Her work assesses the processes and practicality of the integration of indigenous knowledge systems, which include religious beliefs and practices, with modern ecological conservation strategies, and she also outlines the ethical implications of this. She employs the theoretical lens of consequentialism, which prioritises acts in which the results will produce the greatest level of happiness for the greatest number of people. The theory is in line with the need to come up with effective sustainable ecological conservation strategies to save vulnerable communities. Her findings are that there is a need to deconstruct and reconstruct the values embedded in the two approaches for meaningful integration to occur. This work provides some insights that help my exploration of the Ndau indigenous religio-cultural notion of communal existence and sustainable environmental conservation strategies.

Awuah-Nyamkeye (2014) examines the methods of knowing and transmitting indigenous knowledge in the Berekum traditional area of the Brong Ahafo region in Ghana. He argues that a society's level of development, in terms of its socio-cultural political and economic lives, depends on how knowledge is generated and disseminated within that society. Employing a qualitative methodology, he identified the main means through which indigenous ecological knowledge is transmitted to students, namely proverbs, myths, folk tales and rituals. His findings indicate that indigenous ecological knowledge is a potential resource that can complement scientific means of dealing with the region's environmental problems. In another related work, Awuah-Nyamkeye (2009) is concerned about the rate at which Ghana is experiencing environmental degradation. He posits that researchers, individuals, eco-conscious groups and governments have made tremendous efforts trying to salvage the situation over the years without success. In his view, the failure can be attributed to the neglect of two important related areas, namely African religious traditions and cultural values. Awuah-Nyamkeye (2009) brings to the fore some of the means that Akan indigenous religion and culture have used over the years to sustain the balance of the ecosystem. He argues that there has to be an integration of the perspectives of science and of indigenous spiritualties and culture to provide a lasting solution to Ghana's environmental problems.

Amoah (2006), in a preface to a work titled *African women, religion, culture and health: Essays in honour of Mercy Amba Ewudziwa Oduyoye*, describes the circumstances of Mercy Oduyoye's birth and the historical context in which she grew up as having shaped and directed to a large extent what she ultimately became. According to Amoah, Mercy's life was marked by a bumper yield of yams, which followed the planting of seed together with her placenta and umbilical cord on the Yamoah farmstead (Phiri & Nadar, 2006:xviii). This cultural and religious practice of planting an umbilical cord and the afterbirth of a newly born baby together with a food crop is still practised amongst the rural Akan. Amoah (2006: xviii) says that the "ritual act symbolically links and spiritually identifies individuals with the land, the family and the entire community". Her conclusion is that through this act, nature in its infinite wisdom was already carving a path for Mercy Oduyoye's role in religion and society. This work provides some insight into how in most African traditional religious and cultural beliefs nature is intricately entwined with human life. This kind of relationship means that from the African indigenous perspective, nature is not lifeless and material; it is alive. The belief cultivates a relationship of reverence for nature that is positive for the environment.

Taringa (2014) offers a critical comparative study of Shona and Christian attitudes to nature. He sets out to review the existing attitudes to nature in the two religions. This has important implications for the formulation of a public environmental ethic in which traditional Shona and Christian adherents participate in the context of the deteriorating ecological situation in Zimbabwe. The work raises the issue that the environmental crisis in Zimbabwe, as in many places throughout the world, could be fundamentally a moral and religious problem. He examines various beliefs and concerns that are central to attitudes to nature in the two religions. He does this in order to establish the possible reference points for an interreligious discourse aimed at formulating a framework for an interreligious environmental ethic. For him, this framework is open to redefinition and reorientation of traditional attitudes and even to the evolution of new attitudes to nature. The flexible traits of the framework resonate with the focus of the theory of the re-imagination or re-enchantment of nature that I utilise in this chapter in a bid to find some effective sustainable environmental conservation strategies.

Chirongoma (2012) discusses the critical challenge of ecological degradation confronting the Zimbabwean community from an ecofeminist perspective. She looks at the gendered impact of ecological degradation, highlighting that women suffer most when the water source dries up or when firewood becomes scarce, because they need to walk long distances to fetch water and firewood to prepare food for the family. Her views resonate with those of Merchant (2005:213), who argues that "[t]hird world women have borne the brunt of environmental crises … As subsistent farmers, urban workers, or middle-class professionals, their ability to provide basic subsistence and healthy conditions is threatened." Chirongoma (2012) notes the patriarchal nature of Shona society and highlights the twin domination by men of nature and women in patriarchal settings. Chirongoma argues that if nature is to be saved, there is a need for a change of heart and attitude, especially on the part of some men who are on the forefront of exploiting both women and the ecological order. Chirongoma posits that men have to learn a new kind of maleness that puts up with some qualities that they have always deemed fit only for women, which include empathy and yielding in love. She sees women, especially mothers, as the best teachers. Chirongoma is reflective of the living reality in patriarchal societies where nature and women often suffer domination by men much to the disadvantage not only of the victims but of humanity in general, since women and nature are at the centre of life. However, the work is silent on the weaknesses of the ecofeminist perspective in ecological discourse. For example, ecofeminism assumes that "women and men … have an essential human nature that transcends culture and socialization. It implies that what men do to the planet is bad, and what women do is good" (Merchant, 2005:204). Secondly, the ethic of care associated with women falls prey to the essentialist critique that women's nature is to nurture. In this regard, ecofeminism essentialises the caretaking and nurturing traits that are assigned by patriarchy. It would appear that by these actions women cement their own oppression in a patriarchal society. Chirongoma (2012:121) seems to concede to this view when she says: "It is women who stand out in this ecological ministry because they have been ascribed the role of mothering, preserving and nurturing mother-earth, which is the main source of their livelihood."

Maposa and Mhaka (2013) examine the role and significance of the Shona culture in relation to the management of water resources against the backdrop of the challenges posed by climate change in Zimbabwe. They are concerned that in the postcolonial era, no African country has done enough to salvage whatever has remained of the indigenous environmental culture to address the water management techniques. Arguing from the perspective of indigenous knowledge systems (IKS), they aver that in the indigenous Shona culture, water management technology hinges on the proper and sustainable management of the environment. They concur with Rusinga and Maposa (2010), who argue that prior to the colonisation of Zimbabwe in 1890, the indigenous methods of natural resources management imposed little stress on the environment. Some political, economic and social developments in Zimbabwe have led to the country's deep environmental crisis in recent years. This work advances the agenda of returning IKS to the centre, integrating it with the modern ways of conserving the environment for the good of human and nonhuman lives.

Murove (2009) notes that much of the African continent is experiencing levels of environmental degradation and wildlife depletion that are alarming for the welfare of future generations. His argument is that environmental degradation is an ethical problem that, therefore, should look to ethical principles for its solutions. He thinks that African ethics, as espoused in the concepts of *ukama* (kinship/relatedness) and *ubuntu*, offer a plausible paradigm that can help the present generation, and humanity at large, to harmonise their behaviour with the natural environment. He concurs with Ramose (2009), Bujo (2009) and Prozesky (2009). The concepts that Murove (2009) raises are important in that they provide the basis for understanding the themes of embeddedness, reciprocity, interdependence and interconnectedness that I deal with in this chapter in the context of the Ndau to find effective sustainable environmental conservation strategies.

The Ndau people

The Ndau people are a minority ethnic group found in the Manicaland Province in the eastern parts of Zimbabwe. They are concentrated in Chipinge and Chimanimani, sprawling into the central parts of Mozambique (Konyana, 2014). The Ndau have always been grouped together with other Shona ethnic groups, which include Manyika, Korekore, Karanga, and Zezuru, but scholarship on the Shona has often focused on these other ethnic groups, sidelining the Ndau. Ndau had been a dialect of Shona prior to the adoption of a new constitution in 2013. The new constitution of Zimbabwe (chapter 1, section 6), recognises Ndau as an official language independent of the Shona (Zimbabwe, 2013). This has increased interest in research on the Ndau. The Ndau had wanted this separation for a long time. For example, they had for long lamented the imposition of a language on them, especially through the school system, where Ndau children were expected to learn some Shona dialects at the expense of their own Ndau dialect. For the Ndau, it was dehumanising to have a language imposed on them.

Secondly, the use of the term 'Shona' for the people living in Zimbabwe and central Mozambique is problematic. Shona is neither an ethnic nor a tribal label, as often assumed, but it is an accepted linguistic term that identifies speakers of the Shona language, which falls within the south-central zone of the Bantu language group. Doke (cited in MacGonagle, 2007), the linguist who recommended the term, however, noted the challenges associated with the term. According to the Doke's report:

[i]t has been widely felt that the name 'Shona' is inaccurate and unworthy, that is, it is not the true name of any of the peoples whom we propose to group under the term 'Shona-speaking people', and further that it lies under a strong suspicion of being a name given in contempt by the enemies of the tribes. It is pretty certainly a foreign name and as such is very likely to be uncomplimentary.

(MacGonagle, 2007)

Settling on a specific group in this chapter limits confusion that might be caused by the ambiguity of the term 'Shona'. The Chipinge area comprises seven Ndau chiefdoms, namely Garahwa, Gwenzi, Mahenye, Mapungwana, Mupungu, Musikavanhu and Mutema, while the Chimanimani area is home to five Ndau chiefdoms: Chikukwa, Mutambara, Muusha, Ndima and Ngorima (Sithole, 2019). This chapter focuses on three chiefdoms in Chipinge on the Zimbabwean side, namely chiefs Gwenzi Mapungwana and Musikavanhu. These chiefdoms were selected because of their accessibility in the aftermath of the devastating cyclone Idai that destroyed the road network in Chimanimani and some parts of Chipinge in 2019.

Ndau indigenous religion

The value system of the Ndau, like in many African societies including the various Shona subgroups, is underpinned by an elaborate indigenous religion (Gelfand, 1973). It is imperative, therefore, to outline the Ndau indigenous religion for this will help in identifying the synergies between the Ndau religio-cultural values and sustainable environmental conservation.

The Ndau world view, like many other African indigenous religious world views, is a three-tier structure that comprises the spiritual world, the natural world and the human world. The spirit world (*Vari kumhepo* literally meaning "those in the atmosphere") constitutes the community of the unseen spiritual beings that include Mwari (God), ancestral spirits, alien spirits and many others. The exact location of this world is not clear, but it is believed to exist in the midst of the community of the living (Mhlanga, 2019). The human world is the realm of human beings and their social interactions located in the physical world. It is Nyika, meaning the land of the living. The natural world is part of the physical world that comprises all forms of natural resources that include land, rivers, mountains, flora, fauna and many others that can operate as the objects of the manifestation of the spirit world in the human world.

The three worlds are intertwined and make up the cosmic totality of the Ndau conception of life. The existence of each world is dependent on the other, but ultimately the spiritual beings are more powerful than the physical beings, because Mwari created all things. Okoye (2006) puts it succinctly when he says that amongst

Africans nature, persons, ancestors and the unseen world are bound together in cosmic oneness. They cannot talk of well-being unless there is harmony in the cosmic totality. The Ndau have respect and a strong belief that the natural world provides a habitat to the spiritual world and it is the provider of foods, minerals and other resources. The sacred shrines, wetlands and woodlands are spiritual habitats and the foundation of survival.

Ndau society depends heavily on the spiritual world for guidance. The spirit world also punishes and blesses the human world in cases of misbehaviour and obedience respectively. Like many African societies, the Ndau hold that every plant, animal and natural phenomenon is a bearer of the divine. It is taboo amongst the Ndau to pass negative comments about any aspect of natural phenomena lest one provokes the ire of the divine. This means that everything in the universe has life. Therefore, the world is not lifeless and material; it is alive. To maintain the balance, the Ndau have to relate meaningfully to both the natural and spirit world. The flora and the fauna are entities in the natural world that play a hierophantic role as they indicate the route through which messages are transmitted between the spiritual and human world.

The spirit world is fashioned in a way that reflects how the society is structured. In Ndau society, the most senior person, usually the chief, is at the top. He is approached through a mediator and only in cases of emergency is he addressed directly. Requests to the chief or the most senior person go through a process known as *kusuma* (presenting a request). The most junior member in attendance is the one who is told what the request is all about. Mwari (God) is at the apex of the hierarchy, followed by the royal ancestral spirits down to the level of the family in a way that mirrors the hierarchy of power present in Ndau society. For the Ndau, Mwari (God) is not perturbed by the petitions of the people; rather the family and territorial spirits are the busiest of the constituents of the spirit world. It is the duty of the living to maintain a relationship with those in the spiritual world. This is underpinned by the belief that life continues in spiritual form after death, during which the dead continue to influence the community they left behind (Mbiti, 1969).

The notion of ancestral spirits expresses the common African idea of the increased power of the dead in their role as the guardians of the land and the people (Schoffelers, 1979). They are at their best when they have been accorded proper funeral rites by their living descendants, which include decent burial and traditional ceremonies in their honour. Amongst the Ndau, as in most African societies, ancestral spirits are the kingpins of the society. They influence the activities and lives of the living descendants of their community. Ranger (1991) concurs when he posits that "African religious ideas were very much ideas about relationships, whether with other living people or with spirits of the dead or with animals or with cleared bush

6

or with the bush". The involvement of the ancestral spirits in the life of the living constitutes the spiritual nature of the Ndau community.

Ndau religio-cultural values as the bedrock of their communal existence

African Indigenous Religions, in general, are all about relationships. The Ndau are not an exception. They have a value system that clearly outlines virtues and vices in society. The Ndau regulate conduct and mould commendable human character (Ndau: *Untu*; Shona: *Unhu*; Ndebele/Zulu: *Ubuntu*) intricately linked to religious beliefs. *Untu/Botho/Buthu* are Bantu words that denote the same concept. The notions of *Botho/Ubuntu/Buthu* provided by Gaie (cited in Dube, 2009:200) are defined as "the capacity to live responsibly and respectfully with and among other people", which also applies to *Untu*. These concepts emphasise relationships, as these concepts are about concern for others. This is expressed in Mbiti's (1969:108-109) axiom: "I am because we are; since we are, therefore I am." A person with *Untu/Ubuntu* is referred to as *muntu kwaye* in Ndau, meaning a good person. *Untu/Ubuntu* and other Bantu variations entail the capacity to live humanly with others in accordance with beliefs held by the community. *Muntu kwaye* (a good person) exhibits good behaviour towards others and every element that constitutes the cosmic totality of the Ndau community. Murove (2009:315), writing about the Shona, says that "human well-being is indispensable from our dependence on, and interdependence with, all that exists and particularly with the immediate environment on which all humanity depends".

The web of relationships amongst the Ndau goes beyond the living beings. It is rather a cosmic totality that includes the living, the living-dead, the unborn, the flora and the fauna, and the rest of other inanimate elements comprising the environment. This interconnectedness is best explained by the Ndau concept of *Ukama* (kinship/relatedness), shared with the Shona groups (Murove, 2009). *Ukama* (kinship/relatedness) expresses the interconnectedness and interdependence of the human and nonhuman within their environment. The Ndau do not talk of well-being when there is no harmony in this cosmic totality. It is not uncommon for the Ndau indigenous communities to call nonhuman living beings 'people' or confer human traits on nonhuman entities. For example, birds may be referred to as 'winged people' and the Earth may be personified as having a sharp appetite for food: *pashi ari guti* (the Earth has an insatiable appetite) or *pasi panodya* in Shona (the Earth eats) (Taringa, 2014). In this sense, the Ndau cosmology is biocentric as opposed to being anthropocentric. This means that the Ndau indigenous religion embraces the interconnectedness and ultimate identity of all life. A good person owes their sound character or personality to their parents, but principally to their family spirits. This means that the source of values amongst the Ndau is the effective social institution and an elaborate indigenous spirituality. The religious-cultural values of the Ndau, therefore, are the bedrock for the communal existence expressed through interconnectedness, reciprocity, reverence and embeddedness with all elements that constitute their community.

Ndau communal existence expressed through interconnectedness

The theme of interconnectedness assumes a strong sense of kinship with all aspects of the Ndau cosmic totality. As has been said before, the world of the Ndau is not lifeless but is very much alive. As a result, all aspects of the Ndau community are just as alive and conscious as humans, and with humans form a single community that enjoys unity in diversity. The nonhuman aspects include land, fauna, mountains, rocks/stones, flora, air and water bodies. I find Young's (2013) writing about the Native Americans resonates with the Ndau cosmology. Young (2013:310) posits that

> [a] sense of kinship with all beings has caused Native Americans to approach other beings as brothers and sisters. Other animals are considered fellow 'people' whose rights must be honoured and who have a great deal to teach those who are attentive. Stones, trees, mountains and all other 'natural objects' also are alive, and can educate those willing to listen to them.

Like other African indigenous communities everywhere, the Ndau develop a spiritual relationship with particular animals, plants or even inanimate objects.

The principle of totem animals amongst the Ndau, for instance, summarises this interconnectedness in a convincing manner. Ndau clans identify with particular animal species as their *mutupo* (totem animals). For example, the Muyambo clan is associated with aquatic species, especially the Mvuu (hippopotamus). Additionally, the water body, in this case Dziya (Great Pool), is viewed as the source of their origins. Other totem animals include Dhliwayo (termites), Simango (monkey/baboon), Dube (zebra), Mtetwa (birds/chickens), and many others. Each clan has its own taboos and restrictions related to their particular totemic animals. The Ndau believe that if they partake of their totem animals, their teeth will fall out, and that if totemic animals are killed, the culprit will experience *mashura* (mysterious occurrences) that include mysterious diseases. Besides the totemic principle, the Ndau hold that animals are hierophanies through which spirits manifest in the human world. They convey both negative and positive 'messages' depending on the circumstances. Some 'messages' may be a warning of impending danger and the Ndau may ignore them at their own peril. Baboons and snakes are some of the most reliable spirit mediums. Totem animals have a mythical and religious significance, and because of that, they feature in praise poetry of respective clans.

Domestic animals are equally important. Besides their social and economic value, domestic animals amongst the Ndau are also important in the spiritual sense. Death is the fundamental human problem amongst the Ndau and they are always keen to identify the enemies of life to defeat death. Bujo (2009:282) concurs when he says that "Africans believe life to be most sacred but life is permanently threatened by death. The human person's task is to identify the enemies of life to defeat death". Witchcraft is often suspected as lying behind any inexplicable health challenges. The Ndau believe that livestock provide a buffer between them and anti-life forces. Mysterious deaths of livestock are construed as warnings from enemies or offended ancestral spirits and appropriate ritual action is taken to avoid a further deterioration of the situation (Mhlanga, 2019). As a result, for the Ndau, there has to be a justification that meets the approval of the spirit elders for slaughtering a beast or chicken.

Ndau communal existence expressed through reciprocity

Another important aspect of the communal existence of the Ndau indigenous world view is reciprocity, a theme that assumes a sense of living in harmony. It is inspired by the underlying belief that the cosmos exists in a delicate balance. The only way to ensure sustenance of this balance is through forging and maintaining a relationship of reciprocity with all the aspects of the cosmos that include nature. Young (2013:311) avers that "reciprocity means that if humans show proper respect, the spirit beings will respond favourably and assist humans as they seek to live harmoniously".

The Ndau's interaction with the wetlands/water bodies expresses a sense of reciprocal exchange with the spirit world. The 1971 Ramsar Convention (cited in the Environmental Management Authority [EMA], 2014) defines wetlands as

> including a wide variety of habitats such as marshes, peat lands, flood plains, rivers, lakes, coastal areas such as salt marshes, mangroves, sea grass beds, coral reefs and other marine areas no deeper than six metres at low tide, as well as human-made wetlands such as waste water treatment ponds and reservoirs.

The EMA (2015) defines wetlands as "areas of land that are flooded with water, either seasonal or permanently". It further categorises wetlands into three types, namely inland wetlands, coastal wetlands, and man-made wetlands. Inland wetlands include marshes, ponds, lakes, fans, rivers, floodplains, and swamps. Coastal wetlands comprise mangrove, salt-water marshes, estuaries, lagoons, and coral reefs. Man-made wetlands include fishponds, salt pans and rice paddies.

For the Ndau, *matoro* (wetlands) are sacred places since they provide habitats to animals and reptiles associated with the spirits. For example, some pools in wetlands are the abode of *njuzu* (mermaids or water spirits) and some big snakes like the python. They are the guardians of the wetlands on behalf of the spirit world. The

Ndau approach such places with caution and strict observance of the taboos. Earthenware, gourds and wooden containers are the only utensils allowed to be used to draw water. Metal utensils and any items that have been used for cooking are not permissible there. Use of such items may cause the water to dry up because it angers the guardians of the wetlands. Nature will have spoken. This assumes that nature has a voice and can share a message that all human beings can hear (Bauman et al., 2011). Fragrant toiletries are not permissible in these places in the same way that emissions from combustion engines are unwelcome in the sacred space because they choke the spirits (Lan, 1985).

The wetlands are not always dangerous to the Ndau. The wetlands around the Murimbira pool in Chief Mapungwana, Bonyongwe village are a source of livelihood for the Ndau. The Ndau hold that if proper conduct is observed through respecting taboos and prohibitions, the wetlands will provide rich supplementary foods (Machowiro, 2019). For example, they are a source of fish and other small aquatic animals, especially in the dry season, but only if people take what is truly needed and spare the rest to meet future needs. This partnership ethic is also applied to wild fruits and other edibles in the forest. The Ndau also cultivate yam, banana, sugarcane (grass crop) and a variety of vegetable crops that help them in times of drought. They believe that they owe their success to their ancestors.

River valleys and flood plains are also regarded as sacred. These are habitats of the ancestral spirits. Amongst the Ndau, children who die before the teething stage are buried in river valleys. They are believed to have been returned to the spirit world to regenerate the lost life. The burial is conducted exclusively by postmenopausal elderly women who are believed to be in clean ritual condition. Writing on gender flexibility and African Indigenous Religions in general, Grillo, Van Klinken and Ndzovu (2019:196) express this belief:

> As persons age, they are believed to take on greater spiritual power. Female elders past menopause occupy a transcendent status as human beings who have surpassed gender. This widespread conception of their special nature is most clearly expressed in ritual performance.

From a gender perspective, we have to employ a hermeneutic of suspicion when engaging with this belief because of the patriarchal privileges that often lurk behind such beliefs. The Ndau, like many other African societies, also struggle with overt and covert privileges extended to men courtesy of patriarchal structures. The belief may be a patriarchal ploy to 'accept' women elders past menopause as 'men'. They have ceased to be 'women' but have become 'men' and, therefore, can preside over ritual practice without threatening men's monopoly of power. In this sense, ritual performance by this category of women is a duty ascribed to them by patriarchy to advance patriarchal interests. Be that as it may, unsanctioned movements in sacred river valleys and flood plains often put the 'trespassers' at risk of *chahwihwi* (losing direction temporarily and wandering about in the valleys) (Salani, 2019). Proper behaviour by a selected category of elderly women keeps the sanctity of these sacred places intact.

Ndau communal existence expressed through reverence

As noted earlier, the communal existence of the Ndau indigenous world view holds that all of life is interrelated and therefore spiritual. The spiritual aspect of the cosmic totality of the Ndau draws a response of reverence in all interactions between humans and nonhumans within the community. It is from this perspective that the Ndau are not only biocentric, but more importantly ecocentric. Forests, mountains, caves, rivers, big trees, rocks and many other aspects of nature are alive. This belief in pan-vitalism inspires deep respect for nature. In the Ndau community, for example, big trees are regarded as resting places for ancestral spirits. On such premises, the Ndau are wary about the language they use as they want to avoid offending ancestral spirits. Big trees are often meeting places for rituals. *Muhacha/Muchakata* (*Parinari curatellifolia*) is the most commonly used tree for rainmaking rituals. *Muhacha* thrives throughout drought spells owing to their deep roots that access the water table. So, it symbolises abundant life, since it nourishes life during drought through the provision of fruit. The ancestral spirits are believed to stay in the forests. The forests become a place of refuge for the Ndau in times of an attack from enemies (MacGonagle, 2007). Dumping of litter and relieving oneself in the forests is prohibited. The Ndau hold a belief that anyone who breaches the taboo would be followed by the litter and/or human waste wherever they go.

Access to the sacred forest that is not sanctioned is dangerous, because it may result in death. Unwarranted comments about the quality of trees and vegetation, let alone wanton destruction, are believed to infuriate ancestral spirits who may respond with the disappearance of the culprit (Taringa, 2014:53). Gluttonous behaviour is punishable by endless uptake of the resource regardless of being full. The Ndau are encouraged to take only what is needed to avoid embarrassment by the vengeance of ancestral spirits.

Ndau communal existence expressed through embeddedness

The notion of the communal existence of the Ndau emphasises embeddedness in all aspects of their spiritual community, and in particular the land. The land is alive and must be treated with respect. Young (2013:310) avers that "although sometimes male, or often sexless, the earth is indeed widely linked to femininity and motherhood". The Ndau are a people with a strong sense of belonging to their territorial space. They identify with everything that is on it. The name 'Ndau' means not just a place, but a sacred geographical territory entwined with the Ndau people's sacred history. For the Ndau in particular, and many Africans in general, the land symbolises belonging, connectedness and continuity. In support of this conception of land use and importance, Bakare (1993) thinks that "[l]and (house) is a place of connection with mother earth, where one's roots are, where one's umbilical cord has been buried, where one's ancestors are deposited, a place of connection and orientation". For the Ndau, land is priceless; it offers them an identity, a livelihood, and it is sacred because it forms a close and enduring bond between the living and the dead (Mbiti, 1969). For this reason, the Ndau believe they have a sacred duty to protect the land and work responsibly on it to bequeath it to future generations in good shape. Most Ndau men prefer to be buried on their piece of land as a guaranteed indigenous title deed for posterity. Their women would be buried by their husbands' sides.

The Ndau share a particularly strong relationship with vegetation. Several tree species serve various purposes in the Ndau community. Some tree species scare away witches, wizards, lightning and all forces with evil intentions. They are employed in rituals to protect homesteads. Such trees are grown around the homes. The healing paraphernalia of the Ndau traditional healers often include various ingredients from nature to express this holistic approach to life. As a result, unpleasant comments on nature are unwelcome and it is feared that nature will respond through some punishment in the form of disappearances or insanity.

Synergies between Ndau communal existence and the agenda for environmental sustainability

Themes of interconnectedness, reciprocity, reverence and embeddedness espoused in the Ndau notion of communal existence provide neat synergies with the United Nations' (2015) call for sustainable environments enshrined in its Sustainable Development Goals (SDGs) 2030 vision as well as the tenets of some environmentalist movements.

The Ndau's notion of communal existence and the United Nations' SDGs

The United Nations' SDG number 13 calls for climate change action to mitigate one of the worst environmental crisis of our times. Climate change gives rise to extreme weather, including intense rains and stifling temperatures. The increase in the concentration of atmospheric carbon dioxide is the main cause of climate change. The mitigation efforts are enshrined in SDG number 15, whose main objective is to ensure the conservation, restoration and sustainable use of terrestrial and inland freshwater ecosystems and their services, in particular forests, wetlands, mountains and dry lands (United Nations, 2015). Wetlands vegetation helps in mitigating climate change as it acts as a carbon dioxide reservoir and assists in reducing the amount of carbon dioxide in the atmosphere, mitigating the greenhouse effect and leading to a more stable climate. Proper management of wetlands is, therefore, crucial as they offer a variety of ecosystem services that contribute to human well-being. These services include, but are not limited to, climatic stability, flood control, erosion prevention, fire control and improvement of water quality, as well as cultural services such as aesthetic satisfaction and spiritual values (EMA, 2014).

Wetlands control floods in that their vegetation regulates stream and river flow. Vegetation in and adjacent to wetlands and rivers slows water flow and holds soil together, preventing soil erosion. As a fire control mechanism, the soil and vegetation in the wetlands are wet most of the time and discourage the spreading of veld fires. Wetland ecosystems also improve water quality, as they filter pollutants and break down decaying material. They are the kidneys of the ecosystem (EMA 2014). There is a rich synergy between the Ndau attitude to wetlands and the United Nations' call for proper management of the same. The Ndau attitude to wetlands provides a spiritual resource that can partner with the agenda for a healthy environment for all by 2030.

The Ndau's attitude to aquatic life, in particular fish, finds resonance in the United Nations' SDG number 14 that calls for the conservation and the sustainable use of oceans, seas and marine resources for sustainable development. Target number 4, in particular, aims to regulate harvesting, and end overfishing and other destructive fishing practices by 2030. The Ndau ethic on harvesting natural resources, which include fishing, is that people must take what is truly needed and spare the rest for future needs. The Ndau's attitude to forests and flora, in general, encourages the spirit of protecting and maintaining ecosystems. The spirit implicit in this attitude coincides with the United Nations' SDG 15, whose aim it is to manage forests and to combat desertification, as well as halt and reverse land degradation and halt biodiversity loss or the extinction of threatened species.

The Ndau's notion of communal existence and the tenets of Deep Ecology

The Ndau's attitude to aspects of nature echo some tenets of some environmentalist movements such as radical ecology. Within this movement are various sub-environmentalist movements that include Deep Ecology, Earth First, Eco-Feminism, Social Ecology, Animal Liberation and environmental liberation. The bottom line is that these versions have a common point of contact in that the environment is in a deep crisis that requires urgent action. Bornhill and Gottlieb (2010) assert that Deep Ecology is an ecological and environmental philosophy promoting the inherent worth of living beings, regardless of their instrumental utility in meeting human needs. Carter (1999) posits that "the movement describes itself as 'deep' because it regards itself as looking more deeply into the actual reality of human relationship with natural world arriving at philosophically more profound conclusions than of the prevailing view of ecology as a branch of biology". Like the Ndau's communal existence, Deep Ecology's basic principle is that the natural world is a subtle balance of complex interrelationships in which the existence of organisms is dependent on coexistence of others within ecosystems.

Deep Ecology's core principle is the belief that the living environment as a whole should be respected and regarded as having basic moral and legal rights to live and flourish, independent of its instrumental benefits for human use. The movement does not subscribe to anthropocentric environmentalism that is concerned with the conservation of the environment only for exploitation by humans for human purposes. The movement holds that the ecological problems faced by the world today are a result of the loss of traditional knowledge, values and ethics of behaviour that celebrate the intrinsic value and sacredness of the natural world and that considers the preservation of nature of prime significance. They posit that learning how to live in harmony with the surroundings is beneficial, because stopping the global extinction crisis and achieving ecological sustainability requires rethinking our values as a society (Daniel, 1980). Taylor (1998) contends that radical environmentalism is best understood as a new religious movement that views environmental degradation as an assault on a sacred, natural world.

Challenges of the Ndau's communal existence in advancing sustainable environment

The Ndau's communal existence is based on a metaphysical dimension that mobilises respect for the environment. The argument is plausible and deserves respect, but the premises on which it is based are only accessible to believers and may not be accepted by people who do not subscribe to the religious, cultural and ethical values and beliefs of the community. Some tenets of the Ndau communal existence are detestable and offensive to people who profess other religious beliefs. Need and greed are lethal forces that are detrimental to the environment. The poor do damage to the environment out of need and the rich do the same out of greed. The killing of game and destruction of forests and wetlands for monetary gain are also prevalent amongst the Ndau community. The Ndau's notion of communal existence has been shaken over the years. *Untu/Ubuntu* and *Ukama* (kinship/relatedness) are home-grown values on which this communal existence is based. These values can inspire the emergence of strong and vibrant communities, but they are overwhelmed by an emerging society that is obsessed with a "rapid material advancement of the few with no great concern for the rest" (Prozesky, 2009:302). In this stampede for material advancement, the environment is the greatest loser.

6

Conclusion

The chapter has discussed themes of interconnectedness, reverence, embeddedness and reciprocity with nature in the Ndau cosmology that are inspired by the Ndau's notion of communal existence. This communal existence is based on the religio-cultural and ethical values of *Untu/Ubuntu* and *Ukama* (kinship/relatedness). What has emerged from this chapter is that these themes have several points of synergy with the wider agenda for environmental sustainability espoused in, for example, the United Nations' SDGs and some environmentalist movements such as Deep Ecology. Like many Africans, the Ndau are characterised by a holistic type of thinking in which they conceive of themselves as being in close relationship with all aspects of the entire cosmos. This thinking does not recognise any dichotomy between the sacred and the secular. Their self-consciousness is incomplete without peaceful coexistence with the land and everything on it that includes vegetation, animals, water bodies and many other aspects of their biosphere. The chapter has also highlighted challenges with the Ndau's notion of communal existence. I concur with Chirongoma (2012:142), who notes that "most of the problems affecting the country are a result of the economic difficulties that force people to engage in activities that damage the ecological order". The current incessant power outages experienced across the country promote massive destruction of forests and woodlands for alternative sources of fuel. Firewood has become a brisk business in towns and cities of Zimbabwe. Notwithstanding these challenges, the chapter concludes that, in the face of a threatening environmental crisis, there is a critical need for the revitalisation of an awareness of the interdependence of human beings and the natural environment – a type of thinking that does not dichotomise the sacred and the profane, but is more like the views espoused in the Ndau's notion of communal existence.

References

Amoah, E. 2006. Preface. In: I.A. Phiri & S. Nadar (eds), *African women, religion and health: Essays in honour of Mercy Amba Ewudziwa Oduyoye.* Pietermaritzburg: Cluster Publications. xvii-xxii.

Awuah-Nyamkeye, S. 2009. Salvaging nature: The Akan religio-cultural perspective. *World Views Environment Culture Religion,* 13(3):251-282. https://doi.org/10.1163/13635240 9X12535203555713

Awuah-Nyamkeye, S. 2014. Indigenous ways of creating environmental awareness: A case study from Berekum traditional area, Ghana. *Journal for the Study of Religion and Culture,* 8(1):46-63. https://doi.org/10.1558/jsrnc.v8i1.46

Bakare, S. 1993. *My right to land in the Bible and in Zimbabwe: A theology of land in Zimbabwe.* Harare: Zimbabwe Council of Churches.

Bornhill, D.L. & Gottlieb, R.S. (eds). 2010. *Deep Ecology and world religions: New essays on sacred ground.* Boston, NY: State University of New York Press.

Bujo, B. 2009. Ecology and ethical responsibility from an African perspective. In: M.F. Murove (ed), *African ethics: An ontology of comparative and applied ethics.* Durban: University of KwaZulu-Natal Press.

Carter, A. 1999. *A radical green political theory.* London: Routledge.

Chirongoma, S. 2012. Karanga-Shona women's agency in dressing Mother Earth: A contribution towards an indigenous eco-feminist theology. *Journal of Theology for Southern Africa,* 142:120-144.

Chitando, E., Mapuranga, T.P. & Taringa, N.T. 2014. On top of which mountain does one stand to judge religion? Debates from a Zimbabwean Context. *Journal for the Study of Religion,* 27(2):115-136.

Daniel, B. 1980. *Discordant harmonies: A new ecology for the twenty-first century.* New York: Oxford University Press.

Dube, M.W. 2009. "I am because we are": Giving primacy to African indigenous values in HIV and AIDS prevention. In: M.F. Murove (ed), *African ethics: An ontology of comparative and applied ethics.* Durban: University of KwaZulu-Natal Press.

EMA (Environmental Management Authority). 2014. *World Wetlands Day 2014.* Harare: Environmental Management Authority.

EMA (Environmental Management Authority). 2015. *World Wetlands Day 2015.* Harare: Environmental Management Authority.

Gelfand, M. 1973. *The genuine Shona: Survival values of an African culture.* Salisbury: Mambo Press.

Grillo, L., Van Klinken, A. & Ndzovu, H.J. 2019. *Religions in contemporary Africa: An introduction.* London: Routledge. https://doi.org/10.4324/9781351260725

Konyana, E.G. 2014. Euthanasia in Zimbabwe? Reflections on the management of terminally ill persons and the dying in Ndau traditions of Chimanimani and Chipinge, South-East Zimbabwe. In: D.O. Laguda (ed), *Death and life after death in African philosophy and religions: A multidisciplinary engagement.* Harare: African Institute for Culture, Dialogue, Peace and Tolerance Studies.

Lan, D. 1985. *Guns and rain: Guerrillas and spirit mediums in Zimbabwe.* Berkeley, CA: University of California Press.

MacGonagle, E. 2007. *Crafting identity in Zimbabwe and Mozambique.* New York: University of Rochester Press.

Machowiro, C. 2019. Personal interview. 20 May, Village D, Bonyongwe Village, Musirizwi Resettlement, Chipinge.

Mack, N., Woodsong, C., MacQueen, K.M., Guest, G. & Namely, E. 2005. *Qualitative research methods: A data collector's field guide*. Durham, NC: Family Health International.

Maposa, R.S. & Mhaka, E. 2013. Indigenous culture and water technology: A reflection on the significance of the Shona culture in light of climate change in Zimbabwe. *Greener Journal of Art and Humanities*, 3(2):24-29. https://doi.org/10.15580/GJAH.2013.2.022613495

Mbiti, J.S. 1969. *African religions and philosophy*. Oxford: Heinemann.

Merchant, C. 2005. *Radical ecology: The search for a liveable world*. 2nd Edition. London: Routledge.

Mhlanga. D. 2019. Personal interview. 25 May and 30 August, Village 2, Ndamera Village, Musirizwi Resettlement, Chipinge.

Michael, A. & Isaac, L. 2000. *Quantum computation and quantum information*. Cambridge: Cambridge University Press.

Murove, M.F. 2009. An African environmental ethic based on the concepts of *Ukama* and *Ubuntu*. In: M.F. Murove (ed), *African ethics: An Ontology of comparative and applied ethics*. Durban: University of KwaZulu-Natal Press.

Okoye, J.C. 2006. *African theology*. http//www.uni-tuebingen.de/INSeCT/ [Accessed 21 January 2019].

Okyere-Manu, B. 2018. Integrating African Indigenous Knowledge Systems into Current Ecological Conservation Strategies: Ethical Implications for Policy Makers. In: B. Okyere-Manu & H. Moyo (eds), *Intersecting African indigenous systems and Western knowledge systems:*

moral convergence and divergence. Pietermaritzburg: Cluster Publications.

Peter, C.B. 1994. *A guide to academic writing*. Eldoret: Zapf.

Phiri, I.A. & Nadar, S. (eds). 2006. *African women, religion and health: Essays in honour of Mercy Amba Ewudziwa Oduyoye*. Pietermaritzburg: Cluster Publications.

Prozesky, M.H. 2009. Well-fed animals and starving babies: Environmental and developmental challenges from process and African perspectives. In: M.F. Murove (ed), *African ethics: An ontology of comparative and applied ethics*. Durban: University of KwaZulu-Natal Press.

Ramose, M.B. 2009. Ecology through Ubuntu. In: M.F. Murove (ed), *African ethics: An ontology of comparative and applied ethics*. Durban: University of KwaZulu-Natal Press.

Ranger, T.O. 1991. African traditional religion. In: S. Sutherland & P. Clarke (eds), *The study of religion, traditional and new religion*. London: Routledge. 864-872.

Rusinga, O. & Maposa, R.S. 2010. Traditional religion and natural resources: A reflection on the significance of Indigenous Knowledge Systems on the utilization of natural resources among the Ndau people in south-eastern Zimbabwe. *Journal of ecology and natural environment*, 2(9):201-206.

Salani, J. 2019. Personal interview. 25 May, Village K, Kondo Village, Musirizwi Resettlement, Chipinge.

Schoffeelers, J.M. 1979. *Guardians of the land: Essays on Central African territorial cults*. Gwelo: Mambo Press.

Sithole, L. 2018. An exploration of the interface between Shona traditional religious beliefs and practices and human rights: A case study of Ndau religion of Chipinge. Master's thesis, University of Zimbabwe, Harare.

Taringa, N.T. 2014. *Towards an African-Christian environmental ethic.* Bamberg: University of Bamberg Press.

Taylor, B. 1998. *Ecological resistance movement: The global emergence of radical and popular environmentalism.* New York: State University of New York Press.

United Nations. 2015. *United Nations Development Goals 2030.* https://sustatinabledevelopment.un.org/?menu=1300 [Accessed 21 January 2019].

Watling, T. 2009. *Ecological imaginations in the world religions: An ethnographic analysis.* New York: Bloomsbury Publishing.

Young, W.A. 2013. *The world's religions: Worldviews and contemporary issues.* Hoboken, NJ: Pearson.

Zimbabwe. 2013. *Constitution of Zimbabwe.* Harare: Government Printers.

7

THE IMPACT OF URBANISATION ON BURIAL RITUALS IN SOUTHERN AFRICA

Abednico Phili[1]

Abstract

The purpose of this chapter is to explore the significance of burial rituals and land amongst Africans. This will be done through examining burial rites and rituals. For Africans, the significance of land goes beyond the physical activities taking place on it. It is a place to which one has an attachment from the time of the birth rituals that are performed in order to seal the individual to his or her ancestral land. The ancestral land symbolises the relationship between the individual and the clan, the land and the spiritual world. However, the quest to get jobs and formal education has made many Africans move to urban areas, where they established permanent homes and leading eventually to burials in urban areas. Hence, this chapter argues that urban burials have severed Africans from their ancestral lands. The chapter acknowledges that burial in ancestral land always made exceptions for married women who are separated from their ancestral lands by marriage, and their graves linked to their marital homes. Though it would appear it does not matter where married women are buried, the literature suggests that there are rituals performed to reconnect them to their ancestral lands. The chapter adopts the social theories outlined by Wirth (1938), Marrall (2006) and Ayiera (2012). Their social theories provide a framework within which we can understand social communication and forms of connections in urban areas. In the light of the aforementioned theories, urban burials have the potential of severing the ties that Africans have to their ancestry. As a result of this, some Africans have repatriated the remains of their loved ones to rural areas to be buried in their ancestral lands amongst their consanguine as a way of reconnecting them to their ancestral lands.

---

1   Mr Abednico Phili is a master's candidate in the Department of Theology and Religious Studies, University of Botswana. [Email: phili594@yahoo.com]

Introduction

> Land is the greatest heritage of the African people. The health and wellbeing of
> the people is intertwined with the health and wellbeing of the land.
>
> (Naidu-Hoffmeester, 2018)

This epigraph is relevant to the chapter because it highlights the fact that, for Africans, the significance of land goes beyond the physical activities taking place on it. It is a place one has an attachment to because of the birth rituals that are performed in order to seal the individual to his or her ancestral land. The ancestral land symbolises the relationship between the individual and the clan, the land and the spiritual world. Africans are connected to land at birth, a fact that Naidu-Hoffmeester (2018) describes succinctly thus:

> From the time they are born, babies are rooted in their ancestral land by means
> of a ritual of burying the placenta. From birth till death and beyond, land
> represents people's spiritual and economic livelihood.

Therefore, Africans desire to be buried in their ancestral land upon death. Biwul (2017) noted that, while the exact location of the ancestral abode may not be clearly defined in the African conceptualisation, it is generally believed that it is not far from the domain of the living. Burying a family member outside their ancestral land is deemed an offence against the spirits of the land and commonly believed to be akin to 'throwing away' the dead by completely separating them from their lineage or clan. Mbiba (2010) concurs with this point when he says that urban burials are frowned upon and stigmatised.

This chapter argues that the interconnectedness described above is severed by the mass movement of the African rural people to urban areas. This is because urban centres have become loci of all income-generating activities, leading to people building permanent homes in urban areas. A consequence has been that Africans bury their loved ones in those areas, highlighting the impact of urbanisation on African burial rituals.

Theoretical framework

This chapter adopts Marrall's (2006) and Ayiera's (2012) social theories of belonging and urban burials. Marrall (2006) and Wirth (1938) describe social theory as a vehicle through which we can explain the social communication and connections formed in urban areas. The diversity of cultures found in towns creates what Wirth (1938) refers to as superficial relationships, which are prevalent in cities to promote social cohesion. Ayiera (2012) describes the theory of belonging as having historical connections to established spaces such as settlements that have a cohesive sense of community and stable social institutions. The theory emphasises that people belong to a place because they are tied to it by ancestry and the history of residing there. Belonging, therefore, invokes a sense of a claim to a physical space because of defined interests and common identities of culture, nationality, history, and sometimes race and religion. Yet at the same time, urban burials have the potential of severing ties that Africans have to their ancestry, thereby impacting on their burial rituals.

Marrall (2006) used the idea of a social frame to carry out a study on the impact of urbanisation on death and funerary practices in the United States of America. Her findings were that urbanism affects the rituals and ceremonies around death. She gave an example of Muslims who, during burial ceremonies, put emphasis on the body coming into physical contact with the soil, which is not permissible in urban areas as the body must be enclosed in a coffin. Marrall (2006) points out that urbanism attracts people from all walks of life with diverse cultures. In such circumstances, traditional social cohesion is impossible compared to rural settlements, where people live more homogeneously. According to the social framework, urban dwellers then acquire aspects of other cultures that were not inherently part of their traditional norms and values. This theory is important for this chapter as it will help us to identify whether there are burial rituals Africans have adapted from other cultures that have impacted on their original rites. It is argued here that when people move to urban centres, the family structure and ways of doing things are bound to change because of heterogeneity as people are removed from their extended families, which creates a social distance. Following Ayiera's (2012) position, it can also be argued that Africans' strong sense of belonging binds them to their ancestral land. Davison (2000) also argues that people may transport their culture, symbols and rituals to the new place; but all these are watered down as they create new affiliations that lead to significant cultural transformations. Ayiera's (2012) and Davison's (2002) assertions affirm and validates the social theory as appropriate for this research study, because as Africans move to urban cities, elements of their culture such as burial rituals are likely to undergo cultural transformation.

The importance of being buried in ancestral lands

The desire to be buried in ancestral lands is as old as humankind and a phenomenon that is prevalent in many societies the world over. The book of Genesis 23:1-20 highlights a scriptural prescription to be buried in one's ancestral land as a proper burial in Jewish culture. This implies that if one is not buried in one's ancestral lands, then one would not have been accorded a proper burial. It seems a matter of great shame, from a biblical point of view, not to be buried in the land of the forefathers. Walaza (2014) points out that, for Africans, the burial of the umbilical cord, placenta and hair that the child was born with is a ritual that seals the baby to its ancestral home. The burial of *inkaba* (umbilical cord), according to Walaza (2014), denotes the location of one's ancestral home and symbolises the relationship between the individual and his or her clan, the land and the spiritual world. Buttressing the importance of the ancestral land as a place where people should be interred upon their demise, Walaza (2014) notes that the highest honour usually bestowed upon an accomplished African who has acted in a manner befitting a born leader is to call the person a daughter or son of the soil. Walaza (2014) continues to show that amongst the amaXhosa it is very important that when such a person dies, then he/she be brought home to be buried to join a lineage of ancestors who came before him/her. For this reason, former President Nelson Mandela's last wish was to be buried in the soil near where his *inkaba* (umbilical cord) is buried. This is Qunu, the village Mandela called home (Walaza, 2014).

Post-independent South Africa saw the remains of those who died in exile being exhumed from their host countries and repatriated for reburial in their home country. Feni (2018) points out that the reburials were done so as to reconnect the dead with their ancestors and with the ancestral land. As a result, the remains of Duma Nokwe were exhumed from Zambia for reburial in South Africa, where one of the speakers said, "so let his bones rest back in his ancestral land (Feni, 2018). Moeti (2006) noted that the remains of Onkgopotse Tiro, Mnyele, and Essau Mokgethi were exhumed from the Gaborone Extension cemetery and repatriated to South Africa to accord the deceased persons proper burials with their clan and have family rituals performed to connect them to their ancestors. It is this connectivity that is severed when people are buried outside their ancestral land, as in the case of those who died in exile. The ancestral land is an important abode for the dead and the living in the African world view; connection with the land of one's birth after one's death is spiritually significant. Thus, as Tafira (2015) observes, in the African view, the significance of land extends beyond its economic aspect, because land belongs to the living, the dead and the unborn, making it inalienable. Hambira (1999) also postulates that, for the entire African world view, life is a continuum that links people: the unborn, the living and the departed. This idea is implicit in this chapter: the African world view and spirituality have strong links to their ancestral lands.

Ayiera (2012) thinks that many communities place great emphasis on where and how community or family members are buried. Ayiera (2012) further notes that family members of the deceased would strive to repatriate the remains of their loved ones for burial in ancestral soil, and the performance of burial rituals that reaffirm membership of the community. She describes this as follows: "Burial rituals and customs allow the individual to claim affiliation and express solidarity with a defined community. They give the individual a link that perpetuates his social identity in connection with his ancestors, the living and the unborn."

Ayiera (2012) continues that the experience of losing a loved one away from home (in exile) and burying them in a foreign land does not allow for the performance of the requisite rituals. This evokes a sense of alienation and an acute awareness that the exiles do not belong to the host country. This assertion by Ayiera (2012) affirms what this chapter seeks to show: that African burial rituals cannot be adequately performed in foreign urban centres as a result of many factors, including foreign cultural influences, that limit the performance of traditional death rites. Amanze (2002) also highlights the importance of ancestral land amongst the Basarwa of Central Kgalagadi Game Reserve (CKGR), who have a sentimental attachment to their land, hence making the CKGR their spiritual home. Amanze (2002) argues that relocating them to areas outside the CKGR impacted heavily on their spirituality. The argument raised here is that Basarwa's livelihoods are anchored to their ancestral lands.

The Midweek Sun (Sun Reporter, 2017) published a story in which 69-year-old Modise Motshoge exhumed his mother's remains from Mogoditshane cemetery to be reburied at Phomolong Cemetery in Phakalane. He was quoted as saying: "I want my mother's remains next to mine." The reasons as to why he preferred to be buried in Phakalane next to his mother are not provided, but it can be argued that his decision may have been influenced by the African world view of family members being close together, even in death, to maintain the social bond that existed in their lifetime. However, one notes that Phomolong is a burial site marked by social class and it is a status symbol. As a result of having achieved a high social status and economic advancement, this man wishes not to be buried in a common graveyard that may be his ancestral home. Yet he seems to believe that his spirit would be isolated in Phomolong, hence his desire to exhume his mother's remains and rebury them in Phomolong. Would that not isolate his mother from her ancestral land and lineage? The issue of one's economic advancement as a factor that has possibly influenced and impacted on Southern African burial rites is one of the questions addressed by this chapter.

However, it is worth mentioning that economic advancement and change in one's social status do not necessarily sever people from their ancestral lands. For example, great statesmen such as the former presidents of Botswana, the late Sir Seretse Khama and Sir Ketumile Masire, were laid to rest in their villages of Serowe and Kanye, respectively, despite being known to be some of the greatest leaders of the world. This may suggest that the cultural practice of being buried at home is clearly significant for Africans.

It is important to note that it is not only the aforementioned societies that have their spiritualties and religiosity completely connected to the ancestral land.

7

Amanze (2007) and Kamenju (2011) both observed that the link between people and land is not only an African issue, but one that cuts across societies because land in many parts of the world is seen as spiritual holding to both ancestors and the living. Manatsha (2012) highlights an important aspect of Bakalanga history when the remains of Chief Madawu Nswazwi (*She*) were exhumed and repatriated from Zimbabwe to be reburied in Nswazwi village in Botswana. Though Manatsha (2012) makes no mention of the ancestral home, it can be argued that home for the Bakalanga means a place to which one has a spiritual connection, a place of identity and belonging as is the case with other societies. Motshwari (2008) corroborates this view by describing Nswazwi as home, a place where Bakalanga ba ka Nswazwi from Zimbabwe reclaimed their rightful place in the land of their forefathers and reconnected with their roots. The aforementioned description of a home points to the fact that, for the Bakalanga, home means far more than the physical structures of houses and huts.

The effects of urbanism on burial rituals

Komoki (2005), who has written on the burial rituals of the Ovambanderu of Sehithwa, observed that death rituals have been affected by modernity, hence changes in all steps or processes of death have been affected in many cultures. Inferring from the above, it may be postulated that African burial rituals may have been affected by this strong wave of urbanism, which is an aspect of modernity. Wirth (1938) posits that the beginning of Western civilisation was marked by permanent settlements in cities of nomadic people from rural areas. According to Wirth (1938), urban life becomes a cosmopolitan condition controlling the locus of economic, political and cultural life, drawing the most remote parts of the world into its orbit. This he calls urbanisation. The shift from a rural to a predominantly urban society is always accompanied by profound changes in virtual every facet of social life. Sharing Wirth's (1938) sentiments, it is argued here that urbanisation has brought people of different cultures, norms and values together, which creates a heterogeneous society. Wirth (1938:10) summarises this new way of life as follows: "[T]he city has thus historically been a melting pot of races, peoples and cultures, and most favorable a breeding ground of new biological and cultural hybrids."

This point is very important to this chapter, because the peoples of Southern Africa are not an exception to rural-urban migration, which I argue contributes to the loss of cultural elements such as burial rites. Marrall (2006), like Wirth (1938), also defines urbanism as a way of life for those who reside in a densely inhabited area with a heterogeneous human population. She further observes that urbanism is a conglomeration of diverse cultures, world views and practices found in urban areas, which combine in a form of cultural mixing. The study by Marrall (2006) is very important and relevant to this research, because it is about how urbanism has affected funerary practices. Although her research is set within the context of North America, it highlights how urbanism as a global phenomenon affects cultural practices. Marrall (2006) further posits that urban dwellers have different funeral needs than their rural counterparts, owing to the heterogeneity of ethnically diverse residents. This is also true on the basis of my own observations made during funerals I attended in Francistown and Selibe Phikwe, which are urban areas, and Jackalas 1, which is a rural area. In the two urban areas, there was no fire at the entrance; windows were not smeared with ashes to symbolise death, as is the case in rural areas. It was also not easy to separate the chief mourner from the rest of the people who attended the funeral. But in the rural areas the distinctions were clear. This shows that when people move to urban areas, some of the rituals supposed to be performed are watered down. In addition to the aforementioned points, I observed that important rituals like grave identification performed in rural areas are not done in urban areas. This is because in urban areas graves are bought from the council, making a grave identification ritual impossible.

Marrall (2006) seems to have made similar observations when talking about Islamic burials, where the faith decrees the necessity of the body touching the soil when buried. She notes that the federal law in the United States of America insists that the body must be enclosed in a box for public health reasons. Therefore, for Muslims, this raises a cultural conflict of how to bury their loved ones following their religious rituals. Marrall (2006:13) highlights and describes the resolution to this conflict: "They followed the federal laws of burying in urban area using caskets but removing the bottom slats of the coffin upon burial so that the body would touch the soil yet be enclosed by US standards."

The aforementioned views by Marrall (2006) are a clear indication that when people move to urban areas, their burial rituals are affected. Therefore, by inference, the Bakalanga who bury their loved ones in urban areas may have their burial rituals altered to accommodate city councils' requirements. Newel (2010) observes that when a *Hosanna* (*Kalanga*, rain dancer) of the Bakalanga in Botswana dies, they are not buried like ordinary people. They are buried in a niche and this is a ritual that cannot be carried out in urban areas, thereby showing that these exceptions may be hindered by council laws affecting the burial of such special people.

Mbiba (2010) observes that burial at home in Zimbabwe is a crucially important concern. Zimbabweans in the diaspora save money through insurance schemes and burial associations to ensure that they will not rest forever in the foreign soil, but be repatriated to their homes. But Mbiba (2010) raises some pertinent questions about

7

what it means for Zimbabweans when they talk about home, also asking whether they choose to be buried in overcrowded urban cemeteries in Zimbabwe, or want to be buried in rural homes. Mbiba (2010) further argues that the preference for burial at rural homes is an ideal expressed by both Zimbabweans in the diaspora and Harare. The main reason, as pointed out by Mbiba (2010), is that the desire to be buried in a rural area as opposed to an urban centre hinges on the notions of identity and belonging. Above all, he noted that one reason for the desire to be interred at their rural home is the overcrowding and inadequate capacity for urban burials. To underline the importance of being buried at the rural home, Mbiba (2010) has this to say: "Baba Chiendambuya of East London would like to be buried in what he considers home, next to his father's grave in Gokwe."

Assuming the above to be the world view of Africans, then it can be argued that the assertion by Mbiba (2010) resonates well with what this chapter aims to demonstrate. When one is buried not at 'home' then one would be alienated from one's ancestors, hence the desire to be buried next to their consanguineous kin. Showing Africans' preference for rural burials as opposed to urban burial, Mbiba (2010:150) says that "[i]n Harare Zimbabweans from the countryside often considered themselves to be sojourners and often remained anti-urban in outlook, such that urban burial could be stigmatised and associated with failure or with foreigners labelled derogatorily as *mwidi* or totemless".

The stigmatisation that comes with urban funerals has seen urbanised African Zimbabweans continuing to ferry their dead loved ones for burial in the rural lands that are their homes. According to Mbiba (2010), even those who die in Britain are repatriated to be buried at home. The idea of repatriating loved ones highlights the effects of urban burials, which Mbiba (2010) argues lack proper rituals. The significance of this lack of rituals, as indicated by Mbiba (2010), is what my research seeks to understand amongst the Bakalanga. Mbiba (2010) highlights the effects of being buried away from home as being akin to "[g]uerrillas who died during the liberation struggle in the bush and buried away from home without proper funeral rituals [and who] were exhumed for proper burials at home".

Emphasising the importance of home burial amongst the Igbo of Nigeria, Smith (2004) posits that rural burials are opportunities that assure continued identity with the place of origin. This he captures as follows:

> The strength of the obligation that relatives of the deceased come home to bury their dead is exceeded not only by the power of the expectation that the dead should be buried at home. For the Igbo who die abroad the journey home involves the literal transportation of the corpse back to the village.

The above quotation forms the basis of this research study as it captures the importance of home for most African ethnic groups and their continued identity if they are buried at home. Therefore, the Bakalanga are not an exception as they also subscribe to the same view. One important issue that Smith (2004) raises is that the journey home for the Igbo also symbolises status and wealth, even flamboyance, that is displayed by those who reside in the cities or abroad. This is the material dignity that Golomski (2015) noticed when dealing with urban burials in Swaziland. He argues that death in the urban spaces of Swaziland has become a subject of material display in the form of tombstones and flamboyance that signifies the funeral as successful (*ukulunga kahle*). Also of interest, Golomski (2015) notes that a ritual of tombstone unveiling has been infused into Swazi burials. This is important for this chapter as it illustrates ritual aspects that Africans have also embraced as a result of their migration, urbanisation and adoption of other aspects of modernity.

Burials of married women

The question that this chapter is also interested in is how the spirit of a married woman is reunited with her ancestors if she is buried outside her ancestral territory or domain. Does it matter where a woman is buried? I am aware that burial at one's ancestral home had always had exceptions for married women, who upon marriage relocate to their husbands' homes. This, therefore, implies that marriage separates a woman from her ancestral land', as her grave will be in her marital home. There is a Setswana saying, "*bitla la mosadi le kwa a nyetsweng teng*", meaning "a woman's grave is at her matrimonial home". Literature from Southern Africa, specifically Botswana, testify to this saying but also points out that the burial rituals are performed by her people according to her father's lineage. For example, Mhaka (2014) posits that a married woman's burial ritual is done according to her father's lineage because the deceased married woman's spirit is interested in its clan and, as such, her people are the ones who dig her grave and lead the burial and subsequent rituals to ensure her spirit is reunited with her family. Jung (2019) observes that amongst the Zulu, when a woman is married, she brings with her a kist or box to her in-laws, which symbolises a coffin. This marks a separation from her family and indicates that upon her demise she will be buried at her husband's place. According to my Kalanga informants, in Botswana, a girl child is separated twice from her mother: at birth when the *mbeleko* (umbilical cord) is cut and upon marriage when a cloth (*mbeleko*) the mother used to strap/carry her in is also cut to symbolise the separation. Furthermore, they pointed out that at death the married woman is buried according to her father's ritual practices. In one of the funerals of a married woman I attended in Natale, a village in the central district of Botswana, I observed that when the coffin was

7

lowered, there was chanting of a totemic poem by the maternal uncle. The poem is quoted verbatim as follows: "*Ngwena isi nga je ngoabilila tjayo tjozha nge longa. A badzimu bedu ba amutjile nlandankadzi iwoyo*" (translated literally as "You are a crocodile that does not struggle to get food. Your food comes with the flowing water. Let our ancestors receive you").

It is noted from the above that marriage severs women from their ancestry and, as such, they are not reunited with their clan upon death the way in which men and unmarried women are. That is, they are not buried in the land where they were born, where their umbilical cords were buried, and where the spirits of their forefathers dwell. This goes to show the extent to which marriage is a vital gender contract that ensures gender inequality between men and women. A married woman's subservience to her husband is discursively constructed by her relocation to his village in body and spirit. Masenya (2016) confirms the above by noting that amongst the Sotho there is a proverb which states that "a woman's grave belongs to her husband's home village". The implication of the proverb is that a woman must stay in her marriage and be buried at her husband's place to show that she belongs to the man. Although efforts are made to mitigate against the loss of a married woman's spirit by having her people perform burial rituals, there are limitations to that as they had ceded control of her upon marriage. Therefore, it is not uncommon for her people not to dig her grave, as they may not live in the same village, while others are caught up in work commitments. Because of the traditional practice of *lobola* (bride price), a family that has received *lobola* for their daughter bequeaths responsibility to the man and his family; hence, her natal family usually works on the fringes upon her death.

However, it needs to be noted that women have grown increasingly aware of their rights and not all married women are buried at their matrimonial homes. Some married women I interviewed pointed out that they had relocated to towns and they wish to be buried there. Others reasoned that they have worked hard and attained a high socio-economic status for themselves and, as such, have bought pieces of land at Phomolong in the Phakalane estates, where they will be buried. These social changes do not only affect married women but also rural people, who are looked upon as the custodians of culture. The development of cemeteries means that the burial spaces for men and women are no longer separated as was the case in the past. Amanze (2002) has pointed out that, in the past, Bakalanga men and women were not buried in the same place, as men were buried in kraals and women in the compound, which has implications for burial rituals.

This chapter has alluded to the fact that when people are buried in urban areas, certain rituals are not performed. This shows that urbanism and other aspects of modernity have affected burial rituals of the African people. This same has been observed by

Mothetho (1999), who points out that most Ikalanga burial rituals in Botswana were affected by Christianity. This chapter confirms this, because Christians in rural area do not perform certain traditional rituals as per the convictions of their faith. However, data and observations made amongst Bakalanga in North-East have shown that there are rituals that have survived the formidable wave of modernity such as urbanism and Christianity. These are rituals such as smearing windows with ashes, the fire at the gate and grave identification when death has occurred are still practised in rural areas despite modernity.

Conclusion

Moyo (2017), when talking about *ukugqiba inkaba* (burying of the umbilical cord), highlights the fact that when people want to know where one comes from, they ask *"ikuphi inkaba yahko?"* (where is your umbilical cord buried?). According to her, the burial of the umbilical cord by the Ngoni of Malawi signifies one's connection to Mother Earth, the place of one's roots and belonging. Moyo (2017) draws an important analogy by arguing that as the baby is connected to its mother's womb through the umbilical cord for sustenance and survival, in a similar fashion when burying the umbilical cord, the baby is connected to Mother Earth for belonging and sustenance for life. In conclusion, when we are young, we sleep on our mother's bosoms, and after death we find comfort in Mother Earth.

7

References

Amanze, J.N. 2002. *African traditional religions and culture in Botswana.* Gaborone: Pula Press.

Amanze, J.N. 2007. Land and the spirituality of indigenous people in Africa: A case study of the Basarwa of the Central Kalagari Game Reserve in Botswana. *Boleswa Journal of Theology, Religion and Philosophy*, 1(3):97-115.

Ayiera, M.E.A. 2012. "Burying our dead in your city": Interpreting individual constructs of belonging in the context of burial of loved ones in exile. Master's thesis, University of Witwatersrand, Johannesburg.

Biwul, J.K.T. 2014. The African tradition of burial in the ancestral land and its implications for the African church today. *TCNN Research Bulletin*, 61(September):16-30.

Davison, A. 2000. *Citizenship and migration: Globalisation and the politics of belonging.* New York: Red Globe Publishers.

Feni, L. 2018. Nokwe's bones to come home. *Dispatch Live*, 21 September. https://bit.ly/2Ci3viF [Accessed 20 March 2019].

Genesis. 1946. *Holy Bible Revised Standard Version.* New York: Bible Society Resources Ltd.

Golomoski, C. 2015. Urban Cemeteries in Swaziland: materialising dignity. *Anthropology Southern Africa*, 38(3-4):360-371. https://doi.org/ 10.1080/23323256.2015.1087322 [Accessed 20 July 2019].

Hambira, R. 1999. Those who do not know the village they come from will not find the village they are looking for … *Land and Spirituality in Africa*, Echoes series. http://www.wcc-coe. org/wcc/what/jpc/echoes-16-06.html [Accessed 17 February 2019].

Jung, D. 2019. Zulu weddings. *KIVA*. https://www.kiva.org/blog/zulu-weddings [Accessed 20 July 2019].

Kamenju, J. 2011. Land and spirituality in Africa. *The Christian Science Monitor*, 9 February. https://bit.ly/2ZJ9JB6 [Accessed 9 March 2019].

Komoki, N. 2005. A study of death and burial rituals of the Ovanbanderu of Sehitwa in Botswana. Bachelor Degree dissertation, University of Botswana, Gaborone.

Manatsha, B.T. 2012. The historical and politico-cultural significance of Nswazwi Mall in Francistown. *Botswana Notes and Records*, 44:70-80.

Marrall, R. 2006. Urbanism and North American funerary practices. *PSU McNair Scholars Online Journal*, 2(1):186-205. https://doi. org/10.15760/mcnair.2006.186 [Accessed 28 February 2019].

Masenya, M.J. 2016. Navigating a gender-unconscious Biblical studies academic context: One African woman's reflection. *Lectio Dificilior: European Electronic Journal for Feminist Exegesis*, 2. https://bit.ly/2WCovHH [Accessed 20 July 2019].

Mbiba, B. 2010. Burying at home? Negotiating death in the diaspora and Harare. In: J. McGregor & R. Primorac (eds), *Zimbabwe's new diaspora: Displacement and the cultural politics of survival.* New York: Berghahn Books. 144-163.

Mhaka, E. 2014. Rituals and taboos related to death as repositories of traditional African philosophical ideas: Evidence from the Karanga of Zimbabwe. *Academic Research International*, 5(4):371-385. https://bit.ly/3fO4h5m [Accessed 20 February 2019].

Moeti, M. 2006. Botswana: Dead and forgotten. *Mmegi*, 24 March. https://allafrica.com/stories/200603240749.html [Accessed 24 March 2019].

Mothetho, P.L.G. 1999. Tjilenje: Buzwele ne Buthumbi zwe Bakalanga. Francistown: Mukani Action Campaign.

Motshwari, S. 2008. Botswana: Bakalanga ba ka Nswazwi at home in Botswana. *Mmegi*, 30 May. https://allafrica.com/stories/200806020762.html [Accessed 15 February 2019].

Moyo, F.L, 2017. *"Ukugqiba inkaba"* – Burying the umbilical cord: An African indigenous ecofeminist perspective on incarnation. In: G.J-S. Kim & H.P. Koster (eds), *Planetary solidarity: Global women's voices on Christian doctrine and climate justice*. Minneapolis, MN: Fortress Press. 179-192. https://doi.org/10.2307/j.ctt1pwt42b.15

Naidu-Hoffmeester, R. 2018. Land is the greatest heritage. https://bit.ly/2OGEVdD [Accessed 19 February 2019].

Newel, K. 2010. Hosanna, the Bakalanga rainmaking dance. *Mmegi Online*, 22 October. https://bit.ly/33giRPR [Accessed 20 March 2019].

Smith, D.J. 2004. Burials and belonging in Nigeria: Rural-urban relations and social inequality in a contemporary African ritual. *American Anthropologist*, 106(3):569-579. https://doi.org/10.1525/aa.2004.106.3.569

Sun Reporter. 2017. I want my mother's remains next to mine. *The Midweek Sun*, 6 February. https://bit.ly/2OFsyP3 [Accessed 1 May 2019].

Tafira, K. 2015. Why land evokes such deep emotions in Africa. *The Conversation*, 27 May. https://bit.ly/3jhiwlf [Accessed 14 February 2019].

Walaza, N. 2014. Exploring traditional African belief systems and their relation to the understanding of death and afterlife. *Dharma World Magazine*, July-September. https://bit.ly/2CJLIRb [Accessed 18 February 2019].

Wirth, L. 1938. Urbanism is a way of life. *The American Journal of Sociology*, 44(1):1-24. https://doi.org/10.1086/217913

THE BELIEFS AND RELIGIOUS PRACTICES AND THE ENVIRONMENT AMONGST THE KALANGA IN NORTH-EAST BOTSWANA

Fidelis Nkomazana[1]

Abstract

The chapter examines how beliefs and religious practices have influenced communities in dealing with the environment in Botswana. The chapter demonstrates how religious practices and beliefs have in various ways promoted ecological sustainability. The chapter observes that attitudes and perceptions, especially those influenced by religion, are important determinants of ecological behaviours. Rural communities are particularly seen as possessing certain cultural contexts, attitudes and world views that have contributed positively towards environmental protection and sustainability. An examination of the role played by religious practices and beliefs, in the contexts of the Kalanga in the north-east of Botswana, reveals that religion contributes immensely towards positive public attitudes, perceptions and understanding of the environment.

Introduction

Grim and Tucker (2014:62-63) define the word 'environment' in relation to ecology as referring to the dynamic interactions of humans with nature. They also observe that, consequently, the interaction between religion and environment provides a framework for exploring diverse religious world views, symbol systems, rituals and ethics in relation to the processes of the Earth and the universe. The environment, according to Grim and Tucker (2014), is to be nurtured and refers to the Earth and the land on which everything stands and where humans and animals dwell and plants grow, as well as the water and food which are so essential for life. The Earth, therefore, gives life and eventually everything returns to it with deep connections through religious practices and rituals. They use the Latin word for religion, *religio* meaning "to bind back" or "to bind together", to stress this. In this

---

1   Dr Fidelis Nkomazana is affiliated to the University of Botswana. [Email: nkomazaf@mopipi.ub.bw]

way, religion orients humans to the universe, grounds them in the community of nature and humans, and nurtures and transforms the processes and experiences of the environment (Grim & Tucker, 2014:37, 39).

Empirical studies show how beliefs, religious practices and world views amongst the Kalanga in the north-eastern part of Botswana contribute towards addressing environmental challenges and problems. The qualitative methods of collecting and analysing data were used to understand the dynamic interactions and relationship between the environment and religion.

The traditional ways through which ecological knowledge was imparted to subsequent generations are examined. Their effectiveness as methods are examined in the context of modernity and the influence of Western education and culture. The Kalanga strongly believe that indigenous ways of addressing ecological problems were relevant. The challenge is that these indigenous beliefs and religious practices are waning, with many people influenced by Christianity and Western education. Despite this new development, these beliefs and religious practices remain active in the life and thought of the people. The conclusion of the chapter is that neither traditional nor modern scientific modes are adequate on their own in addressing ecological problems. Synergy between the two is necessary.

The chapter argues that religious practices and beliefs significantly influence a community's understanding and experience of climate and adaptation to change, indicating the need for an inclusion of such information in education addressing such adaptation. Certain beliefs and practices were identified from the interviews with participants in north-east Botswana that contributed towards implementing positive environmental conservation measures. It was found that indigenous communities regarded themselves as religious, saw climate as a natural process that is governed by God, and thus influenced members of the community to do those things that will impact on the environment positively.

Objectives of the study

The objectives of the study are to

1. discuss the origins and development of sacred places and identify their locations in the Kalanga region of the north-eastern part of Botswana;

2. examine the impact of beliefs and religious practices associated with sacred places and how they contribute to the conservation of the environment; and

3. assess critically how the introduction of Christianity and modernity have affected and weakened indigenous beliefs and religious practices, and the implications of this for the environment.

Methodology

This study on sacred sites was conducted using qualitative methods as well as interviews and observations. In some instances, a questionnaire was used to investigate how the ideas and stories people tell about the origin, development and purpose of the sacred sites developed (Carmichael, Hubert, Reeves & Schanche, 1994). This involved visiting some of these sites, observing their religious operations where possible, examining the religious objects associated with them and investigating how some of these were used to perform important rituals at these locations that are regarded as sacred (Carmichael et al., 1994). The study also provides an understanding of people's views and perceptions of the objects associated with the sites. During the interviews, I asked the respondents to either relate their experiences of these practices or what they were told by their parents about the religious significance of these sacred sites (Carmichael et al., 1994). They were asked to elaborate on the procedures in performing ritual practices at or near these sacred sites and their understanding of the social, political and religious significance of this. The statements, which are belief systems expressed in terms of practices, were collected through interviews with participants, as well as through observations of rural communities in the Kalanga region with reference to the sacred sites.

Literature review

Amanze (2002) pointed out that religion sees the Earth as very important in human lives. It is on the Earth that people plant their seeds for food and bury the dead, especially the *badimo* (ancestors), who are buried in her bosom. It is for this reason that religion is believed to punish those who abuse the Earth. Amanze (2002) states the name for the Supreme Being amongst the Batswana is *Modimo*, who they say is the Creator and Sustainer of the universe (Mbiti, 1977; Nkomazana, 2005; Setiloane, 1976). He goes further to make a close link between religion and the environment, saying:

> The environment is the area of action of both spiritual as well as physical beings supposed to interact with one another in harmony and reverence. By and large, the environmental processes are essentially a result of the activities of the spiritual forces especially the ancestors, which impinge on the physical world in an intermittent way. Any form of defilement of the environment, it is believed, has its own consequences unless special rituals are performed to pacify the anger of the ancestors, who are the guardians and custodians of what God has created.
>
> (Amanze, 2002:302)

Another important scholar who discusses the relationship between religion and the environment is Parrinder (1969), who argues that in Africa land is generally considered sacred, because it is believed to belong to the *badimo*. It is for this reason that in Africa land was not to be sold, because doing that would displease the *badimo*. For both Amanze (2002) and Parrinder (1969), sacred sites as well as their environments such as mountains, hills, rivers, trees and special rock formations are not only associated with spirits, but are also believed to be endowed with sacred mystical powers. Discussing the religious significance of land amongst Africans, Kenyatta in his book *Facing Mount Kenya* (cited in Amanze, 2002) says that Africans depend entirely on the land as it not only supplies them with the material needs of life, but also provides spiritual and mental contentment. Amanze (2002) observes that African religions have the tendency to promote close contact with the cosmos. For him, nature – which refers to the sun, the moon, the stars, the Earth, animals and plants – greatly influences people's religiosity. He sees nature as possessing spiritual powers and providing a platform for people to communicate with the divine, which is done by turning to the natural objects such as trees for the worship of God. Amanze (2002) argues that it is for this reason that certain trees are highly respected and preserved. He argues that these objects cannot be cut or used for purposes other than for ritual performance. To support his argument, he quotes Zahan (1979), who writes:

> The African believer does not willingly isolate himself from nature; nature must act without intermediaries or obstacles on the officiants and those who participate in the mysteries. As regulators of liturgical cycles, the sun, moon, stars, earth, animals, and plants directly influence people in prayer. That is why the idea of a temple as a place of worship is foreign to the African beliefs.
> (Amanze, 2002:299)

Gelfand (1962) also makes an important contribution to this discussion. He suggests that trees have great religious symbolism and that they are a symbol of life, steadfastness, permanency, immortality and fertility. He observes that certain ritual activities take place under a tree for its shade and other benefits, thus playing an important role in the religious life of the people. He therefore concludes that the environment is a sacred phenomenon.

Amanze (2002) takes the issue of the religious significance of the environment further by citing Zahan (1979), who writes that

> [i]t is curious to note that while in geographical terms the hydrography of Africa makes it a land of contrast (humidity and dryness being found there to extremes) Africa can also reveal an astonishing uniformity if we consider the purely religious value of water ... men consider it with respect. Springs, streams, rivers, lakes and ponds constitute the great "aquatic temples" of African religions. Each possesses its own meaning. (Amanze, 2002:300)

Gelfand (1962) draws our attention to the fact that water had religious significance everywhere in Africa. It is life and the source of life for plants, animals and human life. It purifies, restores, cleanses and regenerates.

Finally, it must be mentioned that a wide range of literature has confirmed this connection between religion and environment (Amanze, 2002; Campbell, 1968; Larson, 1971; Livingstone, 1857; Mackenzie, 1971; Setiloane, 1976). Mbiti (1977) and Setiloane (1976) take the matter further and observe that in African traditional religions humanity and religion are interwoven. In their view, the natural phenomena and nature itself are inextricably part of African beliefs and religious practices.

Theoretical framework

Identifying a theoretical framework for the relation between religious beliefs and environmental protection and conservation is critical for this chapter. You have nature/environment, on the one hand, and beliefs and religious practices, on the other. Bell (1992:v, quoting Geertz) concludes that "[i]n ritual, the world as lived and the world as imagined … turn out to be the same world".

Mbiti (1977), in his book *African religions and philosophy*, observes that religious beliefs are so strong and influential that communities will conduct certain rituals and practices in order to reconcile with the ancestors. These rituals, according to Mbiti (1977), are a way of cleaning the environment where it has been polluted or desecrated. Religion warns of the consequences of disobedience in human plunder and greed in the usage of the environment and nature, and exploration of the Earth. Mbiti (1977) also points out that African traditional religions hold the view that there is reason to safeguard and protect the Earth, because people share it with the ancestors who are forever its guardians, defenders, and protectors. Ancestors are committed to see how the Earth is handled and treated. Both Mbiti (1977) and Setiloane (1976) point to the fact that in African traditional religions, humanity and religion are interwoven. They point out that natural phenomena and nature are inextricably part of African traditional religious beliefs.

African traditional religions therefore suggest a strong relationship between religious beliefs and the environment. Nature, which is an important part of the environment, forms part of God's creation. The relationship between nature and humanity is a pragmatic one. It must be a relationship of care, responsibility and stewardship. The concepts that can be drawn from these authors give the impression that there is a strong connection between humanity and nature. The responsibility that humanity has towards nature/environment is that of stewardship, which is about responsible use, no indiscriminate cutting of trees, no pollution of water sources, etc. The view expressed in this literature is that humanity cannot dominate nature negatively, that is, use it for personal gain and in a greedy way. A greedy use of nature has no care for what the consequences are. The *badimo* are believed to demand that humanity be caretakers and guardians of the resources of the Earth. All the aforementioned writers underscore this relationship, where humanity is appointed and called upon to take care of the environment, which embraces both nature and the climate.

Religious beliefs and practices amongst Africans, therefore, show a strong or binding relationship between humanity and the environment. Failure to act responsibly as the stewards of nature is not only regarded as abuse of the environment, but can also result in punishment by the *badimo*. Humanity and African communities will not risk any conflict with the ancestors, who are believed amongst the Batswana to be agents of *Modimo*, the name of the Supreme Being, the Maker and Creator of the universe. The literature shows that there is a demand for obedience and that disobedience is followed by punishment. This framework or understanding summarises the fundamental principles governing the religious beliefs and practices as well as the functions and operations of the sacred sites.

Presentation of the research findings about sacred sites

This section presents research findings on selected sacred sites identified in the north-eastern part of Botswana. Four sacred sites were studied: the Nzeze Shrine, the Tegwi Hill sacred site, the Luswingo (also known as Nlisi or Ntogwa) site, and the Lutambo Daka sacred site. The Mwali cult and their rainmaking practices and beliefs are very important to demonstrate that the environment is central to the functions of the sacred sites.

The Mwali cult

The key finding of the research is that the Kalanga, who populate much of the north-eastern part of Botswana, are predominantly connected closely to the Mwali cult, the dominant element in their rainmaking practices. Some scholars regard *Mwali* as a Supreme Being, equivalent to *Modimo* (Amanze, 2002; Nkomazana, 2005), while others see him as a spirit medium, acting as a link between the Supreme Being and the community, but higher in authority than the ancestors. Grand (1984:125), for instance, writes:

> The general observation is that Mwali is an intermediary through whom people's complaints, gratitude and messages of any kind are conveyed to the high God. In other words, all matters pertaining to the welfare of the society are addressed to him. Thus, it is a common belief amongst societal members that he helps in times of need, for example, in times of natural disasters, plague and other forms of epidemics (which include pertinent poverty). In this respect he is the central figure in the Bakalanga socio-religious life, hence he is regarded a sacred figure.

The Mwali cult was for many years the strongest element that has kept the Kalanga closely connected in terms of religious traditions, especially when it comes to the rainmaking rites introducing important environmental and ecological factors. Bhusumane (1985:34) writes that

> [t]he Kalanga are well known for their proclamation and profession in one Supreme Being whom they call Mwali. They regard him as the Supreme, the Highest and He is the Creator of all things and manifests His power in the situations of the people. He can express His dissatisfaction about His subjects through suffering and other cosmological phenomena. He is the sole authority (and is also) a lawmaker and sustains the life of his subjects. He is the bringer of rain and all life comes from Him. He expects all His subjects to obey His law or otherwise suffer the consequences. The failure to observe these laws may result in cessation of rains most people believe. This can also be seen through a curse, famine, illness, death [of] livestock and so forth.

Both Grand (1984) and Bhusumane (1985) point out that there are several sacred sites connected mainly to the Mwali cult, which have heavily influenced the beliefs and religious practices of the Kalanga people. These ceremonies and practices were generally held during the summer season (Bhusumane, 1985).

- ### The role of the messengers and the mediator-priests

Another important finding is the role that was played by the messengers and the mediator-priests of Mwali. In the 1970s, my own village Jackalas 2[2] used to participate actively in the Mwali rainmaking rites and ceremonies. At that time, the village religious leader was a highly respected old man by the name of Mtshaywa. He was regarded as the village messenger of Ntogwa. Whenever a delegation was sent to inquire from Ntogwa about a variety of issues, especially in matters pertaining to rain, he was always the leader of the team. Before they left, there would be a week of rain *indazula* dances, prayers and ceremonies accompanied by the singing of traditional rain songs in preparation for the visit to the Siviya Shrine,[3] where Ntogwa was presented with the people's requests. Before the delegation set off for the journey, it was obligatory that traditional beer be brewed as part of the rainmaking ceremonies and carried by women who walked behind the village messenger. On arrival at the Siviya Shrine, the beer was presented as an offering to Mwali. Led by Mtshaywa, the women were instructed to leave the calabashes full of traditional beer at the entrance of the cave (shrine). As they walked towards the cave, the women and the men accompanying them were expected to walk backwards, with eyes focused on the ground. It was believed to be a taboo to look directly at the cave or in the direction from which the voice of the mediator-priest was coming. These rules were

---

2   Jackalas 2 is some 30 km north-east of Francistown. It is located along the Botswana-Zimbabwe border. It is a predominantly Ndebele-speaking community.

3   The Siviya Shrine was located at a hill along the Ramokgwebana River, along the Botswana-Zimbabwe border. It is located east of the Siviya village, which is about 16 km north of Jackalas 2 village.

8

to be strictly observed.[4] The common dances performed at the *kgotla* included *ndazula*, *hooso/woso/hoso*, and *hosanna*.[5] The dances were a way of preserving the cultural heritage of the community. They were accompanied by *ingoma* (traditional songs) and drums. The dance starts with a man dancing alone, but is then joined by others as the intensity of the drumming, singing and dancing gains momentum during the rainmaking ceremonies.

Another prominent messenger of Mwali, who actively worked in the villages of Mathangwane, Gulubane, Tlhalogang and Borolong, was Mokobo Mongwa (Tobela) (Grand, 1984). Mongwa and his children were accused of exploiting people by collecting gifts in the name of Mwali. This resulted in succession power struggles between Mongwa's children (Grand, 1984). In Senyawe, Mbage, through visions and dreams, rose to the position of a messenger-priest of Mwali in the 1980s. The messengers are believed to possess the spirit and power of Mwali to be able to perform these spiritual functions, such as interpreting messages and addressing people in their language and conducting rituals. For the appeasement of Mwali, they did not only offer traditional beer, but also offered tobacco snuff, which was left at the entrance of the shrine. After the death of Ntogwa, snuff was replaced by money collected from the people. From this, it would appear that Mwali's taste was dynamic, changing with time. The use of money led to selfishness and greed on the part of the messengers and medium priests, which has contributed to the loss of interest in these beliefs and religious practices. Greed and selfishness were believed to pollute the environment and cause poverty, while enriching the medium-priests and the messengers. This resulted in curses and punishments in the forms of drought, pestilence, and other societal challenges.

The late 1960s and early 1970s saw the coming of Ntogwa, a famous medium priest of the Mwali rainmaking cult, whose invigorating leadership led to new hope and interest amongst the north-east Kalanga people. He started as a dancer, after which he became a messenger and he was later promoted to the office of a medium priest. It was during Ntogwa's time that the practices of the Mwali cult were revived and reinstated with strict religious observation. Through his leadership, people were encouraged to adhere to certain religious rules (Monyatsi, 1984).

With the coming of Ntogwa as the medium priest, coupled with the long distance to Njelele, new oracles were found, and old ones revived in the area. Elderly men and women, as well as virgin girl dancers carrying calabashes of traditional beer, visited the shrines as part of the rainmaking ritual and to consult Mwali's medium

---

4   Personal observation.

5   The Ndebele people settled amongst the Kalanga. This was not a Nguni acquisition of the dominant group, the Kalanga (Chebanne, 2019).

priest. Gifts were presented to the medium priest with thanksgiving, praise poems, and *woso* and *ndazula* dances as part of the offerings and sacrifices as demanded by Mwali, followed by their petitions. The following section briefly discusses four major shrines devoted to the Mwali rainmaking rites.

■ The historical development of sacred sites

The section shows that there is a relationship between the rituals, the place or location in which they are performed, and the environment. Moser and Feldman (2014:1) in their book, *Locating the sacred*, confirm that

> [r]eligious ritual cannot be studied as a disembodied event or series of events – removed from its location and separate from the physical of its performance. Instead the ritual must be examined in its specific material and topographical context in which ritual action impacts its physical setting while, simultaneously, the location in which the ritual is enacted informs and guides the religious practice.

To localise the study of the relationship between religion and the environment, we will first examine the Nzeze sacred site, also known as the Mapoka Great Sacred Shrine (*daka*). The Nzeze shrine, which gets its name from the *nzeze* tree, is situated five kilometres from the Mapoka village. The shrine is just an open space where people meet for their religious practices. It lies under a big *nzeze* tree, which is of great religious significance in the rainmaking practices throughout the Kalanga region. It signifies fertility, knowledge, life source and resilience. It is said that at the official opening of the Nzeze Shrine, Mwali appeared in the form of a snake, an incident that is not only vividly remembered, but also highly regarded and repeated with great conviction by older members of the society. It is also said that the occasion was signalled by the ringing of bells, which was followed by heavy winds from which they say a big and mysterious snake suddenly appeared and was seen for some minutes before disappearing into the whirlwind again. This, they say, was immediately followed by a heavy rainfall.

It must be mentioned that the *nzeze* is a protected tree, believed also to possess important medicinal value. It is also believed to contribute towards creating climatic conditions that contribute to the formation of rain clouds. This is essential in that it encourages the community to preserve indigenous trees for purposes of enhancing positive climatic conditions and the general environment. Monyatsi (1984:26) has described the usefulness of the *nzeze* tree as follows:

> Nzeze is originally a tree but has great significance with regard to rainmaking especially in the Bokalanga area. People of this area use Nzeze branches to remove the foam of beer from the calabashes when they consult Mwali. Sometimes the branches are used as *maabe* (a kind of skirt usually made of beads) for the virgins who collect mud from any place where rain might have

8

fallen, and splash the mud right through the village. They use Nzeze branches for splashing the mud and it is believed that rain is being attracted. There is a belief that during the hunting of *zwamwi* (things that are believed to stop rain by bad omen). Nzeze branches are collected and burnt with whatever they would be burning. The smoke is believed to bring new life or luck and as such, rain can fall. They value nzeze so much that they built a great daka (worshipping place) under a big nzeze tree in Mapoka.

Noli Gunda, one of my interviewees, described the Nzeze Shrine as follows:

> When I grew up, I found people going to the Nzeze Shrine. A *hosanna*, called Gogo, used to regularly perform religious activities from this very place. Due to her old age, she had to be transported on a sledge to this place. After her death, she was succeeded by Njejema and later on by Ntogwa, who originated from Zimbabwe, and became a mediator-priest of the Mwali cult at the Tegwi hill, near Mapoka. Ntogwa was accompanied by a leading *hosanna* called Machakaile, who helped him in the performance of religious functions. As a mediator-priest, Ntogwa could pray for rains, predict the future and heal people from different diseases. In due course, a hut was built there for this purpose, but as time went on, especially with the death of Ntogwa, it was neglected and destroyed by cattle. There were many mysterious stories told about Ntogwa. Some were to the extent that at first nobody knew if he was a woman or a man because of his voice, which was like that of a woman. However, his gender was later realised when he impregnated a woman.[6]

The messenger was usually accompanied and assisted by both male and female dancers called *dziwosana* and young virgins who carried calabashes of traditional beer during ceremonies. The medium-priest praises Mwali and presents the people's petitions. This is accompanied by different rain dances: *dantshiwa, woso, kobodolo, ndazula* and *mayile* that are believed to cause rain. The dancers wear feathers and *nzeze* branches, which symbolise wind and rain. Following the dance, the wind is said to begin to blow to induce nucleated particles and condensation that form raindrops. Coupled with this, rain dances are believed to cause thunder that also results in rain formation. Ritual dances, therefore, are believed to influence the modification of the weather. The whistles and drums are believed to produce sounds that attract the attention of Mwali. Music and dances are generally believed to have special powers that control the formation of rain clouds and consequently forming raindrops.

The second sacred site studied is the Tegwi Hill that is situated at the Ramokgwebana village, which is about thirty kilometres east of the Mapoka village. The sacred place is beside the Tegwi Hill, about 200 metres from the Botswana-Zimbabwe railway line. The Tegwi Shrine was established by Vumbu Ntogwa, who originally came from Zimbabwe. The development of the shrine had greatly been influenced by

---

6   Noli Gunda, Mapoka Village Kgotla, interviewed in 1995 and reviewed in 2018.

a place in Zimbabwe called Manyagwa, named after a man, called Manyagwa. The Manyagwa people are said to have believed in Mwali whom they accepted as a Kalanga, Ndebele and Shona God at the time. Ntogwa came to the Kalanga of Botswana and established his own shrine at Ramokgwebana on the Tegwi Hill. The Kalanga in Ramokgwebana welcomed this development and respected the Tegwi Hill Shrine, because they believed that their god stayed at that mountain. Prayers and sacrifices were, from that time until today, held annually at that place. However, the headquarters of the Mwali cult are still believed to be at Venda, at the Njelele Hill. The shrine came into existence because Ntogwa claimed that he had been sent by Mwali through a dream to be his messenger amongst the Kalanga of Botswana. He therefore claimed to have been given immense power and information from Mwali.

When asked how old the place was, one of my interviewees said:

> I don't know how old the place is as everybody found the place in existence. Even John Mackenzie and David Livingstone found it in existence. Some people argue that Ntogwa did not establish the Tegwi Hill Shrine, but simply revived what was already known to exist among the Kalanga before he came as a mediator-priest.[7]

This could imply that the Kalanga people at Ramokgwebana were worshipping Mwali long before the advent of Ntogwa. They only went to the Njelele Shrine in Zimbabwe for major celebrations, which occurred only once or twice annually.

The third sacred site is known by any of the three following names: the Luswingo / Nlisi / Ntogwa Daka site. It is situated on a cave ten kilometres west of Jackalas 1, a village in the north-east district near the Ramokgwebana border. The sacredness of this place is said to have originated from the time when Vumbu Ntogwa, who was a *wosana* dancer, came from Zimbabwe and settled at Jackalas 1. Inspired by Mwali, he directed the people to that sacred place. Some huts were built by the community near the place to accommodate the visiting *Dziwosana*. The sacred place is now said to be in ruins, since Ntogwa left Jackalas 1 some years ago and settled in a different area of the north-east district. The status of the shrine declined even more after his death. Greed, negligence and irresponsibility on the part of his successors have been the major contributing factors. As a mediator-priest, he was seen as providing a link between the people and Mwali. The people would follow this man to this place and when they got near it, they would face in the direction of the sunset, that is, away from the sacred place. It was a rule. No one was supposed to face the cave. Disobedience was believed to lead to blindness or some other severe punishment. The people claim that Ntogwa used to get into the cave and present the petitions of the people to Mwali. It is said that the people could identify his voice from

---

7   Mushabi Thela, Mapoka Village Kgotla, interviewed in 1995 and reviewed in 2018.

that of Mwali. Ntogwa travelled with women and dressed like them; they danced together for rain and it is believed that it would rain immediately.

Lutambo Daka is the fourth sacred site, which is situated on a hill in the eastern part of Botswana within Jackalas 1 village. The sacred place developed when people went to the hill to ask for rain, thinking that the ancestors had forsaken them. A man named Nsinamwa, who was once one of the messengers of Ntogwa, led the people to the sacred place and told them what to do when they got there. They brought traditional beer, tobacco, beads and crushed grain for the ancestors. When their prayers were accepted, it is said to have rained heavily afterwards. It therefore became a practice for people to go there for sacrifices and prayers.

■ Religious objects, stories and events

These religious objects, stories and events demonstrate the power of sacred sites. The spirits of the ancestors are believed to manifest themselves in the environment in the form of wind, rain, etc. (Carmichael et al., 1994).

There are many stories and occurrences associated with sacred sites. One of the popular stories is about two people who went to the shrine without permission and disappeared until a black ox was sacrificed at the sacred place. Rituals performed in honour of Mwali were accompanied by dancing and singing. They included the following:

1. The brewing of traditional beer and placing some in a special calabash at the entrance of the sacred place to collect the empty container the following day, which is a sign that Mwali has accepted the offering.

2. The collection of money from the community for Mwali has become very popular, especially after the death of Ntogwa. This has become a source of conflict because of suspicions that the messengers are enriching themselves.

3. Animal sacrifice is an essential element of ritual performance in the Mwali rainmaking cult.

4. Thanksgiving ceremonies for the rains and harvest. Before or at harvest time, the messenger cuts corncobs from the fields and ritually gives some of them to Mwali as first fruits (Grim & Tucker, 2014). It is for this reason that Grim and Tucker (2014:92) write: "The nurturing powers of Earth are displayed in all the world religious traditions that celebrate food with rituals of planting, harvesting and thanksgiving" (cited in Carmichael et al., 1994:173).

When asked to describe what takes place at the Tegwi Hill Shrine, Mr Muchoko (interviewee) said:

> The only thing, which I heard when I went there because of sickness, was the voice that I could not tell whether it was from Mwali or somebody else in the cave. The voice was very soft and directed to the mediator. Rocks, trees and

other objects around the place are associated with the shrine and cannot be cut or removed. Everything in the vicinity of the shrine is said to be sacred. Nothing should be touched without the permission of the mediator-priest or his messengers. When the *dziwosana* dance during the ceremonies and other occasions, their dresses are not blown by the wind. They dance until they fall into a trance. Whenever Ntogwa finished asking for rain from Mwali, it immediately fell to clear his footprints. Although the rain falls behind and before him, he does not get wet. Ntogwa is said to have died at the age of about three hundred years old.[8]

For Carmichael et al. (1994), caves and mountains are regarded as the abode of spirits and source of life, shelter and protection. They are also often regarded as the entrances to the underground and places of origin of fertility spirits. The Nzeze Shrine has two important arenas nearby. The first is a flat rock, where the *maele* dancers have performed for years. The place of dancing, called *nonga*, has become visible. The second arena is used by men to roast the meat of the wild animals they killed during *zwamwi* hunting,[9] while the women dancers underwent ritual cleansing exercises. This is performed as an offering to appease Mwali. This sacred place of worship was located by a man called Sikhuthu after people saw two snakes cross each other at that spot and then stand upright to face the people. From that time onwards, the people believed that the shrine was an abode of the ancestors and that it was to be treated as sacred, thus highly reserved and protected.

▪ Rituals, ceremonies and festivals

Rituals, ceremonies and festivals conducted at the sacred sites continue to create a positive atmosphere and assert the relevance of the religious dimension in human life. Each major village was expected to brew traditional beer and take it to the shrine for a big ceremony. According to Mr Mushabi Thela,[10] participants went there in the morning accompanied by the mediator-priest. All had to put on black blankets and clothes, the colour associated with the worship of Mwali. Ceremonies and rituals are held there several times a year. This takes place when the rains come, when the people prepare for ploughing, and when crops are ready to be harvested. People also visited the shrine when there were problems like famine, sickness and drought. During the prayers, dances and ritual practices, people faced the direction of the sun, which is away from the hill. On arrival at the shrine, they would squat with their backs to the entrance of the cave to avoid annoying Mwali. In fact, to reach that position they would have had to walk backwards and advanced until they sat facing away from the entrance of the shrine (cave).

---

8   Mr Muchoko, Mapoka Village Kgotla, interviewed in 1995 and reviewed in 2018.

9   *Zwamwi* hunting will be fully discussed in the following pages.

10   Mushabi Thela, Mapoka Village Kgotla, interviewed in 1995 and reviewed in 2018.

The mediator-priest enters the cave where he communicates the greetings and the requests of the community. Immediately afterwards a voice, usually thought to be that of Mwali, is heard. There are, however, allegations that the mediator-priest himself speaks with a deep voice from the cave using a drum, pretending to be Mwali. Critics give this as the reason why people are not allowed to sit facing the cave, when Mwali is supposed to be still speaking. They also see this as disrespect to Mwalithe and the cause of the current drought. The older generation, however, still insists that it is the voice of Mwali (Monyatsi, 1994). They regard those who question the authenticity of the voice as committing blasphemous acts punishable by death. They also believe that disobeying rules, such as looking towards the direction of the cave, might have, for instance, sand thrown into their eyes or they might experience bad omens (Grand, 1984). As Mwali spoke, the elders responded in praise and thanksgiving saying "*eh Thobela*" or "*Mbedzi*" (Bhusumane, 1985:36-39).

Special traditional beer and porridge were also brought as gifts to Mwali when people consulted the oracle. The calabashes were found the next day full of froth but without beer. The top layer of the porridge is also found removed, which is believed to be a sign that Mwali has accepted the offering. All these have played a major role in influencing the people's attitude towards the sacred places, as well as to the environment around the sacred place.

▪ Precautions and measures

There are precautions and measures to be observed before going to the sacred place. The messenger goes there first to report the visitors to Mwali before the people could come closer to the shrine. In addition, gifts and sacrifices of a goat, a cow, sheep or any other domestic animal have to be taken to the shrine to appease Mwali. After that, the *dziwosana* must dance to clear the way for the visitors.

The punishment for breaking the rules, such as climbing the Tegwi Hill without permission or for leisure, is believed to be a mysterious disappearance or some other misfortune that affects the person for life or sudden death. Carmichael et al. (1994) confirm that the landscape near or around the sacred places are deemed sacred, hence cannot be utilised for personal use, cut or burnt. These places are to be respected, preserved and protected by all. They use cemeteries and tombs as a typical example. These are places of power, which points to the intersection between the material world and spiritual world (Carmichael et al., 1994). My interviewee also observed that

> [o]ne person actually lost his sense of sight and hearing after he went there without permission. He had to be led to the village by someone, who found him struggling to find his way home. He was blind and deficient in his hearing ability.

Another person, a white photographer, also went there without the permission from Mwali and became blind.[11]

It is also believed that the anger of the ancestors may cause the whole community to face the wrath of Mwali. The consequences may be famine, sickness, drought, etc. Another interview pointed out that breaking the rules governing the shrine, exposed the person and the community to danger.[12] Because of the rules governing the usage and operations of the sacred place, only two elderly people in Jackalas 1 village were allowed to go there. The sick or people with problems could only go there with the consent of the elders or the mediator-priest himself.[13]

When a person broke the rules governing the sacred place for the first time, he/she was given a warning from Mwali. If the person failed to heed the warning, Mwali could punish him/her with blindness before getting to the site or by sending a violent storm to confuse their sense of direction. Those who accompanied the mediator-priest were supposed to remove their jewellery, glasses and shoes, since these items were said to offend Mwali. The headmen were responsible for granting people permission to visit the shrine after consulting the mediator-priest. Going there without permission is believed to be dangerous, since big and dangerous snakes are believed to guard the shrines against intruders. The rules, precautions and measures governing the sacred shrines therefore contributed towards conserving the environment. Sacred sites become part of people's culture over course of time, gaining more sacred significance and promoting ecological preservation (Carmichael et al., 1994).

▪ Effects of modernity and Christianity

Before the advent of Christianity, Friday was generally observed as a religious day reserved for the worship of Mwali by the majority of people in the north-east. The coming of Christianity, especially the Seventh Day Adventists (SDA) and the Roman Catholics in this region, led to new religious practices and observances. The SDA refused to observe Friday and declared Saturday as their day of worship and rest. The Roman Catholics insisted on Sunday instead of Friday, hence breaking Mwali's orders. *Dziwosana* used to receive gifts but at present things have changed. They now gain nothing from performing these duties. In the past, an ox was slaughtered and the *dziwosana* would be offered the blood and other parts of the animal as gifts. Today this has changed. One of my interviewees blamed these changes on modernisation and Christianity, which have affected the essence of community

11   Mr Muchoko, Mapoka Village Kgotla, interviewed in 1995 and reviewed in 2018.
12   Mr Nkawo, Mapoka Village Kgotla, interviewed in 1995 and reviewed in 2018.
13   Jingo Mpofu, Mapoka Village Kgotla, interviewed in 1995 and reviewed in 2018.

8

and togetherness. He urges government to encourage people to persist with their traditional culture so that the nation could return to prosperity. He further suggested that Friday be declared as a day of rest, totally dedicated to the worship of Mwali.[14] During the era of Ntogwa, many people, in addition to observing Sunday as their day of worship, also accepted Friday as a religious day. In recent years, however, the impact of Christianity has led to many changes and the decline of the Mwali cult activities. The increase in the number of churches in the region has greatly contributed to the decline of the worship of Mwali. With many people influenced by Christianity, traditional religious practices are today seen as unchristian and a hindrance to development. On the other hand, the elderly is reluctant to change their beliefs.

The forces of modernity have also greatly contributed to changing the spiritual landscape. The Tegwi Hill Shrine is gradually losing its religious importance. In the past, children were not allowed to go to the shrine or even climb that hill, but nowadays there are no such prohibitions. Rules of sexual relations during the rainmaking rites were strictly enforced, but today the adherents of the Mwali cult admit that these rules are deliberately broken. Western medicine is also said to have interfered with the practices as people now go to hospitals. The sacred places, which were also visited for health reasons, are said to be failing to meet their physical needs. The old people see this disobedience as having brought about many problems for the nation. The government is being blamed for encouraging people to despise their past. The complaints are that young people go there for entertainment and picnics which, they say, has led to chronic diseases such as HIV and AIDS as a punishment from Mwali for these dishonourable acts.[15]

The observation is that today there is a preference for the Christian practices and beliefs rather than the traditional religious beliefs and practices. The traditions of the past, especially the Mwali rainmaking cult, are resented. There is, therefore, a tendency for people to ask for rain from the Christian God (Bhusumane, 1985). The syncretistic view of Christianity, education and technology generally favour Christian beliefs and religious practices over the Mwali's rainmaking practices and beliefs.

■ *Zwamwi ritual practices and environmental stewardship*

Zwamwi are things that are believed to stop rain. The removal of these things involved what is here referred to as the hunting of *zwamwi* ritual, which was accompanied by a wide variety of traditional dances called the *dantshiwa, woso, kobodolo* and *ndazula*

---

14   Mr Gunda, Mapoka Village Kgotla, interviewed in 1995 and reviewed in 2018.
15   Mr Thumuku, Mapoka Village Kgotla, interviewed in 1995 and reviewed in 2018.

dances. These dances were performed by men, with women clapping their hands and beating drums of different sizes to produce a mixture of different sounds. The *mayile* dance was performed by women, while a group of men went into the forest to hunt *zwamwi* (Bhusumane, 1985). They dance in circles imitating *Njelele*, which Monyatsi (1984) refers to as the fish eagle, while Bhusumane (1985) describes it as the bird of rain. A variety of rites is performed before the ploughing begins to usher in sowing season. It is a practice whereby men go round a locality to clean the environment by collecting scattered bones, nests of crows and other big birds, dead animal skins, bird feathers, stones, sticks, cloths, papers and plastics hanging on trees and removing trees struck by lightning. All of these objects are seen as malignant and should be hunted and removed around August and September to prepare for the rain season. After the wood and other waste materials have been heaped together, a calabash of water is broken on them and branches of the *nzeze* tree added before the heap is set on fire. The smoke produced from this was believed to purify the air, dispel bad odours that pollute the atmosphere, and cause the formation of clouds laden with rain.

Ruined and abandoned huts are also destroyed because they are believed to harbour evil spirits, which prevent the formation of clouds and falling of rain. They also hunted wild animals and, if they killed any, they roasted the meat upon reaching the place where the girls were performing the *mayile* dance. The roasting of the meat was carried out as a sacrificial rite with strong religious meaning and implications. It was a process in selling the relationship between the community and Mwali (Carmichael et al., 1994). Upon the arrival of the hunting party, the girls performed a special dance called *tshukwi* to welcome the men (Bhusumane, 1985; Monyatsi, 1984). This is the climax of their dance. At this point, their faces and bodies are painted with a white paste made of fine powder from white stones. Their performance involved running around the village, singing and dancing until the "rain washed off the white paste on their bodies" (Monyatsi, 1984:27). The white colour is here used as a symbol of rain clouds. It is also believed to attract rain. If it fails to rain, which is believed to be unlikely, the old women ritually wash the girls with ordinary water in the veld outside the village.

This practice was followed by the *dziwosana* dance, which is performed by the devotees of Mwali. It was performed at the *daga*, a special dancing arena where the traditional beer was brought in calabashes. There are stories that some calabashes mysteriously reach the *daga* empty, yet there is froth at the rim of the calabash as though they were still full. This is said to remain a mystery even to the women carrying the calabashes, because they are also unable to feel changes in the weight of the calabash (Bhusumane, 1985; Monyatsi, 1984).

As already pointed out, *zwamwi* are believed to be things that cast a bad omen or spell on the environment that is believed to stop cloud formation and rain. The *zwamwi* ritual practice, therefore, is the removal of malignant/malevolent spirits that are evil in nature and effect. As stated above, the practice involves men going around cleaning the environment by collecting everything malignant and that should be hunted and removed around August and September to prepare for the rain season. What happens is that certain big birds are fond of collecting dead animals, their skulls and bones, and keep them on top of trees. These are believed to pollute the environment and prevent the formation of rain clouds. They are also believed to produce an odour that affects the dissolving of clouds and moisture formation in the atmosphere; therefore, it must be removed and destroyed. When all these waste materials are heaped together and ritually destroyed by burning, the smoke from this was believed to purify the air, dispel bad odours, and cause clouds laden with rain to form. Ruined and abandoned huts are also destroyed because they are believed to pollute the environment and offend Mwali. Overall, the hunting of *zwamwi* is believed to support environmental stewardship through combatting pollution, dumping of waste materials and decomposition of waste that produces a smell which pollutes the air. It also relevant to fire, which destroys nature. It is like throwing petrol bombs on a bush fire. Religion, especially in the context of the traditional religion, places humans at the centre of all things to be stewards who accommodate, protect and conserve the environment (Amanze, 2002).

Both female and male *dziwosana* dress in black skirts and black beads. The black colour is believed to be favoured by Mwali. As they danced, the rest of the people, men and women, sang and clapped their hands in support of their performance. During this celebration, it was a taboo for them to engage in sex or talk about sexual relations. Immoral conduct, such as sexual activities, were avoided during the dance week. Even married couples participating in the dance were expected to avoid sexual relations until the end of the ceremony. Mwali was believed to punish disobedience by death. It must be mentioned that the *dziwosana* dance and singing marked the climax of the rainmaking rites. At the end of the dance, the elders went to the shrine to present their petitions and sacrifices, and to listen to the voice of Mwali. Only the elders were allowed to enter the shrine and listen to Mwali speaking. As part of ritual practice, traditional beer was poured and some food put on the ground for Mwali. It is said that when Mwali is pleased with the performance of the rituals, he sends the rain to wash away the footprints of the *dziwosana* that very same day (Monyatsi, 1984).

■ The reasons for the Zwamwi cleansing ritual

The community believes that the *zwamwi* cleansing ritual is carried out in order to cool, cleanse and protect the land, animals and the general environment. Pollutants were believed to cause the Earth to become hot, impure, poisonous and desecrated, resulting in what is today referred to as global warming, causing climatic changes, including irregular rainfalls (Collier, Conway & Venable, 2009:125-141).

The Kalanga religious practices, therefore, call on the adherents of the Mwali cult to be caretakers of the Earth, to save Mother Earth, and protect the environment from pollution that destroys trees and grass as well as pollutes the air and water, and eventually kills humanity. Failure to observe the necessary land-cleansing rituals (i.e. *zwamwi*) was not only believed to lead to rain failure and drought, but also affected land fertility as well as crop and animal production, as the drought would lead to premature births and deaths.

The Kalanga traditionally found it difficult to disregard the *zwamwi* cleansing ritual, because the community demanded it and they ensured that ritual procedures were strictly followed every August/September. During this period, there is a wide range of taboos to be observed. The practices emphasise that certain trees are not to be used as firewood or cut for any purpose. Trees such as *nzeze, mogonono, mosetlha, morula* and *mokgalo* are not to be cut, because they are believed to be connected to very important ritual practices. Certain animals and reptiles, such as pythons, are not to be killed during this period or at any other time when they are found in the vicinity of the sacred site. These trees and animals are regarded as taboos. Failure to observe the taboos will also lead to crops being destroyed by heavy hailstorms. Observance of the taboos and performance of ritual practices create harmony between the ancestors and the people.

▪ Results and further discussion of the zwamwi ritual

It is important to note that *zwamwi* and other causes of pollution are believed to result from the negative activities of human beings and their failure to act as stewards of the environment. Environmental pollution was seen as having the greatest impact on human health, climate change and weather patterns. The major forms of pollution relevant here are those affecting air, water and soil. Several studies have already provided evidence that connects air pollution, human health and climate change (Parsons, 1995:141-166).

The *zwamwi* ritual practice also represents the view that the wild fires that are sometimes started by humans also contribute to the lack of rain. It is for this reason that any signs of wild fires are removed as part of the cleaning process of the environment. Most important are the measures that are put in place to ensure that wild fires will not occur in the future. These fires cause high levels of pollution, which is associated with inadequate levels of the moist air that contributes to cloud and rain formation. Burnt wood, grass and other remains causing any form of environmental pollution are therefore collected and removed. The burning of trees

8

and grass is therefore believed to pollute the environment, for example the air, the water sources, etc. Wild fires also emit a terrible smell that pollutes the air and water.

The *zwamwi* ritual cleansing therefore also addresses water-quality problems. The concern of the community, which is the pollution of the environment that results in water-quality problems and other challenges, remains relevant today. If this were not resolved, it will escalate as the population grows and eventually the waste problem could not be resolved.

Conclusion

This chapter has contributed to the ongoing discussion about the role of religion in the conservation of the environment. It has done this by investigating the indigenous religious beliefs and practices of four sacred sites of the Kalanga of the north-east region of Botswana and the strategies adopted by these communities to address the problem in the environment. As part of the rainmaking activities and the preparation for the coming of rain, the aim of the *zwamwi* practice is to combat the pollution disturbs geographic and atmospheric conditions. Its strategy is therefore to identify specific polluting agents that could become sources of emissions and then come up with measures to cleanse and protect the atmosphere. It must be mentioned that what makes the role of the sacred sites important in the conservation of the environment is the centrality of religious beliefs and practices that revolve around a supernatural power and the spirits of the ancestors. The value is that these beliefs and religious practices are intrinsically tied to the everyday activities of the people. In addition, these activities are believed to be governed by the supernatural. This is why prayers are said and ceremonies performed before important activities such as planting, harvesting, dancing, and singing (Carmichael et al., 1994).

The other important point that needs to be made is that *zwamwi* hunting also works towards removing water-polluting agents that would normally destroy animal and plant life. Water pollution causes many deaths, mainly due to the contamination of drinking water, which results in diseases and conflicts. The *zwamwi* laws address growing global climate challenges because pollution has become a global problem. It imposes health and clean-up costs on the whole society. Polluted air can kill many organisms, including humans. Ozone pollution can cause respiratory diseases, cardiovascular diseases, throat inflammation, chest pains and congestion as well as sleep disturbance amongst elderly people.

Finally, it must be mentioned that the *zwamwi* practice helps to increase the consciousness of the community about the negative effects of pollution and indiscriminate dumping of waste materials. It also helps with awareness education.

The Kalanga beliefs and religious practices have for years promoted environmental conservation and strategies contributing towards sustainability. The forums on the importance of tree planting, environmental care, the dangers of depleting scarce natural resources, air and water pollution are promoted. At *kgotla* meetings, climate change and the need for biodiversity are discussed and strategies to protect the environment are adopted by the community. Ancestors are believed to view the Earth as rich and bountiful, but in need of stewardship. For African communities, therefore, there is an inseparable bond between man and nature.

It is also interesting to note that pollution was the theme for the World Environmental Day on 5 June 2019, which concluded that the quality of the environment depends on people's lifestyle choices, which corresponds with the purpose of the *zwamwi* ritual practice for restoring nature. Genesis 1:29 states that God created the universe and was pleased by the condition of the plants, flowers and fruits. Grim and Tucker (2014) argue that the role of religion is to orient humans to the Earth. It teaches them that they are not isolated in the universe, but a part of the Earth from which they draw meaning through stories, practices, symbols, meditation, and prayer. These are the means by which humans and communities integrate themselves with the Earth and environment. Creation is understood to be a place that reveals divine sacredness. Humans are invited not only to partake of and share in, but also contribute towards preserving and caring for the Earth as well as using it responsibly (Grim & Tucker, 2014). Grim and Tucker (2014:106) point out: "To abuse nature is to sin against it. Domination of nature is to be avoided. However, humans have a special place in creation. Any abuse of our power, any wanton or wasteful use of the world's natural resources, is repugnant to God."

Bell (1992) has pointed out that ritualised activities based on the experience of previous generations have a great influence on communities. He also agrees with Ranger (1999:1-7, 19-29, 39-66), who observes that activities and values inherited or preserved from the past should be appropriated in such a way that they influence the current strategies in order to benefit society. Bell (1992) further suggests that we need to rethink ritual as practice and proposes a new framework within which to reconsider traditional questions about ritual. In this framework, ritual activities are restored to their rightful contexts, concretising the ways of acting in that particular culture. The point is that the ritual influences people's concepts, cultural world views, and ideological systems, which consequently influence people to regard the rituals as true or reality. Shared cultural interpretations attached to rituals promote social solidarity. A ritual has a transformative effect making the ideological real. Social solidarity is the goal of any and all ritual mechanisms (Bell, 1992).

Land gives an assurance of identity and security. It provides an eloquent mark of continuity between past, present and future, and is a source of food that can be relied on from year to year. The land is regarded as sacred, a symbol of the ultimate fount of being. The Earth is living, as are the trees, animals and rivers. To harm the Earth, to divert the rivers, to destroy a tree, are to heap contempt upon the Creator and the creative process (Dillistone, 1986). The land, the plants and animals together form a sacred whole. Land and its resources are not only a huge economic commodity; they are to be cherished by people as the sacred organism through which the blood of their own veins flows to maintain its health and productivity (Dillistone, 1986).

References

Amanze, J. 2002. *African traditional religions and culture in Botswana.* Gaborone: Pula Press.

Bell, C. 1992. *Ritual theory, ritual practice.* Oxford: Oxford University Press.

Bhusumane, D. 1985. The ethics of rainmaking and the twentieth century atmosphere in Botswana. In: A.B.T. Byaruhanga-Akiiki (ed), *Religion in Botswana project.* Gaborone: University of Botswana. 30-40.

Campbell, A.C. 1968. Some notes on Ngwaketse divination. *Botswana Notes and Records,* 1(1):9-13.

Carmichael, D.L., Hubert, J., Reeves, B. & Schanche, A. 1994. *Sacred sites, sacred places.* London: Routledge.

Chebanne, A. 2011. Personal interview. 11 October, Gaborone.

Collier, P., Conway, G. & Venable, T. 2009. Climate Change and Africa. In: H. Dieter & C. Hepburn (eds), *Climate Change & Africa: The Economics and Politics of Climate Change.* New York: Oxford University Press. 125-141. https://doi.org/10.10 93/acprof:osobl/9780199573288.00 3.0007

Dillistone, F.W. 1986. *The power of symbols.* London: SCM Press.

Gelfand, M. 1962. *Shona religion with special reference to the Makorekore.* Cape Town: Juta.

Genesis. 2007. *The Bible.* Carol Stream, IL: Tyndale House Publishers.

Grand, B. 1984. The role played by the Chief Messenger of Mwali usually referred to as 'Mongwa'. In: A.B.T. Byaruhanga-Akiiki (ed), *Religion in Botswana project.* Gaborone: University of Botswana. 124-129.

Grim, J. & Tucker, M.E. 2014. *Ecology and religion.* London: Island Press.

Larson, J.L. 1971. The significance of rainmaking for the Hambukushu. *African Studies,* 25(1):23-36. https://doi.org/10.1080/00020186608707225

Livingstone, D. 1857. *Missionary travels and researches in South Africa.* London: John Murray.

Mackenzie, J. 1971. *Ten years north of the Orange River.* London: Frank Cass.

Mbiti, J.S. 1977. *African religions and philosophy.* London: Heinemann.

Monyatsi, O.M. 1984. The Nzeze Rainmaking ritual among the Bakalanga. In: A.B.T. Byaruhanga-Akiiki (ed), *Religion in Botswana project.* Gaborone: University of Botswana.

Moser, C. & Feldman, C. (eds). 2014. *Locating the sacred: Theoretical approaches to the emplacement of religion.* Oxford: Oxbow Books. https://doi.org/10.2307/j.ctvh1dqff

Nkomazana, F. 2005. Some evidence of belief in the One True God among the Batswana before the missionaries. *BOLESWA: Journal of Theology, Religion and Philosophy,* 1(1):26-49.

Parrinder, G. 1969. *Religions in Africa.* Harmondsworth: Penguin.

Parsons, M.l. 1995. *Global warming.* New York: Plenun Press.

Ranger, T.O. 1999. *Voices from the rocks.* Harare: Baobab.

Setiloane, G.M. 1976. *The image of God among the Sotho-Tswana.* Rotterdam: A.A. Balkema.

AFRICAN IMAGINATION OF TECHNOLOGY AND ENVIRONMENTAL STABILITY

Examples of Kikuyu and Luhya communities in Kenya

Doreen Karimi Nyaga[1]

Abstract

Community and environmental sustainability are a global concern that calls for the civilised, the professional practitioners, the creative thinkers, and the future world to participate in providing, creating and establishing a sustainable environment. This study aims at stimulating and informing the discussion on the concept of community and environmental sustainability, as well as on how technology has influenced it. It explores African concepts of environmental sustainability with relevant examples from the Kikuyu and the Luhya communities in Kenya. The chapter highlights an African imagination of community and its role in the conservation of natural resources, and the creation of sustainable economic conditions for African communities. A survey was conducted in Roysambu, a small village in Nairobi, Kenya. The study picked a sample of 150 respondents in the area, who were selected using random sampling. One stipulation in this selection was that each of the members of the study sample was either from the Kikuyu or Luhya communities. The study also adopted the diffusion of innovation theory, which explains that over a duration of time, an innovation or idea is adopted by users and spreads in a given social system or population (Rogers, 1983). The study established that it is important for communities to live according to their traditions and values despite the intense technological wave, with the support from the government, in order to create a balance between traditional ways and the technological ways of establishing a sustainable environment.

Introduction

The relation between the environment and sustainability is an idea that has been in existence for many decades. Different perspectives on and perceptions of the concept are emerging and this has changed how the communities in Africa respond to the whole issue of environmental sustainability. Shiel (2018) explains the environment

---

1   Ms Doreen Karimi Nyaga teaches Kiswahili and Christian religious education at Cianda High School, Department of Humanities, Kiambu, Kenya. [Email: doreenndegih@gmail.com]

as the sum total of the elements, factors and conditions in the surroundings that may have an impact on the development, action or survival of an organism or group of organisms. Environmental sustainability has been defined as "a condition of balance, resilience, and interconnectedness that allows human society to satisfy its needs while neither exceeding the capacity of its supporting ecosystems to continue to regenerate the services necessary to meet those needs nor by our actions diminishing biological diversity" (Morelli, 2011). The positive and negative growth of Africa is linked to the sustainability of its environment. This makes the study of the African imagination regarding environmental sustainability amongst different communities in Africa of such importance.

This chapter maps out the concept of environmental sustainability in Africa using the examples of the Luhya community, who belongs to the larger linguistic group known as the Bantu, and the Kikuyu community, who come from the central part of Kenya. The examples are based on these groups' methods of conservation of natural resources and creation of sustainable economic conditions. The chapter also explains the challenges facing environmental sustainability by the Luhya and Kikuyu community such as the decline of general culture, lack of government support, undermining of community participation by politicians, and the intense wave of technological development. Moreover, it points out the impact of technology on environmental sustainability as entailing the decline of traditional modes of sustainability and the erosion of culture.

Enhancing environmental sustainability is not only the role of the government and other big organisations, but also of the communities who are the major beneficiaries of that same environment. A sustainable environment ensures good psychological, physical and sociological conditions in the country, which in turn contributes to the quality of the ecological system, health conditions and food security of future generations. The traditional disciplines, values and norms of the society that used to guide management of the environment have been swept away by the rapidly advancing technological wave, an issue that has confused different communities in Africa regarding environmental sustainability. There is always enough that the environment gives us; if we could also give it enough attention, then the problems associated with environmental sustainability in Africa will always attract the best remedies for the good of both the current and the future generation.

Methodology

Since there is quite a substantial number of Kikuyus and Luhyas in Roysambu, self-administered survey research questionnaires were used for data collection in both residential and business premises. The survey included a study sample of

150 respondents, who were selected using random sampling. The stipulations for this selection were that each of the members of the study sample was an active user of WhatsApp and that their primary residence was within Roysambu.

The researcher resides mostly in Roysambu and therefore elected to use the residents of Roysambu as the research population. It was a convenient choice and it meant that the researcher could administer the questionnaire with less difficulty. Since the researcher elected to use a combination of convenience and purposive sampling, selection of the respondents depended largely on the researcher's judgement. For one, not all targeted members of the population could be accessed and so only those who were conveniently available to participate in the study were approached. The business people in shops and those who were by the roadsides were approached to fill in the structured questionnaires to the best of their abilities. Questions were clarified for the respondents when necessary to ensure that they provided reliable information. Given that it is not possible to apply statistical methods in either convenience or purposive sampling, the results lack external validity and are therefore not representative of the entire Roysambu population.

As is required of all survey research, the questionnaire began with a carefully crafted introduction outlining the purpose and procedures of the research study and informing the respondents that the final paper will be published for educational purposes and to provide knowledge about the communities. It not only gave clear instructions to the respondents on how to answer the questions, but also informed them that they were free to decline participation or withdraw at any time.

Theoretical framework

The diffusion of innovation theory explains that, over a duration of time, an idea or an innovation is adopted by users and spreads in a given social system or population. Rogers (1983) defines innovation as a practice, object or idea that is perceived by any adopter as new. The theory is one of the oldest in the social sciences. Rogers (1983) was able to synthesise well over 3,000 previously conducted studies on adoption and diffusion to come up with a good number of generalisations. These generalisations explained the process through which innovations, such as creation of a sustainable environment, spread through the populations of probable adopters. The theory is fitting for the current research study because, at a community level today, people are shifting away from their traditional ways of creating a sustainable environment and adopting new ways of doing this through technological innovations.

The first important generalisation of the theory is that any innovations must possess certain characteristics. They may have a relative advantage, be more compatible, less complex, and their trial ability and observability are less demanding (Rogers, 1983).

The impact of this generalisation amongst the adopters is that it affects perception and eventually determines the rate and patterns of adoption. The second generalisation is that adopters differ in their personal characteristics. Some potential adopters are said to be more innovative compared to others. Such differences are easily observed through their level of education, occupation and tech savvy, amongst other characteristics. The current study will closely investigate the demographics in the dominant phase to see how this generalisation is applied.

Rogers (1983) further noted that any adoption decisions require a series of stages to unfold. The starting point is the knowledge of the innovation and this is naturally followed by persuasion, the decision to adopt, implementation and finally confirmation. As the third generalisation of the theory, it explains how different adopters are predisposed towards varying forms of influence in the different stages.

The fourth generalisation that the theory of innovations makes is that there are individuals amongst any given population who act as change agents and/or opinion leaders and can, therefore, accelerate the adoption of an innovation (Rogers, 1983). This is especially the case in instances where the potential adopters think of such change agents and opinion leaders as possessing characteristics similar to theirs.

Finally, diffusion of innovations theory generalises that, as a process, diffusion will normally start out slowly amongst a few pioneering adopters and will then reach a take-off point when a more established community of adopters will develop. At this stage, there is more peer influence working amongst the adopters. In the course of time, there are no additional adopters and so the growth declines. The end result is a cumulative 'S'-shaped adoption curve.

According to Attewell (1992), there are two distinctive styles that almost all diffusion research tends to follow. These are adopter studies and the macro-diffusion studies. The author defines adopter studies as those whose primary concern is to understand the differences in the innovativeness of adopters. In this case, innovativeness is taken to mean the time of adoption. It concerns itself with the early adopters, early majority, late majority and laggards. On the other hand, macro-diffusion studies are basically concerned with characterising the rate as well as patterns of adoption of a technology across a select community of the potential adopters. It is an approach that largely employs mathematical models of the process.

For the purposes of this study, the researcher elected to take an adopter study approach. Guided by the various generalisations made by this theory, the research will look at the manner in which early adopters, early majority, late majority and laggards fit cumulatively into the adoption curve and establish the dominant phase, which will in turn be examined in relation to various factors.

Literature review

A lot of studies have been done and published to understand the concept of environmental sustainability from a variety of perspectives. This study will focus only on the literature that provides relevant information from the African perspective on environmental sustainability and then narrowed down to the Luhya and Kikuyu communities in Kenya. This chapter explains how environmental sustainability has been perceived by the two communities in Kenya and the changes that the new technology has made to it (Jayne, Chamberlin & Headey, 2014). Various issues affect environmental sustainability in Africa: land pressure, the evolution of farming systems, development strategies in Africa on food policy (Acho, 1998), human interference, environmental instability, the environmental consequences of rapid urban growth in Bamenda (Barnes et al, 2017), and the impact of plastic debris on marine life. I agree with the aforementioned statement that each scholar addressed specific aspects of environmental sustainability in Africa.

In their studies, scholars such as Jayne et al. (2014) synthesised how people, markets and governments are responding to the rising pressures on land. This is the result of rapidly changing demographic conditions and the immense challenges that mounting land pressures pose. These challenges include, in the context of current evidence of unsustainable agricultural intensification, a rapidly growing labour force associated with the region's current demographic condition and limited non-agricultural job creation. They argue that these challenges are manageable but require explicit policy actions to address the unique developments in densely populated areas.

Acho (1998) focuses on urban environmental problems and their different dimensions such as geological, climatic and cultural factors. This study was based in Nigeria. The researcher explained that the cultural factors seem to be more pronounced in the Nigerian context because most of the identified urban environmental issues are so much associated with the way of life of the people, either as reactions to urbanisation or their spatial heritage. Their effects are far-reaching in pursuing sustainable development in the country.

On the other hand, in a study done in the United Kingdom Barnes (2017) points out that environmental sustainability is affected by *technology* and argues that technology has a positive impact on the environment. But there is also a negative side. Our *technological* innovations have the potential to harm our *environment*, but if we use them wisely and develop *sustainable* methods, they could also help solve the *ecological* problems we have created.

The Luhya concept of environmental sustainability

The Luhya, Luyia or Abaluhya, as they are interchangeably called, are the second-largest ethnic group in Kenya, after the Kikuyu. The Luhya belongs to the larger linguistic group known as the Bantu. The Luhya are comprised of several subgroups with different but mutually understood linguistic dialects. Some of these subgroups are Ababukusu, Abanyala, Abatachoni, Avalogoli, Abamarama, Abaidakho, Abaisukha, Abatiriki, Abakisa, Abamarachi and Abasamia.

The ethnic homeland of the Luhya community is located in western Kenya, north of Lake Victoria and stretches from Kisumu to Webuye going north and south, and from Kapsabet on the east to the Ugandan border on the west (Okello, 1977).

In the Luhya community, the conservation of natural resources is a community responsibility. It is not an individual role. The god of the land, *Wele Khakabha*, who is a male, is considered omnipresent in the environment and therefore is in charge of the moral guidelines concerning the well-being of the environment. For someone to thrive in the community, they must be in harmony (*Kumulembe*) with the environment. This peace comprises a person's health, wealth and blessings.

Traditional Luhya livelihood systems conserved natural ecosystems through culturally controlled utilisation strategies such as extensive and rotational grazing, shifting cultivation, and the use of substitutable and complementary resources. These strategies were disrupted by colonialism through the introduction of tenure systems (Wekesa, 2000). Animal bones, crocodile nails and ostrich shells were used to make ornamental objects for different rites (Burt, 1980).

To the Luhya community, the environment will always be protected because of the benefits that the community derives from it. The soil has been the most valuable natural resource amongst the Luhya community since ancient times. It is considered the origin of the human race. One of the most common myths amongst the Luhya group relates to the origin of the Earth and human beings. According to this myth, *Were* (God) first created Heaven, then Earth. The Earth created by *Were* had three types of soil: top soil, which was black; intermediate soil, which was red; and bottom soil, which was white. From the black soil, *Were* created a black man; from the red soil, he created a brown man; and from the white soil, he created a white man. (Kamau, 2013).

The soil is still considered sacred because of the burial ceremonies and growing of food crops. Since the western part of Kenya is considered to have the most fertile soil and experiences rainfall regularly, even people outside the region rely heavily on this area for food. Additionally, soil has been valued as a home of humanity, "where the feet of humanity tread and support the self" (Kenyan saying).

Trees are valued worldwide because of their ability to keep the ecological environment in order. The Luhya community believes that everything that has a good side always has an evil side as well, and so it is for the trees. Trees are valued as much as life, because their presence has the ability to either sustain or kill both human and life.

Mwene (2018), in his story of trees with cultural significance amongst the Luhya community, illustrates the significance of trees to the environment and why they are respected and conserved. The *Kumukhuyu* tree bears small red-orange berry-like fruits that are edible. First, they are only consumed when fully ripe. Secondly, you must only eat the ectoderm, because the endoderm is made of seeds that allows insect to thrive within, without spoiling the fruit. Besides the fruits acting as obvious attractants to other life forms, the *Kumukhuyu* tree also allows bushes, shrubs and climbers to grow under it. This means it acts as a perfect foil for predators. Foxes, particularly, love the *Kumukhuyu* tree.

Foxes use the bushes to waylay prey. They also hide their loot in the bushes and in the tree's hollow (*ekhombe*). Despite the benefits of this tree to the fox, Bukusu folklore is that the fox and the *Kumukhuyu* tree do sometimes have disagreements with each other. When that happens, the fox will defecate in the tree's shade. As a result, the Bukusu saying, *Kumukhuyu kwasinya enjusi*, is used to remind people about the ungrateful, wily ways of the fox (Mulembe Nation, n.d.). The *ekhombe* of *mukhuyu* trees are also used by bees as hives. The *Kumukhuyu* tree continues to give by bestowing surrounding communities with eternal rights to honey (Mwene, 2018).

In the Luhya community, the environment is believed to be under patriarchal care. Men own and are given the responsibility of taking care of the environment. Women are always oppressed by this tradition because it denies them the freedom to own land.

The concept of environmental sustainability amongst the Kikuyu community

The Kikuyu, also known as the Gikuyu, community of the East African country are the largest tribe in Kenya with a population of 6.6 million in 2009. They account for close to 17% of the total population of Kenya (Boyes, n.d.). The Kikuyus are believed to have come from West Africa along with other Bantu and settled around Mount Kenya. They practised farming because of the fertile volcanic highlands. Today, most of the Kikuyus have migrated to the capital city of Nairobi and other towns, but their territories still remain in the Mount Kenya area and the central highlands such as the Nyeri, Murang'a, Kiambu and Kirinyaga regions of Kenya (Jenkins, 2008). The Kikuyu were fortunate to have an attractive country with adequate rainfall, rich volcanic soils, and teeming with flora and fauna except in periods of adversity. They were largely self-sufficient; they grew 49 types of food plants besides keeping livestock (Leakey, 1981).

151

The Kikuyu culture of environmental sustainability and conservation of natural resources has been practised since they settled in Kenya. They still uphold their cultural traditions and are believed to be a tribe that had a lot of political and economic influence in *Kenya* since colonial times (Rothchild, 1969). Because of the political and economic power that they have in the country, their regions are always given the first priority of development by politicians. The community always raises a concern if they do not experience any kind of development in their region. This sometimes forces the leaders to tour the area and ensure that the development plans are initiated and progress is made. This is same way that President Uhuru Kenyatta embarked on commissioning projects in central Kenya a few days after the region's Members of Parliament decried the dismal development track record in the area (Oruko, 2018).

Amongst the Kikuyu community the environment is always given the utmost attention because they believe that their survival depends on how good their environment is. Initially, the sacred *Mugumo* tree was mythically imbued with religio-political power, used by the elders for social and religio-political control of the community. The community was therefore advised not to cut down the tree; instead, the tree was to be conserved and respected (Muriuki, 2005).

The Kikuyu tradition of protecting the sacred *Mugumo* tree is still upheld, despite the fact that traditional beliefs are diminishing in the current generation. Ojukwu and Esimone (2014) explain that youths are exposed to new environments associated with the social changes that come with new cultures that contradict African moral values. Traditional Kikuyu society depends on the use of various medicinal herbs to treat human and livestock ailments. People in Kenya suffering from, for example, erectile dysfunction, hail the advent of Viagra, yet the Kikuyu do not mind consulting herbalists on whether there is anything similar in the traditional pharmacopoeia (Karimi, 2002).

Kenyatta (1938), in his book *Facing Mount Kenya*, stressed that all land was owned by individuals or *mbaris*, and none was held communally in the sense that everyone had equal access to it. This implied that the role of environmental conservation when it comes to land was individual, a view which is maintained until today. The traditional land of the Kikuyu community is not supposed to be sold (Bunche, 1941) and, therefore it is preserved according to their rights and rituals. Leakey (1981) explained that the Kikuyu's traditional law provided for the formation of what would now be called forest reserves. This meant, of course, that much more of the forestland could be left undisturbed.

Today, the Kikuyu community is the most developed in their land usage, and their environment is in a better condition than that of any other community in Kenya.

Most of their traditional methods of ensuring environmental sustainability are still active despite the technological wave.

Land and women in the Luhya and Kikuyu communities

Traditionally, the Luhya and the Kikuyu communities have similar traditions about land ownership and inheritance. In both communities, men are the ones who own and control the land and are therefore held responsible for protecting and creating a sustainable environment. This has led to the oppression of women in these societies. Women have been prevented from owning property, the same property those men control and are authorised to take care of. Women in this community have usufruct rights, but they have been excluded from inheriting land.

It is true that Kenyan women have made tremendous contributions to the overall economic growth through their agricultural practices, but a look at the agricultural sector where women are highly represented reveals a high degree of marginalisation, neglect and outright discrimination against women in the distribution of economic resources (Karanja, 1991). This shows how the traditional laws enslave and oppress women; this situation should be addressed at a community level to ensure that women are given a place in these societies.

In the Kikuyu community, the unmarried daughters had a right to use the land within the paternal homestead, but they can only plant annual crops. Whenever a father decides to allocate land to any unmarried or divorced daughter, these women are likely to be forcefully evicted from the land by their male siblings, who believe that daughters have no right to share paternal land with them (Kilson, 1995).

Women in the community play a very major role by creating a sustainable environment and therefore they should be treated fairly by being allocated land to own and inherit with no man's interference. Perhaps there should be a law in the country that allows women to inherit land, a law that removes that particular tradition that oppresses the major conservators of the environment.

Challenges facing environmental sustainability in the Luhya and Kikuyu community

The digital era has eroded the traditional methods and rules for ensuring environmental sustainability. Today the world has become a global village where everyone is learning from others. There is no one best way of doing things; social media have led to people relying on whatever information that is published as solutions to problems.

In the Luhya and Kikuyu communities, the traditional ways of environmental conservation are no longer in existence. The sacred trees such as the Kumurembe and Mugumo trees in the Luhya and Kikuyu communities are no longer spared. They are cut down because people no longer fear the consequences. The traditional beliefs and cultural values have been eroded by Westernisation.

The social networking platforms such as Google are doing excellent work in the promotion of action to address various issues of environment preservation. Nowadays, instead of people sticking to the traditional ways of creating a sustainable environment, Google is being used as an advanced method of searching for new ways of sustaining the environment. The Kikuyu community, known for having a high economic standard in Kenya, is taking advantage of the new technology in businesses and agricultural practices.

From global warming, climate change to solid waste management and renewable energy news, social media platforms are very active with participation from a large number of people, especially the youth or younger generation (Robelia, Greenhow & Burton, 2011). This generation no longer understands or acknowledges the traditional ways of environmental sustainability; this is because either they have not been taught about them or they have intentionally accepted being swept away by the new ways of conserving the environment that have been initiated by the new technology.

Technology has given communities the ability to change some of their behaviours and conduct clean and green businesses, but still people are not keeping up with the pace of the environmental changes happening locally and globally because of indiscriminate utilisation of natural resources. Social media has become an important tool for providing a space and means for the public to participate in influencing or disallowing environmental decisions made by governments and corporations that affect all. This has developed a mode for people to be connected with local environmental challenges and interpretations to larger-scale stories that will affect the global community (Warner, Eames & Irving, 2014)

Undermining of community participation by politicians

The world we are living in is said to be a global village bringing together isolated people. At local and national levels, the community is always underestimated in politics, discouraging the creation of a sustainable environment. Poor leadership in Africa is the root of a lot of challenges facing the continent and its people.

In Kenya, since the leadership is mainly in the hands of the Kikuyu ethnic group, the community tends to relax and expect that their people will defend them in ensuring that the environment is well taken care of. Currently, President Uhuru Kenyatta is facing a rebellion in the Mount Kenya region over claims that the government has neglected the area, which is overwhelmingly supported by the Jubilee. The rebellion, which has been simmering, boiled over at New Year 2019, when Gatundu South's Member of Parliament, Moses Kuria, openly accused the President of ignoring the region and focusing on developing areas that voted for the opposition (Wainaina & Ndung'u, 2019).

The more things change, the more they stay the same. This means that there has been a misuse of the word 'change' by politicians in society today. In every election, in every change of leadership, the word '*change*' is not far away. It not only conveys the promise of a better future and the removal of a flawed past; it appeals to the desire for something new (Winchester, 2018). Once the politicians get into power, they forget about the promises, the lives of the people in the society, and the environment they promised to work on.

The unfinished long-term infrastructural projects started by the politicians during the campaign periods are left at standstill. This kills the energy and the morale of the residents who are supposed to be the beneficiaries of the same environment. They give up and sometimes, with the poor standards, do not know what to do to complete the projects. In Kenya, when the road construction activities are not completed, roads become worse and impassable for long periods before any action is taken by the government, leading to the citizens suffering.

The intense technological wave

Despite the fact that innovation and technology have led to improvement and new alternatives of environmental sustainability, it has also led to the unstoppable challenges to the environment such as the emission of harmful gases into the atmosphere. This has led to climate change. The challenges of getting a long-term strategy that includes a search for full technological alternatives to the hydrocarbon-based technologies for low- or zero-emission innovations in large-scale technologies for energy production, distribution and use are yet to be resolved. These innovations are difficult to forecast and likely to be radical in the sense that they will go far beyond our current knowledge bases and technological horizons (Smith, 2008).

Findings

The research question sought to establish the rate at which the residents of Roysambu adopted technological methods for ensuring environmental sustainability. The aim was to establish the various phases of adoption and enable the researcher to select

9

identify most intense phase of adoption. As indicated in Table 9.1, the dominant phase of adoption fell occurred with the early majority adopters at 36%, representing the respondents who said they had adopted the use of technological measures for environmental sustainability, about 1-3 years after they learnt about it and they do not remember when they conformed to the traditional ways of doing things. Adoption amongst the other categories was fairly equally distributed, with a small margin of variation. The late majority adopters showed the second highest number at 22%, while early adopters came a close third with 21.5%, and the laggards took the last place at 20.5%.

Table 9.1 The rate of adoption of technology in creating a sustainable environment amongst residents of Roysambu[2]

Adoption rate	Number	Percentage
Less than one year (Early adopters)	30	21.5
1–3 years (Early majority)	50	36.0
3–5 years (Late majority)	31	22.0
Over 5 years (Laggards)	28	20.5
Total	139	100.0

The next research question sought to determine how this dominant group varied according to factors such as demographics and satisfaction. To establish how these factors influenced the dominant phase of adoption, percentages were calculated for each against the dominant group, the findings for which are displayed in Table 9.2 and then discussed.

Table 9.2 How the dominant phase of adoption varied according to demographics and satisfaction

Demographics	Number	Percentage
Gender		
Male	46	46
Female	54	54
Age group		
18–25 years	43	43
26–35 years	45	45
36–45 years	5	5
Over 45 years	7	7
Occupation		
Student	15	15
Part-time employment	14	14

2   Twenty-one respondents either declined to participate in the survey or did not report adoption of technology by answering the core question.

Demographics	Number	Percentage
Full-time employment	38	38
Self-employed	30	30
Not working at the moment	2	2
In training: Internship or apprenticeship	1	1
Education		
Primary School	1	1
High School	11	11
Certificate training	6	6
College diploma	36	36
University degree	38	38
Master's degree	6	6
Main tribe		
Luhya	69	69
Kikuyu	76	76
Others	5	5
Level of satisfaction		
Satisfied	39	39
Very satisfied	57	57
Dissatisfied	3	3
Very dissatisfied	1	1

Gender and age

The levels of adoption amongst the age groups differed significantly between the youth and the older generation amongst Roysambu residents. There were 43% of people aged between 18 and 25 years, while the highest number (45%) was amongst those who were aged between 26 and 35 years old. The lowest number of adopters in the dominant phase were those aged between 36 and 45, at 5%, while those aged over 45 years did not vary much from their closely preceding age set, at 7%.

Occupation

Full-time employees reported the highest number in the dominant phase of adoption, at 38%, which was followed closely by those who are self-employed, at 30%. Students and part-time employees did not differ much, at 15% and 14% respectively. The lowest numbers were recorded amongst those not working (2%) and those doing internships (1%).

9

Education

Respondents with a university degree indicated the highest figure of 38% in the dominant phase of adoption, while those with a college diploma came a close second at 36%. According to the results in Table 9.2, there was a significant drop in these numbers, with high school graduates coming in a distant third with 11% and those with master's degrees fourth at 6% of the respondents in the dominant phase.

Main tribe

It was not surprising that an overwhelming majority in the dominant phase, at 76%, identified as members from the Kikuyu tribe, while 69% were from the Luhya community. The remaining 5% were members of other tribes who participated in the study.

Level of satisfaction with the environment

As expected, the level of satisfaction was very high in the dominant phase of adoption. Respondents who indicated that they were very satisfied were recorded at 57%, while 39% participants were satisfied. A miniscule 3% were dissatisfied, while only 1% were very dissatisfied.

Discussion

In line with the diffusion of innovations theory, the first concern for the researcher was to establish whether the rate of adoption fitted the S curve and how this explained the dominant phase of adoption of technology amongst Roysambu residents. The findings indicate that there is some correspondence with the assumption made by Rogers (1983); there is usually a slow start amongst the pioneering group of adopters and this is often followed by a more established group of adopters. Even though the findings show that in the dominant phase the early majority adopters were high at 36%. The other phases of adoption seemed to vary only slightly. Early adopters were at 21.5%, late majority adopters at 22%, and laggards at 20.5%. This seems to indicate a semblance to the adoption curve, but is too close to call.

To understand these results better, the researcher looked at the outcome of the survey through the prism of yet another generalisation of the theory: the idea that there are differing characteristics amongst potential adopters. Three specific areas of the findings fit with this generalisation: occupation, education and age group. Greater receptivity for technology was found amongst the educated, who have great knowledge about the environment. The results also indicated that those with a university degree and a college diploma featured prominently in the dominant phase of adoption. At 38% and 36%, respectively, this is indicative of the fact that the university and college graduates may have shared expertise informally amongst themselves in the learning institutions they attended and that some social structures formed as a result. In this way, their response to social pressure spiked their adoption of technology, whether or not they perceived it as valuable.

According to Kenneth, Zhao and Borman (2004), this is also about social capital, where adoption correlates with the idea of fitting in. However, those with a master's degree (6%) and those with a PhD (2%) may not fit this generalisation specifically for residents of Roysambu, more because the dominant phase of adoption consisted of a higher number of younger residents who may not yet have attained that kind of educational qualification.

The youth are also an important factor in the dominant phase of adoption. The findings indicated that those aged between 18 and 35 years of age had a combined share of 88%. One may argue that this is largely because younger people are more receptive to new innovations and are willing to try out new things more than the older generation are. There is not a big difference amongst men and women when it comes to the early majority adopters.

Technological ways of creating a sustainable environment at the community level seem to have replaced the traditional ways. People are very satisfied and praising the use of technological innovations to preserve the environment to the extent that they have forgotten their traditional roles of the community. They look to politicians to provide ways in which they can handle the environmental issues.

Conclusion

Tradition existed before technology and every community in the world has its own traditional ways of creating a sustainable environment. In many African countries such as Kenya, Nigeria and South Africa, traditional ways of conserving the environment are still followed, even with the overwhelming intrusion of technology. Achieving a sustainable environment at community level is possible only if clear rules, guidelines and boundaries are stated for both the government and the members of the respective community by clearly outlining the roles of each individual.

The African imagination related to environmental sustainability is evolving every day, with the intense technological wave playing a major role in introducing new ways of conserving the environment through, for example, the use of machines and chemicals. This has led to the fading of traditions. For example, in the Kikuyu and the Luhya communities in Kenya, trees that were of cultural significance such as the Mugumo and Kumukhuyu trees are no longer revered as before. The communities now cut down these trees and use them to make charcoal, build settlements and even use the them for cooking fuel. Other trees that were used for herbal purposes and rituals are no longer preserved. The cutting down of these trees has aggravated the environmental degradation in times of lack of rainfall in the regions.

Women, who are the major environmental caregivers, should be allowed to own the land that they conserve and it should not only be owned by men to impose rules on women. The Kikuyu and the Luhya traditional laws oppress woman when it comes to land ownership. Something that is of concern is that women are not valued in society. My assumption here is that if women were to be given land to own, then their economic status could increase twofold.

Technology is good, but it also has its negative side. Despite the fact that it has led to inventions and innovations that have resulted in better ways to create a sustainable environment, it has killed the traditional ways of conserving the environment. Communities no longer think of the remedies they have at hand; they rely on and wait for the government to donate machines and chemicals to them so that they can maintain the environment. To be on the safe side, the communities need to educate their children about the traditional ways of conserving the environment rather than raising a generation that will depend exclusively on technology.

References

Acho, C. 1998. Human interference and environmental instability: Addressing the environmental consequences of rapid urban growth in Bamenda, Cameroon. *Environment and Urbanization*, 10(2):161-174. https://doi.org/10.1630/095624798101284527

Figuerola, B., Barnes, D.K.A., Brickle, P. & Brewin, P.E.B. 2017. Diversity around the Falkland and South Georgia Islands: Overcoming Antarctic barriers. *Marine Environmental Research*, 126:81-94. https://doi.org/10.1016/j.marenvres.2017.02.005

Boyes, J. 1874. *How I became king of the Wa-Kikuyu*. Nairobi: W. Boyd & Co. https://archive.org/details/howibecamekingof00boyeiala/mode/2up [Accessed 8 June 2007].

Bunche, R.J. 1941. The *Irua* ceremony among the Kikuyu of Kiambu District, Kenya. *The Journal of Negro History*, 26(1)(January):46-65. https://doi.org/10.2307/2715049

Burt, M.R. 1980. Cultural myths and supports for rape. *Journal of Personality and Social Psychology*, 38(2):217-230. https://doi.org/10.1037/0022-3514.38.2.217

Frank, K.A. & Zhao, Y. 2004. Social capital and the diffusion of innovations within organizations: the case of computer technology in schools. *Journal of sociology Education*, 77:148-171. https://doi.org/10.1177/003804070407700203

Jayne, T.S., Chamberlin, J. & Headey, D.D. 2014. Land pressures, the evolution of farming systems, and development strategies in Africa: A synthesis. *Food Policy*, 48:1-17. https://doi.org/10.1016/j.foodpol.2014.05.014

Jenkins, O. 2008. *The Kikuyu people of Kenya: A cultural profile*. http://orvillejenkins.com/profiles/kikuyu.html [Accessed 3 October 2018].

Kamau, S. 2013. *Let's cook Kenya! National ethnic foods*. Nairobi: Sliced Onion Company Limited.

Karanja, P.W. 1991. Women's land ownership rights in Kenya. *Third World Legal Studies*, 10:109-135. https://bit.ly/39bB7uj

Karimi, J. 2002. Vibrant herbs, ancient Secrets. *The East African*. https://allafrica.com/stories/200201290569.html [Accessed 29 January 2002].

Kenyatta, J. 1938. *Facing Mount Kenya*. London: Secker and Warburg.

Kilson, M. 1995. Land and the Kikuyu: A study of the relationship between land and the Kikuyu political movements. *The Journal of Negro History*, 40(2):103-153. https://doi.org/10.2307/2715382

Leakey, L.S.B. 1981. *The Southern Kikuyu before 1903*. London: Academic Press.

Morelli, J. 2011. Environmental sustainability: A definition for environmental professionals. *Journal of Environmental Sustainability*, 1(1):1-10. https://doi.org/10.14448/jes.01.0002

Mulembe Nation. n.d. *Bukusu proverbs and sayings*. https://www.mulembenation.co.ke/luhya-proverbs-sayings/bukusu-proverbs-and-sayings/ [Accessed 12 February 2020].

Muriuki, M.K. 2005. The sacred *Mugumo* tree: Revisiting the roots of Gikuyu cosmology and worship: A case study of the Gicugu Gikuyu of Kirinyaga District in Kenya. PhD thesis, SOAS University, London.

Mwene, O. 2018. *Trees with cultural significance among the Luhya culture*. https://www.mulembenation.co.ke [Accessed 3 May 2018].

Ojukwu, E.V. & Esimone, C.C. 2014. Inculcating morals in adolescents through the Igbo folk music. *WEI International Academic Conference Proceedings*. New Orleans, LA: The West East Institute. 162-171.

Okello, A.H. 1977. *History texts of the Lake Region of East Africa*. Nairobi: Kenya Literature Bureau.

Oruko, M.O. 2018. Uhuru tours central Kenya days after region's leaders complained of underdevelopment. *TOKU*. https://bit.ly/30r6pcP [Accessed 1 November 2018].

Robelia, A.B., Greenhow, C. & Burton, L. 2011. Environmental learning in online social networks: Adopting environmentally responsible behaviors. *Environmental Education Research*, 17(4):553-575. https://doi.org/10.1080/13504622.2011.565118

Rogers, E.M. 1983. *Diffusion of innovations*. 3rd Edition. New York: The Free Press.

Rothchild, D. 1969. Ethnic inequalities in Kenya. *The Journal of Modern African Studies*, 7(4):689-711. https://doi.org/10.1017/S0022278X00018905

Shiel, C.W. 2018. Medical definition of the environment. *MedicineNet*. https://www.medicinenet.com/script/main/art.asp?articlekey=19104 [Accessed 12 November 2018].

Smith, K.H. 2008. *The challenge of environmental technology: Promoting radical innovation in conditions of lock-in*. Final report to the Garnaut Climate Change Review. https://bit.ly/2BeXQcD

Wainaina, E. & Ndung'u, G. 2019. *Mt Kenya MPs fault Uhuru over projects*. https://bit.ly/3fKLV54 [Accessed 3 January 2019].

Warner, A., Eames, C. & Irving, R. 2014. Using social media to reinforce environmental learning and action-taking for school students. *International Electronic Journal of Environmental Education*, 4(2):83-96. https://doi.org/10.18497/iejee-green.53452 [Accessed 19 February 2020].

Weseka, P. 2000. Politics and nationalism in colonial Kenya: The case of the Babukusu of Bungoma District, C. 1894-1963. *Journal of Social Anthropology and Ethnology*. https://bit.ly/3hdUQwn

Winchester, D. 2018. Hope without change: The empty promises of politics. *Vision: Society and Culture*, Winter. https://www.vision.org/is-there-hope-for-political-change-8307

10

THE ROLE OF RELIGION IN SUSTAINABLE DEVELOPMENT

Theological reflections on sustainable development goals and Mother Earth

Mwawi Nyirenda Chilongozi[1]

Abstract

The UN's Sustainable Development Goals (SDGs) build on the Millennium Development Goals (MDGs) (United Nations, 2015). However, there is a shift in the understanding of sustainable development as it was stipulated in the MDGs and how sustainable development is defined in the SDGs. The SDGs are applicable to countries in the Global South and in the Global North, unlike the MDGs that focused mainly on countries in the Global South. The MDGs focused on the eradication of extreme poverty and hunger, gender inequality, as well as on improving education, health and forming global partnerships. However, the SDGs integrate the three dimensions of sustainable development, namely economic, social and environmental. The SDGs, therefore, include building peaceful, just and inclusive societies, protecting human rights, promoting gender equality and the need to protect Mother Earth and its natural resources by combating climate change and protecting oceans and forests.

In analysing the SDGs critically, it is evident that the religious dimension is missing. The religious dimension is nevertheless critical, as Oduyoye (2001) argues that religion determines the shaping of the moral, social, political and economic dimensions of many societies in Africa. Religion influences how people relate to each other and the environment. In the African world view, there is no separation between the sacred and secular as it is holistic in its perspective. Religion is an element of people's identity and it influences the core of the lives of people in Africa. Hence, an agenda for sustainable development should not exclude religion.

This chapter engages Mercy Amba Oduyoye's (2001) four central themes of doing theology in Africa as the theological lens in its analysis of sustainable development goals, with a focus on understanding Mother Earth. Her book, *Introducing African women's theology* (Oduyoye, 2001), addresses theological themes that entail a holistic approach to sustainable development in the African context. These themes are: (1) community and wholeness, (2) relatedness and interrelationships, (3) reciprocity and justice, and (4) compassion and solidarity.

---

[1] Rev. Mwawi Nyirenda Chilongozi is a PhD student at Stellenbosch University.
[Email: rev.m.chilongozi@gmail.com]

These theological themes describe the characteristics of traditional life in Africa of caring for each other and the environment. The care for the environment and the natural resources emerge from the religious belief in the need to ensure harmony between the elemental forces and human beings. Achieving sustainable development, as stipulated in the SDGs, is a challenge if religion and the spirituality of people in different societies are not taken into account.

Introduction

This chapter discusses the role of religion in sustainable development and analyses the UN's Sustainable Development Goals (SDGs) as a developmental framework to achieving sustainable development by 2030. The SDGs build on the Millennium Development Goals (MDGs) (United Nations, 2015). However, there is a shift in the understanding of sustainable development as it was stipulated in the MDGs and how sustainable development is defined in the SDGs. In analysing the SDGs critically, it is evident that the religious dimension is missing. The religious dimension is, nevertheless, critical. Oduyoye (2001) argues that religion determines the shaping of the moral, socio-economic and political life of many societies in Africa.

This chapter provides a historical perspective on, and definitions of, the concepts 'development' and 'sustainable development'. It also discusses the role of religion in sustainable development. It engages Mercy Amba Oduyoye's (2001) four central themes of doing theology in Africa, namely community and wholeness; relatedness and interrelationships; reciprocity and justice; and compassion and solidarity as a theological lens for the analysis of sustainable development goals, with a focus on understanding Mother Earth.

Definition of development and approaches

The concept of development emerged shortly after World War II and during the postcolonial and Cold War eras (August, 2010; Biehl, 2013). According to Biehl (2013:103), the concept of development was an ideology of Western capitalism implying that societies in the Global South were to develop or "catch up" with Western societies in the North. Modernisation theorists defined development as the modernising and secularising of societies deemed as undeveloped and freeing them from ties to religion (Biehl, 2013). Thus financial aid and the provision of technical assistance became the means by which underdeveloped countries would develop. Financial aid flowed from Western countries and financial institutions such as the International Monetary Fund (IMF) and World Bank to the countries in the Global South (August, 2010). Biehl (2013:98) further argues that in their view "religion was predominantly held as responsible for more traditional worldviews which seem to impede development". Modernisation theorists regarded development as progress, evolution and economic growth in the countries of the Global South (August, 2010). These countries were regarded as backward and underdeveloped, and needed to develop like countries in the West. However, this approach was proven a fallacy by the second generation of development practitioners, who pointed out that economic growth was not a measure of development per se, as there were more aspects to development.

Consequently, in the 1970s development practitioners came up with other development approaches to correct the imbalances created by modernisation theory. These approaches entailed the elimination of dependency, global reformism, meeting basic needs and capacity building. Later on, more appropriate approaches of development were people-centred development, a rights-based approach and sustainable development (August, 2010; Biehl, 2013). Consequently, the culture and religion of the people targeted in development projects were taken into account, since culture and religion influence people's world view and the relationship to their environment (August, 2013).

Similarly, issues that concern women were not taken into account in the development agenda. It was Ester Boserup, a development practitioner, whose publication *Women's role in economic development* in 1970, brought into the limelight the fact that women were not taken into account and that they did not benefit from the economic growth. Until that time the status of women was not recognised as essential in the development equation (Momsen, 2010). As a result of Boserup's (1970) third world development work, Women in Development (WID) became a key approach to development. However, the WID approach was criticised because it regarded women as a homogenous group. In the late 1970s, the Women and Development (WAD) approach emerged that was led by white feminist women from the Global North who were fighting for gender equality. Again, the WAD approach was criticised, because it did not take into account the challenges that women in the Global South faced. Thus, the Gender and Development (GAD) approach in the 1990s recognised women's contribution to both public and private spheres, and took into account the different aspects of women's lives. It notes the importance of women and men working together.

In 2000, governments, nongovernmental organisations (NGOs), faith-based organisations (FBOs), and United Nations agencies globally started working towards achieving sustainable development through the MDGs and currently through the SDGs 2030 (United Nations, 2015). Now the focus of development is more on sustainable development.

10

What is sustainable development?

Several definitions of sustainable development have been suggested by different scholars from different academic disciplines. The World Commission on Environment and Development (WCED) (1987) defines sustainable development as development that meets the needs of the present generation without depleting the natural resources so that future generations will benefit from the same. In the same context, Repetto (1986:15) describes sustainable development as a "developmental strategy that manages all assets, natural resources, and human resources, as well as financial and physical assets, for increasing long-term wealth and well-being. Sustainable development as a goal rejects policies and practices that support current living standards by depleting the productive base".

Similarly, sustainable development has to be participatory and people-centred. Participation in development projects becomes a learning process that empowers people to understand their social reality (August, 2010). The essence of participation in development is for the people to take charge of their own lives and be able to solve their own problems (August, 2010). Participation is a people-centred approach that assists people to identify and act according to their own needs and priorities without external ideas imposed on them. Moreover, sustainable development advocates for the bottom-up approach and is inclusive, allowing women and the poorest to participate fully.

As a matter of fact, sustainable development takes gender issues into consideration. According to Braidotti, Charkiewicz, Hausler and Wieringa (1997), women are regarded as environmental managers with specific skills and indigenous knowledge in environmental care. Hence, their involvement in any development is crucial to sustainable development. Women work closer to the environment than men, and women's relationships with the environment entail reciprocity, harmony, mutuality and interrelatedness as they depend on nature for meeting daily needs. Therefore, development is sustainable when it is people-centred, incorporates gender issues and is concerned with future generations.

Sustainable development goals

The SDGs – officially known as *Transforming our world: The 2030 agenda for sustainable development* – were adopted by world leaders at the United Nations Summit in 2015. The SDGs build on the MDGs. The MDGs had a lifespan of 15 years from 2000 to 2015 and they focused on ending extreme poverty and hunger, as well as on improving education, health, gender equality and creating global partnerships. The MDGs concentrated on development in countries in the Global South. Although most countries did not meet the targets of the MDGs, the

MDGs raised awareness of issues that help achieve sustainable development such as gender equality, women's empowerment and universal education.

The SDGs are a set of seventeen goals with 169 targets set to be achieved by 2030. The SDGs integrate the three dimensions of sustainable development, namely economic, social and environmental. The SDGs therefore include building peaceful, just and inclusive societies, protecting human rights, promoting gender equality, and focus on the need to protect Mother Earth and her natural resources by combating climate change and protecting oceans and forests. Although the SDGs are regarded as holistic, integrated and universal, they miss the religious (spiritual) dimension.

Religion and sustainable development

Religion plays a significant role in society as it influences the world view, attitudes and values of individuals and communities (Hitzler, 2013). Religion contributes to the well-being of society in terms of social behaviour, economics and political participation. In the African context, there is no separation between the sacred and the secular, between the physical and spiritual realms (Kanyoro, 2002; Ver Beek, 2002). Thus, religious beliefs and practices have to be considered in the planning and implementation of development if it is to be sustainable.

However, in the 1950s and 1960s, development practitioners and academics had no interest in the role of religion in development and regarded religion as a "development taboo" (Tveit, 2016:4). Thus, Tveit (2016:4) notes that development practitioners and academics avoided the subject of religion in their endeavours, as religion was perceived as "irrelevant for social development and at worst was an obstacle to the advancement of social development and human rights". The religious dimension is, nevertheless, critical; Oduyoye (2001) argues that religion determines the shaping of the moral, social, political and economic dimensions of many societies in Africa. Concurring with Oduyoye (2001), Tveit (2016:4) states that "religion informs peoples' understanding of what constitutes a 'good life', their hope, their self-esteem and belief in their own dignity and rights, their inspiration for asserting their dignity and rights, and their resilience in times of crisis". However, Tveit (2016) also argues that the role of religion has both positive and negative aspects.

Religion influences how people relate to each other and the environment. Thus, Hughes and Bennet (1998) argue that people's world view is determined by their religious beliefs. Religion is an element of people's identity and it influences the core of the lives of people in Africa – hence, the need to include religion in the sustainable development agenda. Therefore, a holistic approach which includes the spiritual aspect can assist to achieve sustainable development.

Mercy Oduyoye's life and work

Mercy Amba Oduyoye is a Ghanaian woman theologian and widely renown as "the mother of African women's theology" (Gathogo, 2010:1). Oduyoye was born in 1934 in Asamankese, Ghana to Reverend Charles Kwaw Yamoah and Mercy Yaa Dakwaa; her father was a minister in the Methodist Church (Gathogo, 2010; Smith, n.d.). She got married to Adedoyin Modupe Oduyoye, a Nigerian, in 1968. Her husband is an Anglican, but Mercy remained a Methodist, even after her marriage, and serves in the Methodist Church as a lay leader. She was educated in Ghana up to graduate level. However, she enrolled for her postgraduate studies at Cambridge University in England (Gathogo, 2010; Landman, 2007).

Oduyoye has been involved in the ecumenical movement since 1966, when she attended the World Student Christian Federation (WSCF) in Ghana (Smith, n.d.; Gathogo, 2010). From 1967 to 1970, Oduyoye was Youth Education Secretary of the World Council of Churches and later served as Youth Secretary for the All Africa Conference of Churches (AACC). In 1987, Oduyoye was appointed as the Deputy General Secretary of the World Council of Churches (WCC) and during her tenure of this office, she initiated the Ecumenical Decade of Churches in Solidarity with Women 1988-1998 (Landman, 2007). She became the first woman president of the Ecumenical Association of Third World Theologians (EATWOT) in 1997. Oduyoye, together with other African women theologians, founded the Circle of Concerned African Women Theologians (the Circle) in 1989. The Circle is a "community of African women theologians who come together to reflect on what it means to them to be women of faith within their experiences of religion, culture, politics, and social-economic structures in Africa" (Phiri, 2008:67). The Circle encourages African women theologians to research, write and publish books on issues that concern them. The first convocation of the Circle held in Accra, Ghana in 1989 brought together seventy women theologians from all over Africa.

Oduyoye has positively contributed towards and influenced the work and writings of African women's theologies. She has written and co-edited several books and articles and her books include *Daughters of Anowa: African women and patriarchy* (1995), *Hearing and knowing: Theological reflections on Christianity in Africa* (1996a), and *Introducing African women's theology* (2001). According to Pui-Lan (2004), the two main tenets of Oduyoye's contribution to African women's theology are inculturation and liberation. Oduyoye has written on several theological topics such as spirituality, anthropology, Christology, gender, poverty, culture and religion. Her main interest is how religion and culture influence the experiences of African women (Pui-Lan, 2004). Apart from being a writer, Oduyoye is also an educator, a poet, a mentor and a keynote speaker at several international conferences. She has received various international awards.

Oduyoye's theological perspective

This chapter engages Mercy Amba Oduyoye's (2001) four central themes of doing theology in Africa as a theological lens in an analysis of the SDGs and their relationship to Mother Earth. Oduyoye's (2001) theological themes, expounded in her book *Introducing African Women's Theology*, which she successfully presented as a holistic approach to sustainable development in the African context, will be utilised here. The themes are: (1) community and wholeness, (2) relatedness and interrelationships, (3) reciprocity and justice, and (4) compassion and solidarity. These theological themes describe the characteristics of traditional life in Africa of caring for each other and the environment. Care for the environment and natural resources emerges from the religious tradition of ensuring harmony between the elemental forces and human beings. Human beings depend on the environment for their well-being, but at the same time people are interrelated with God, other spirit beings and the environment. In this regard, Oduyoye's (2001) theological perspective is relevant to analysing the role of religion in sustainable development.

Community and wholeness

Community and wholeness are two essential components of the way African people live in communities. Human beings are interdependent and everyone is part of the community – the unborn, children, youths, the elderly and the ancestors. Individualism is unknown in the African sociocultural tradition. True humanity is expressed in communal life, where people depend on each other for self-understanding. This is passed on from generation to generation as is expressed in the maxim "I am, because we are" (Oduyoye, 2001:26). Other African scholars have described this as '*ubuntu* philosophy'. Thus, Mbiti (1969:108-109) also states that "I am, because we are; and since we are, therefore I am" (see also Tutu, 1999:31; Musopole, 1994:13).

As life is community-oriented, Oduyoye (2001:17) argues that all are "sensitive not only to the needs of others but also to the well-being of the community as a whole". The communal life leads people to care for the marginalised, the vulnerable and those at the periphery of the community as well as for the environment.

Wholeness means "all that makes for the fullness of life, and makes people celebrate life" (Oduyoye, 2001:34). In the African world view, the secular and the sacred belong together, unlike the Western view, which is dualistic and separates the secular and the sacred. Wholeness celebrates the well-being and wellness of all in all aspects of life – spiritually, physically, socially and emotionally. This is observed in times of harvest, the birth of a child, initiation to adulthood, puberty, marriage and death as people come together to celebrate or express their sadness (Chilongozi, 2017). In this

10

regard, theology done from an African perspective affirms the life-enhancing aspects of the African tradition and religion. At the same time, it resists the exploitation of people and the environment.

Relatedness and interrelationships

As noted above, in African cultures people live a communal life and life is expressed as a whole. Oduyoye (2001:35) states that "in the African religious worldview, God, the source of Being, other-spirit beings … and human beings are in constant communication and interrelationships. This relatedness and interrelationship controls and directs human actions and relationships." Human beings rely on the environment and nature as the source of food, shelter and energy (Oduyoye, 2001), hence, the need for a harmonious relationship with the whole of creation. In the African world view, the natural and physical realms are connected to the spiritual realm and these are interdependent. In other words, the African tradition has a holistic view of life (Oduyoye, 2001).

Oduyoye (2001) further notes that Mother Earth is the home for all living things – plants, animals and human beings. At the same time, it is also the habitat of spiritual beings and the survival of human beings depends on their health and wholeness. Rakoczy (2004) agrees with Oduyoye (2001) when she points out that all nature is interdependent and interconnected. The Earth's web of life and ecosystem is interlocked, diverse and delicate, which means that when one part is disturbed, the whole becomes disturbed.

However, the truth is that things have changed in the African context (Momsen, 2010). There is ongoing depletion of natural resources and environmental degrada-tion due to overpopulation, overgrazing and deforestation (Chilongozi, 2017). This has resulted in food insecurity, increased poverty, droughts and floods. In such cases, it is women who suffer the most as they walk long distances in search of water and firewood. In addition, Dube (2012) points out that globalisation and the coming of transnational corporations (TNCs)[2] also contribute to environmental degradation. Globalisation, with its ethics of maximising profits, exploits the environment through deforestation and sometimes land is taken away from locals to establish companies run by transnational corporations (Dube, 2012; Van Drimmelen, 1998).

Despite these challenges, African women theologians advocate for a spirituality of resistance and reconstruction (Oduyoye, 1996b). African women theologies enhance

---

2   Transnational corporations (TNCs), also known as multinational corporations (MNCs), are international companies working across the globe. Most TNCs originate from the Global North and they establish companies abroad in search of cheap raw materials and labour for maximisation of their profit and elimination of competitors (Van Drimmelen, 1998).

the life-affirming aspects of the African tradition and resist the life-denying aspects. Relatedness and interrelationships are crucial if we are to achieve sustainable development.

▪ Reciprocity and justice

It is important to note that in Africa the principle of relatedness and interrelationships calls for reciprocity and justice (Oduyoye, 2001). Oduyoye (2001:36) argues that "throughout African communities, the moral obligations enforced include reciprocity and justice". The struggle for gender justice, economic justice, social justice and environmental justice is what African women theologians are engaged in. This is evident in Oduyoye's (2001:37) statement that "the injustice of having to struggle to have one's humanity recognised and treated as such, all of this becomes the context of struggle reflected in women's theology".

The exploitation of natural resources, such as trees, has devastating results on the environment and human beings, as noted above. Food insecurity and travelling long distances to fetch water and firewood result in social and gender injustice, as women are the ones who do most of the household chores (Oduyoye, 2001). Women may not get the nutrition they need for their bodies to function properly.

Furthermore, global warming and climate change have resulted from human activities that have destroyed the ecosystems. The effects of climate change are devastating as nations experience droughts, floods and tropical cyclones. Habel (2000:1) argues that "global warming has become a frightening threat and crisis that threatens the very life of the planet earth". In seeking justice, African women theologians in their theologising confront issues of injustice that women experience as well as the exploitation of the environment.

▪ Compassion and solidarity

Compassion and solidarity are aspects of relatedness and interrelationship. It is compassion that leads women to live and to work together in solidarity, to feel hurt with those who are hurting, and to rejoice with those who are rejoicing (Oduyoye, 2001). According to Oduyoye (2001:37), "compassion is the wellspring of women's solidarity that is evident in the many women's organised groups, both in the traditional society and the contemporary women's movements." In the African context, women organise themselves in groups for good causes. They celebrate together in times of joy such as weddings and harvest, and they also mourn together in times of sorrow such as funerals and natural disasters.

Hospitality is one of the important virtues which expresses solidarity. Oduyoye (2001:46) argues that "hospitality is a word that generates themes of caring, providing, helping, sharing and 'ministering' to the needs of others". Caring for all people and even strangers is part of the African way of life. Thus, Oduyoye (2001:93) states that "offering and receiving hospitality is an indicator of the African life-force sustenance that is emphasised by both individuals and communities".

Theological analysis of SDGs

The SDGs are the development frameworks that focus on achieving sustainable development by 2030. The seventeen SDGs are currently being implemented in all countries – developed and developing countries, although each country has its own challenges. The SDGs aim at ending poverty and hunger, protecting human rights, promoting gender equality as well as women's and girl's empowerment, combating inequalities within and amongst countries, building peaceful, just and inclusive societies, and ensuring the lasting protection of the planet Earth and its natural resources (United Nations, 2015). The SDGs are interrelated and intertwined.

In analysing the SDGs critically, it becomes evident that the religious dimension is missing. The goals and the targets are well stipulated, but they miss one important aspect that would help to achieve sustainable development. Hence, Mercy Oduyoye's (2001) theological themes (as listed above) are used in this chapter as the theological lens in analysing the role of religion within the context of sustainable development goals. Although the SDGs are interrelated, they are broad in scope. The SDGs aim at ridding the globe of poverty and hunger, inequalities and protecting the life-support systems of Mother Earth. However, this chapter analyses only four out of the seventeen SDGs and their relationship to Mother Earth. The four goals are selected according to the three thematic areas of the SDGs, namely social, economic and environmental. Goal 3, good health and well-being, will be analysed under the theological theme of community and wholeness, as it is related to the social dimension. Goal 15, life on land, will be analysed under the theological theme of relatedness and interrelationship, since it relates to the environment. Goal 8, decent work and economic growth will be analysed under the theme of reciprocity and justice, as it is related to economics, while Goal 10, reduced inequalities, will be analysed under the theme of compassion and solidarity, since it deals with social responsibility.

Community and wholeness as related to good health and well-being

Community is the way of life in the African context. Communal life entails caring for each other and the environment. The African world view is holistic as it regards life as a whole in all aspects – spiritual, physical, social, cultural and economic. Therefore, Oduyoye (2001:46) argues that the belief in God as the source and centre of all things is the "beginning of women eco-theology". African women's theologies are a form of communal theology done within the African context whose point of departure is the experiences of African women. African women's theologies are life affirming and they resist the exploitation of human beings and the environment, because human beings depend on the environment for their livelihood. This theology recognises the impact of environmental degradation on the lives of people, especially women and children. It affirms the good practices in the communities and critiques the bad practices that are present in some communities that contribute to the degradation of the environment.

Similarly, wholeness is well-being and wellness in all aspects of life – physical, spiritual and emotional. Wholeness regards life as a whole and resists any aspect that threatens the well-being of the community, but rather promotes the life-flourishing aspects. SDG 3 focuses on "ensur[ing] healthy lives and promot[ing] well-being for all at all ages" (United Nations, 2015). In the light of promoting community and wholeness, it is important to note that health and healing cannot be separated from the well-being and wellness of human beings (Marais, 2015). Health, therefore, is understood as "encompassing the physical emotional, psychological and social domains" (Phiri & Nadar, 2006:9). At the same time, health is relational, which means that the healing of broken relations is crucial for the well-being of all members of the community. Therefore, Oduyoye (2001:53) grounds the concern for the health and healing of human beings in what she calls the "spirituality of care". The spirituality of care involves mutual care, sharing, learning together, and nurturing the vulnerable and the less privileged. Thus, religion is complete with resources that can bring healing to the communities (Phiri & Nadar, 2006).

Relatedness and interrelationship as related to life on land

People are connected to each other, to God and to the environment. The theological understanding that God is the creator and sustainer of the whole of creation is crucial. "The earth is the LORD's, and everything in it, the world and all who live in it, for he founded it upon the seas and established it upon the waters" (Psalms 24:1-2). God commissioned people to be stewards of his creation (Hughes & Bennet, 1998). As stewards, Christians need to respect and appreciate the creation, while at the same time having a sense of their interdependence with the environment (Hughes & Bennet, 1998). Caring for natural resources is crucial to achieve sustainable development. Similarly, religion plays an important role in caring for the environment as people appreciate natural resources as God-given.

SDG 15 aims to "protect, restore and promote sustainable use of terrestrial eco-systems, sustainably manage forests, combat desertification, halt and reverse land degradation and halt biodiversity loss" (United Nations, 2015). This goal is analysed in the light of the theological theme of relatedness and interrelationship. Protecting and restoring ecosystems depend on how human beings relate to each other and the environment. Oduyoye (2001:35) argues that "religion that emerged in Africa was developed to ensure harmony between the elemental forces and humans". Oduyoye (2001) further argues that spiritual connectedness arises from the ecological relationship. Therefore, religious observances and practices are key to sustainable development.

Reciprocity and justice as related to decent work and economic growth

Reciprocity and justice are required for peace and harmony in every community. Social, economic and gender justices are crucial in communities to ensure the well-being and wellness of all people and the environment. At times, environmental degradation and depletion of natural resources are a consequence of the injustices that are prevalent in our societies. Koopman (2015) argues that justice is inclusive of both the social and ecological bonds of life. Justice respects the human dignity of women and men who are created in the image of God. The SDGs aim at building peaceful, just and inclusive societies where human rights and gender equality are promoted. Such societies are possible, if the religious life (spirituality) of the people is recognised.

SDG 8 aims to "promote sustained, inclusive and sustainable economic growth, full and productive employment and decent work for all" (United Nations, 2015). Analysing Goal 8 in the light of the theological theme of reciprocity and justice, it becomes evident that sustainable economic growth is only possible when there is economic justice. Trade liberalisation and globalisation are the challenges the world is facing today. Dube (2012) argues that religious fundamentalism is a consequence of globalisation. Dube (2012:384) further states that "fundamentalism supposedly rises due to the social insecurities created by liberalisation and privatisation, which hike living expenses and lead more people to find security in religion". Economic justice is a prerequisite for sustainable development in order to achieve inclusive and sustainable economic growth. There is a need for fair trade between the Global North and Global South, as well as for respect for the economic rights of all people at all levels. In the African context, Oduyoye (2001:36) argues that "the moral obligations enforced include reciprocity and justice".

Compassion and solidarity as related to reduced inequalities

In the African context, compassion and solidarity are important aspects of communal life. Compassion and solidarity are enforced by the relatedness and interrelationships between people and God. Compassion and solidarity promote the interconnectedness of reciprocity and justice. Oduyoye (2001) argues that solidarity in Africa is expressed through hospitality. The gathering together of people on different occasions shows solidarity and compassion, whether it is at funerals or weddings. People share and encourage each other in times of crisis and celebrate together in times of joy. Communities can work together to protect the natural resources using the indigenous knowledge system available in their communities.

SDG 10 aims at reducing inequality within and amongst countries. The gap between the rich and the poor in many countries in the Global South is a consequence of economic policies imposed by the International Monetary Fund (IMF) and World Bank (Dube, 2012). Justice, caring, solidarity and compassion are the expression of the divine image all human beings are expected to reflect (Oduyoye, 2001). Compassion is expressed in care for all humanity without counting the cost or expecting to receive back the same (Oduyoye, 2001). Compassion is the wellspring of solidarity as people organise themselves in groups or organisations that focus on caring for each other in times of need and celebrating together in joyful times. The religious values of compassion and solidarity can assist in reducing inequalities that present within and amongst nations.

Conclusion

This chapter has briefly discussed the historical perspective of the term 'development', what sustainable development is, and the role of religion in sustainable development. It has also discussed Oduyoye's (2001) theological themes, namely (1) community and wholeness, (2) relatedness and interrelationships, (3) reciprocity and justice, and (4) compassion and solidarity. These have been engaged as a theological lens in analysing four SDGs.

In order to achieve sustainable development as specified in the 2030 Agenda for Sustainable Development for people and Mother Earth, it is crucial that a holistic approach that is inclusive of religious realities be followed. Tveit (2016) argues that faith (religious) communities have an obligation to respect human dignity, to serve their communities, to protect creation as good stewards and to bear witness to the Supreme Being. Faith communities are "the key sources of social capital for sustainable change, transformation and hope" (Tveit 2016:6). In addition, Oduyoye (2001) points out that the liberation of Christ covers all creation as Christ restores the whole cosmos (Romans 8:20-23). The groaning of creation as in the pain of labour is to reconcile all things to God. Jesus Christ heals and restores nature, individuals and communities.

References

August, K.T. 2010. *Equipping the saints: God's measure for development.* Bellville: The Print-man.

August, K.T. 2013. How development ethos emerges and is engrained and sustained in contact with the local culture and religion. In: K. Mtata (ed), *Religion: Help or hindrance to development.* Geneva: Lutheran University Press. 69-95.

Biehl, M. 2013. Religion, development and mission. In: K. Mtata (ed), *Religion: Help or hindrance to development.* Geneva: Lutheran University Press. 97-119.

Boserup, E. 1970. *Women's role in economic development.* London: Earthscan.

Braidotti, R., Charkiewicz, E., Hausler, S. & Wieringa, S. 1997. Women, the environment and sustainable development. In: N. Visvanathan, L. Duggan, L. Nisonoff & N. Wiegersma (eds), *The women, gender and development reader.* London: Zed Books. 54-61.

Chilongozi, M. 2017. The role of the church with regard to maternal health: A case study of Church of Central Africa Presbyterian (CCAP), Synod of Livingstonia. Master's thesis, Stellenbosch University, Stellenbosch.

Dube, M.W. 2012. Feminist theologies of a world scripture(s) in the globalisation era. In: M.A. Fulkerson & S. Briggs (eds), *The Oxford handbook of feminist theology.* Oxford: Oxford University Press. 382-401. https://doi.org/10.1093/oxfordhb/9780199273881.003.0019

Gathogo, J. 2010. Mercy Oduyoye as the mother of African women's theology. *Journal of Theology and Religion in Africa,* 34(1):1-18.

Habel, N.C. 2000. The challenge of ecojustice readings for Christian theology. *Pacifica:*

Australasian Theological Studies, 13(2):125-141. https://doi.org/10.1177/1030570X0001300202

Hitzler, E. 2013. Opening remarks. In: K. Mtata (ed), *Religion: Help or hindrance to development.* Geneva: Lutheran University Press. 13-17.

Hughes, D. & Bennet, M. 1998. *God of the poor: A Biblical vision of God's present rules.* Carlisle: OM Publishing.

Kanyoro, M.R.A. 2002. *Introducing feminist cultural hermeneutics: An African perspective.* London: Sheffield Academic Press.

Koopman, N. 2015. Men and women in church and society: Equal in dignity? United in diversity? In: E. Mouton, G. Kapuma, L. Hansen & T. Togom (eds), *Living with dignity: African perspectives on gender equality.* Stellenbosch: African Sun Media. 309-324.

Landman, C. 2007. Mercy Amba Ewudziwa Oduyoye: Mother of our stories. *Studia Historiae Ecclesiasticae,* 33(1):187-204. http://uir.unisa.ac.za/handle/10500/4460

Marais, N. 2015. Imagining human flourishing? A systematic theological exploration of contemporary soteriological discourses. PhD dissertation, Stellenbosch University, Stellenbosch.

Mbiti, J.S. 1969. *African religions and philosophy.* London: Heinemann Educational Books.

Momsen, J.H. 2010. *Gender and development.* 2nd Edition. New York: Routledge. https://doi.org/10.4324/9780203869628

Musopole, A.C. 1994. *Being human in Africa: Toward an African Christian anthropology.* New York: Peter Lang.

Oduyoye, M.A. 1995. *Daughters of Anowa: African women and patriarchy.* Maryknoll, NY: Orbis Books.

Oduyoye, M.A. 1996a. *Hearing and knowing: Theological reflections on Christianity in Africa*. Maryknoll, NY: Orbis Books.

Oduyoye, M.A. 1996b. Spirituality of resistance and reconstruction. In: M.J. Mananzan, M.A. Oduyoye, E. Tamez, J.S. Clarkson, M.C. Grey & L.M. Russell (eds), *Women resisting violence: Spirituality for life*. Maryknoll, NY: Orbis Books. 161-171.

Oduyoye, M.A. 2001. *Introducing African women's theology*. Sheffield: Sheffield Academic Press.

Phiri, I.A. 2008. Major challenges for African women theologians in theological education (1989-2008). *Studia Historiae Ecclesiasticae*, 34(2):63-81.

Phiri, I.A. & Nadar, S. 2006. Introduction: Treading softly but firmly. In: I.A. Phiri & S. Nadar (eds), *African women, religion and health: Essays in honour of Mercy Amba Ewudziwa Oduyoye*. Maryknoll, NY: Orbis Books. 1-16.

Psalms. 1999. *The Bible. New International Version (NIV)*. Grand Rapids, MI: Zondervan.

Pui-Lan, K. 2004. Mercy Amba Oduyoye and African women's theology. *Journal of Feminist Studies in Religion*, 20(1):7-22.

Rakoczy, S. 2004. *In her name: Women doing theology*. Pietermaritzburg: Cluster Publications.

Repetto, R. 1986. *World enough and time*. New Haven: Yale University Press.

Romans. 1999. *The Bible. New International Version (NIV)*. Grand Rapids, MI: Zondervan.

Smith, Y.Y. n.d. Mercy Amba Oduyoye. https://www.biola.edu/talbot/ce20/ database/mercy-amba-oduyoye [Accessed 9 May 2019].

Tutu, D. 1999. *No future without forgiveness*. New York: Random House. https://doi.org/10.1111/ j.1540-5842.1999.tb00012.x

Tveit, O.F. 2016. The role of religion in sustainable development and peace. Speech presented at the Partners for Change: Religions and the 2030 Agenda for Sustainable Development. Berlin, 17 February.

United Nations. 2015. *United Nations Development Goals 2030*. https://sustainabledevelopment. un.org/?menu=1300 [Accessed 23 March 2019].

Van Drimmelen, R. 1998. *Faith in a global economy: A primer for Christians*. Geneva: WCC Publications.

Ver Beek, K.A. 2002. Spirituality: A development taboo. In: D. Eade (ed), *Development and culture*. London: Oxfam. 60-77. https://doi. org/10.3362/9780855986919.005

WCED (World Commission on Environment and Development). 1987. *Our common future: The World Commission on Environment and Development*. Oxford: Oxford University Press.

CONTRIBUTING AUTHORS

Georgina Kwanima Boateng is a reverend minister in the Presbyterian Church of Ghana (PCG).

Mwawi Nyirenda Chilongozi is a PhD student at Stellenbosch University and also an ordained minister in the Church of Central Africa Presbyterian (CCAP), Synod of Livingstonia, Malawi.

Doreen Karimi Nyaga teaches Kiswahili and Christian religious education at Cianda High School, Department of Humanities, Kiambu, Kenya.

Molly Manyonganise is a senior lecturer in the Department of Religious Studies and Philosophy at Zimbabwe Open University.

Nobuntu Penxa Matholeni is a lecturer in the Department of Practical Theology and Missiology at Stellenbosch University, South Africa.

Kenosi Molato is a researcher for the SHINE Africa Project, Botswana.

Bridget N. Masaiti Mukuka is Dean of Research at the United Church of Zambia University, Lusaka Campus. She is also a research associate at Stellenbosch University, South Africa.

Godfrey Museka is a lecturer in the Department of Curriculum and Arts, University of Zimbabwe.

Fidelis Nkomazana is an associate professor in the Department of Theology and Religion at the University of Botswana.

Mercy Amba Oduyoye is a teacher, theologian, author and international speaker.

Abednico Phili is a master's candidate in the Department of Theology and Religious Studies, University of Botswana.

Macloud Sipeyiye is affiliated to the Department of Religious Studies, Midlands State University, Zimbabwe. He is also a research fellow at the Research Institute for Theology and Religion, College of Human Sciences, Unisa, South Africa.

Made in the USA
Las Vegas, NV
19 December 2021

38769327R00109